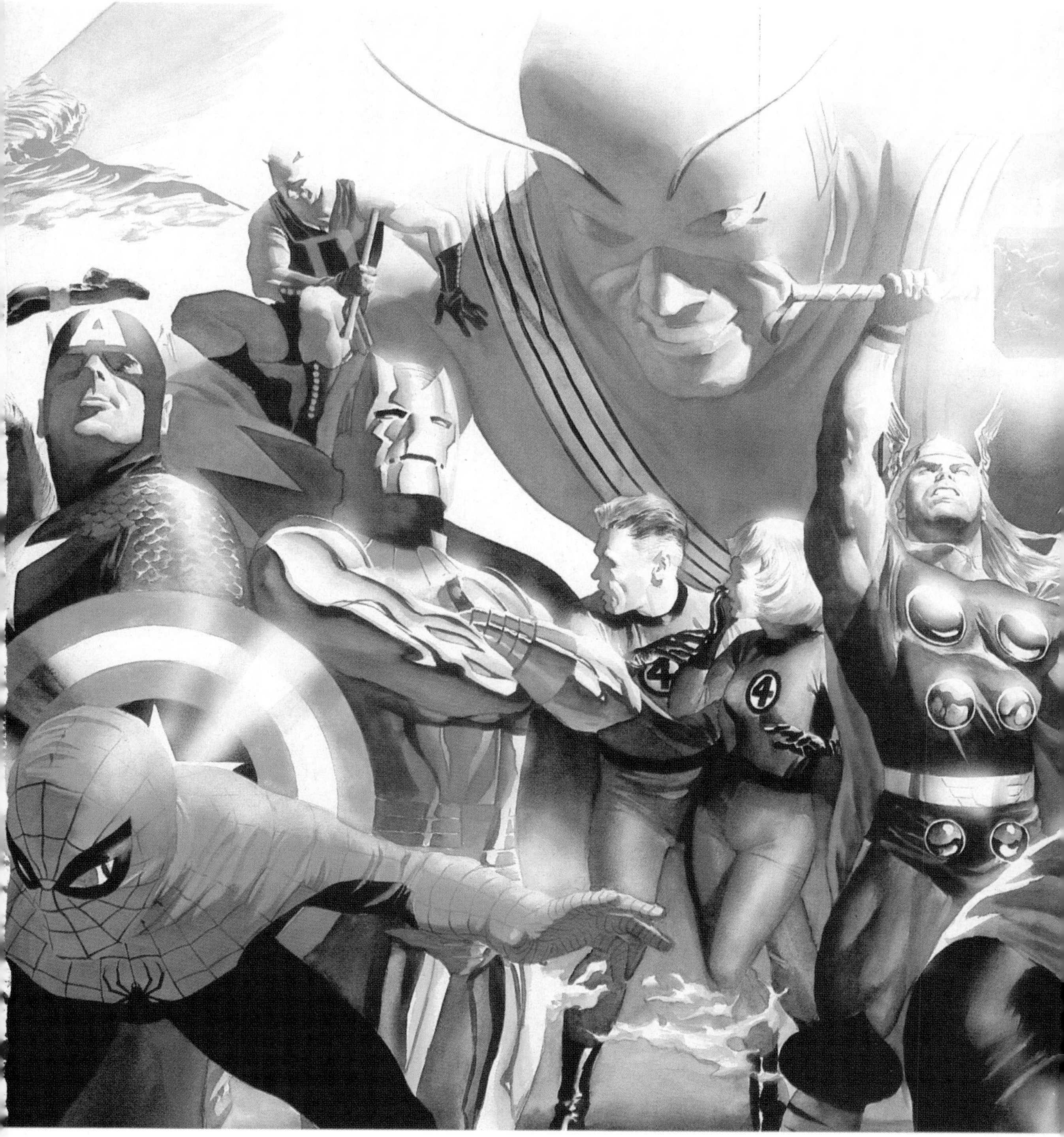

MARVEL

ART OF MARVEL COMICS VOL. 1. First printing 2003. ISBN# 0-7851-1163-8. Published by MARVEL COMICS, a division of MARVEL ENTERTAINMENT GROUP, INC. OFFICE OF PUBLICATION: 10 East 40th Street, New York, NY 10016. Copyright © 2003 Marvel Characters, Inc. All rights reserved. $29.99 per copy in the U.S. and $48.00 in Canada (GST #R127032852); Canadian Agreement #40668537. All characters featured in this issue and the distinctive names and likenesses thereof, and all related indicia are trademarks of Marvel Characters, Inc. No similarity between any of the names, characters, persons, and/or institutions in this magazine with those of any living or dead person or institution is intended, and any such similarity which may exist is purely coincidental. **Printed in Canada.** ALLEN LIPSON, Chief Executive Officer and General Counsel; AVI ARAD, Chief Creative Officer; GUI KARYO, Chief Information Officer; DAVID BOGART; Managing Editor: STAN LEE, Chairman Emeritus. For information regarding advertising in Marvel Comics or on Marvel.com, please contact Russell Brown, Executive Vice President, Consumer Products, Promotions and Media Sales at rbrown@marvel.com or 212-576-8561.

10 9 8 7 6 5 4 3 2 1

THE ART OF

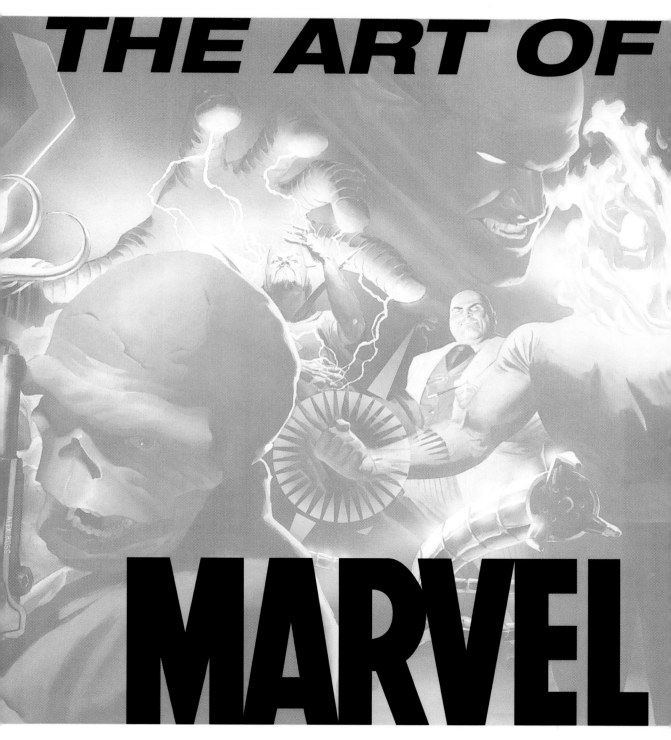

MARVEL

Alex Ross
Cover Art

Jeff Youngquist
Editor

Cory Sedlmeier
Associate Editor

Jennifer Grünwald
Assistant Editor

Johnny Greene
Director of Creative Services

Tom Marvelli
Creative Director

Matty Ryan
Book Designer/Art Director

Joe Quesada
Editor in Chief

Bill Jemas
President

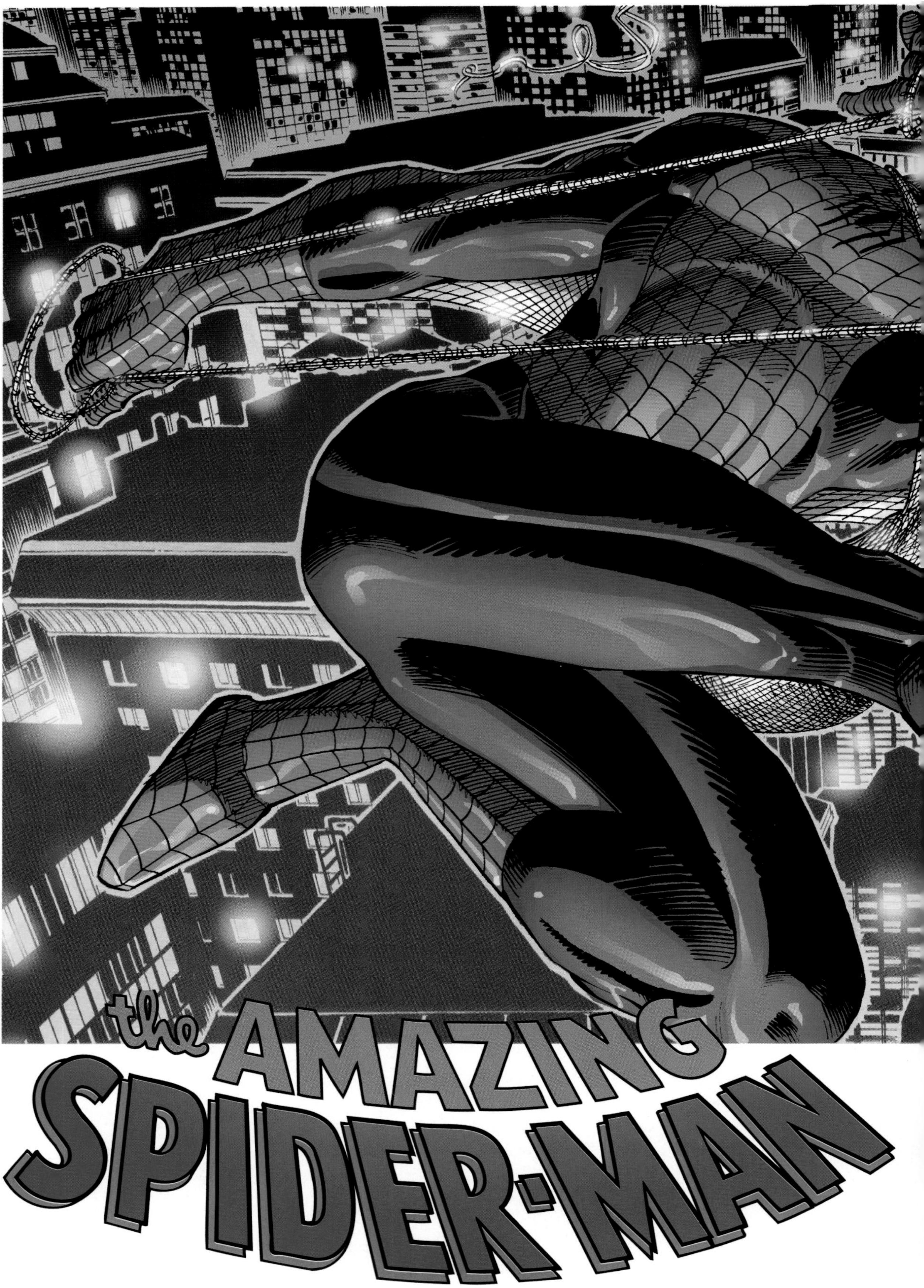
the AMAZING
SPIDER-MAN

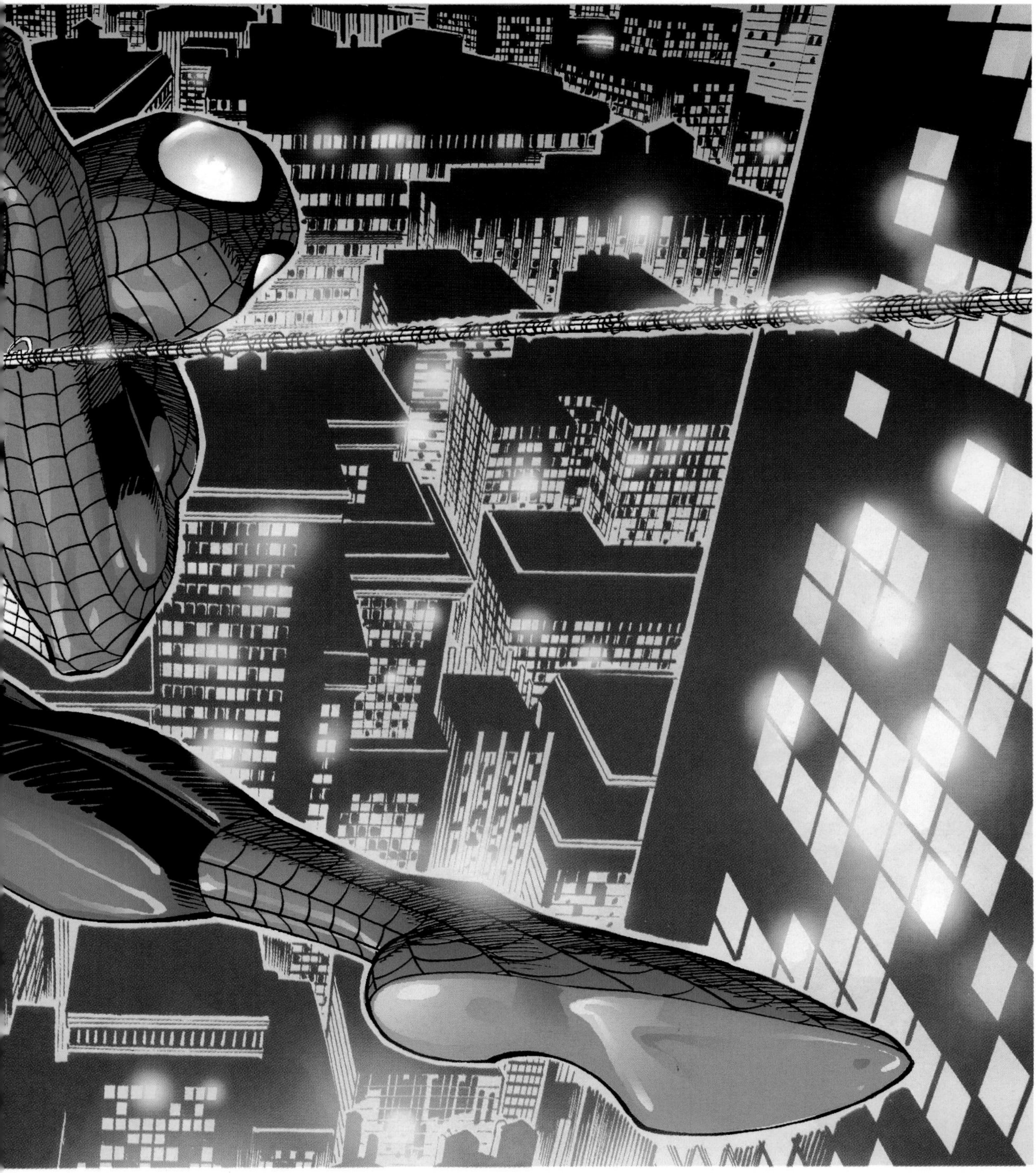

Art by John Romita Jr.

At a demonstration on radiation, high-school student Peter Parker was bitten by an irradiated spider, from which he gained the arachnid's incredible abilities. When a burglar killed his beloved Uncle Ben, a grief-stricken Peter vowed to use his great powers in the service of his fellow man. He had learned an invaluable lesson: With great power, there must also come great responsibility.

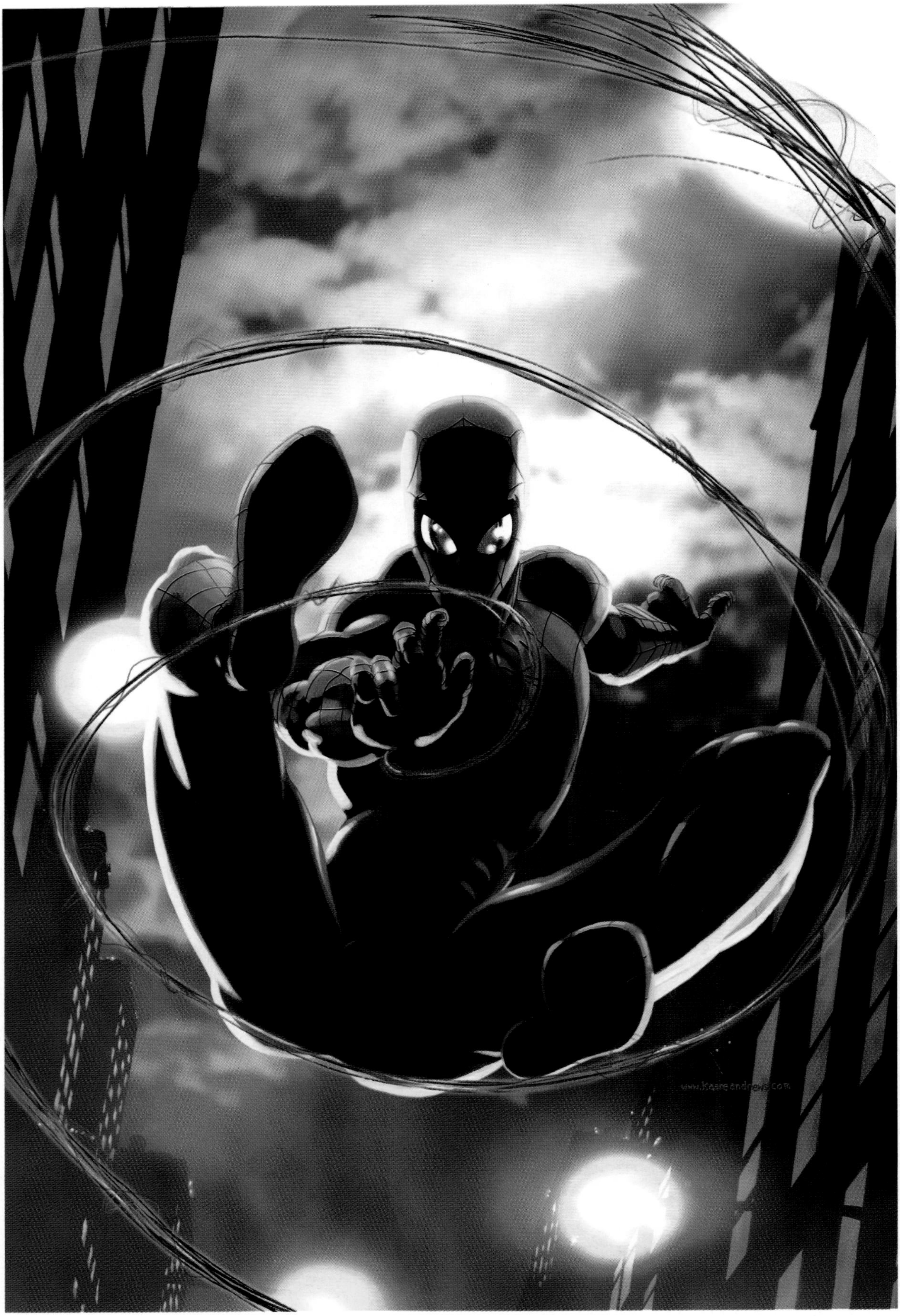
www.kaareandrews.com

Art by Kaare Andrews

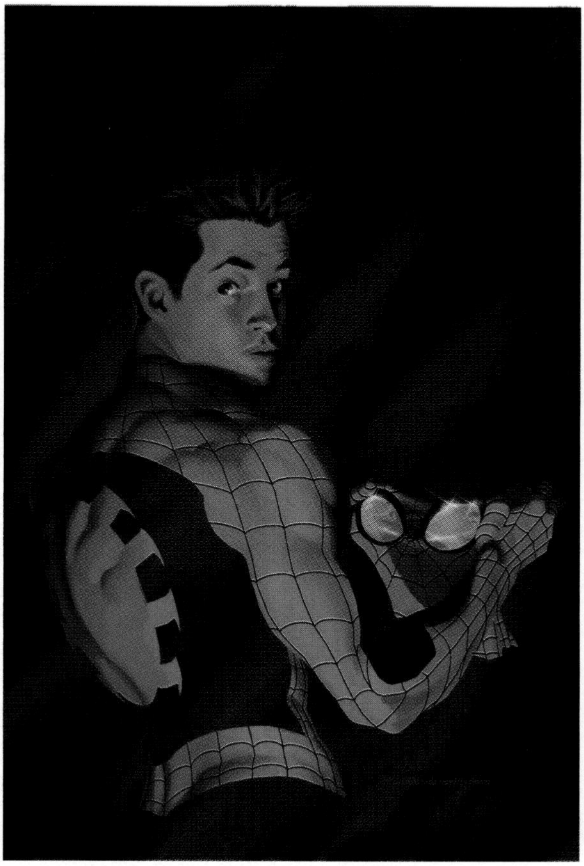

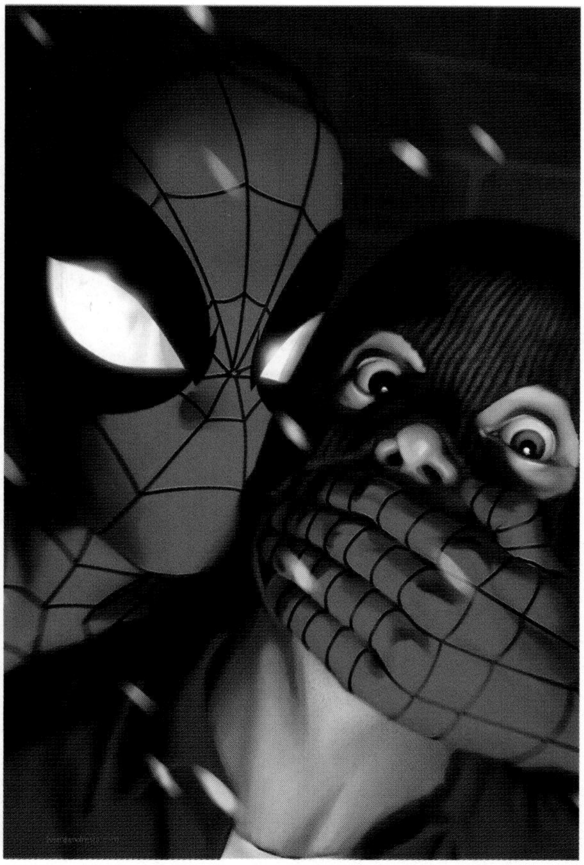

"No matter how many times Spider-Man clocks Doctor Octopus or saves the damsel in distress, it is the ongoing saga of his life that fascinates us most. Beneath the tights and beyond the famous mantra lies a guy like any of us ... just doing his best to be his best, for himself and those he loves."

Axel Alonso
Editor
Amazing Spider-Man

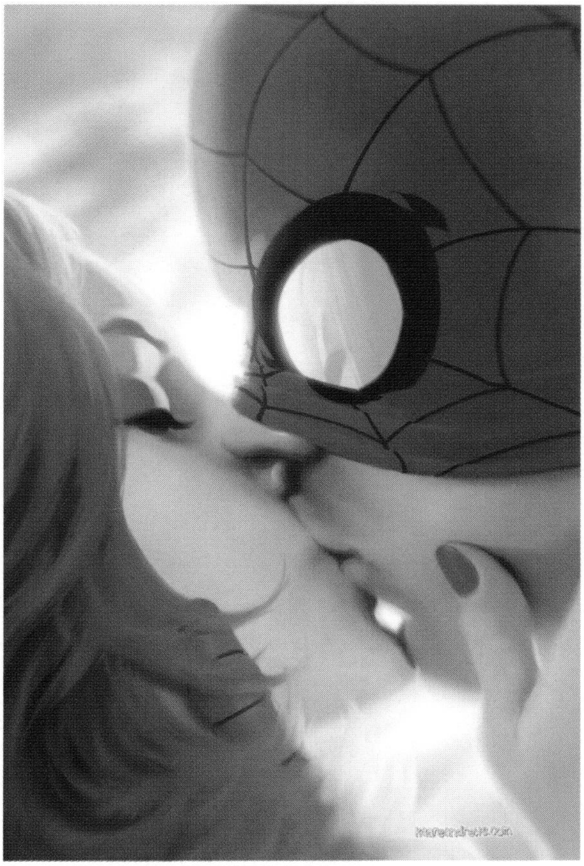

Art by Kaare Andrews

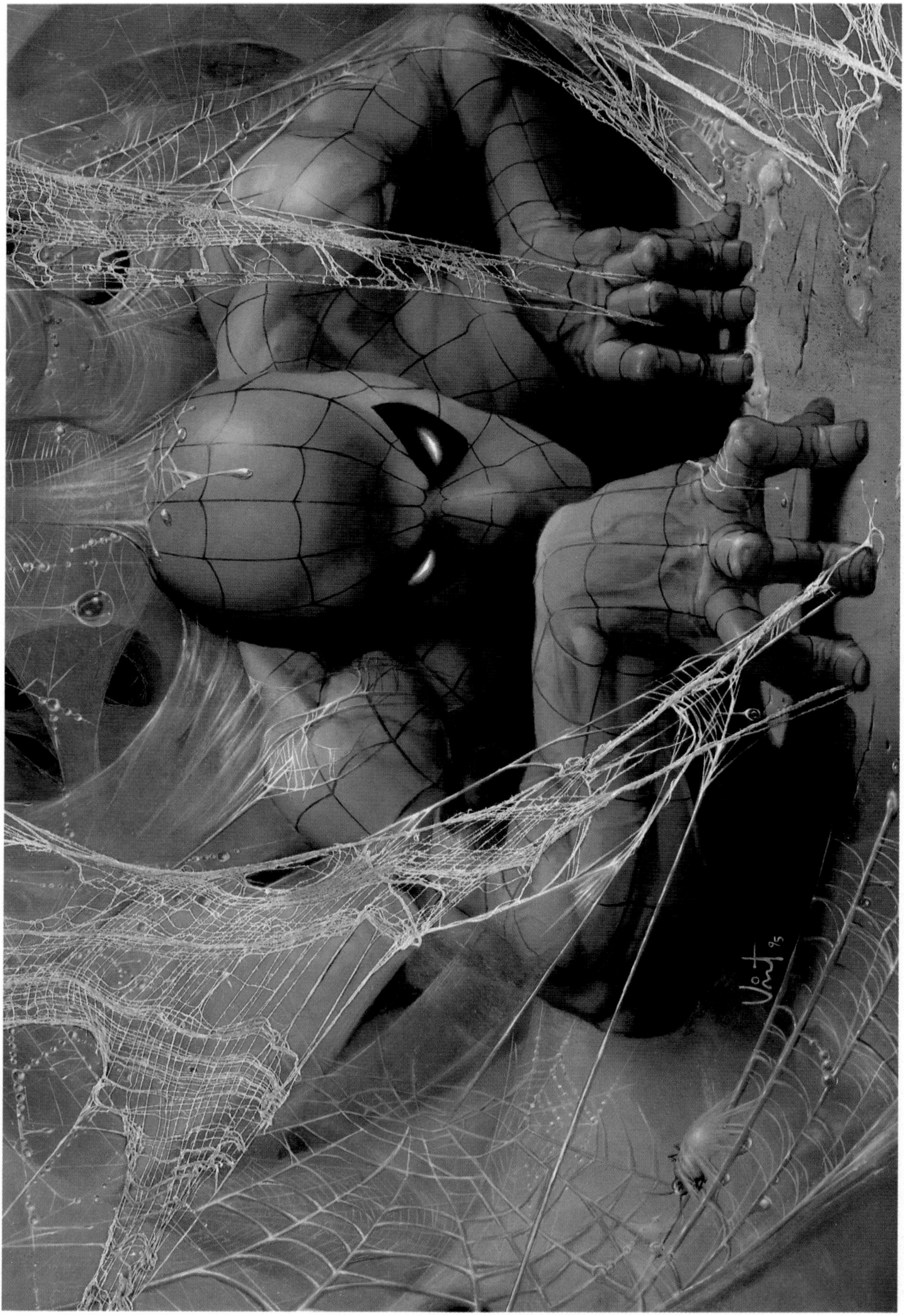

Art by Vince Evans

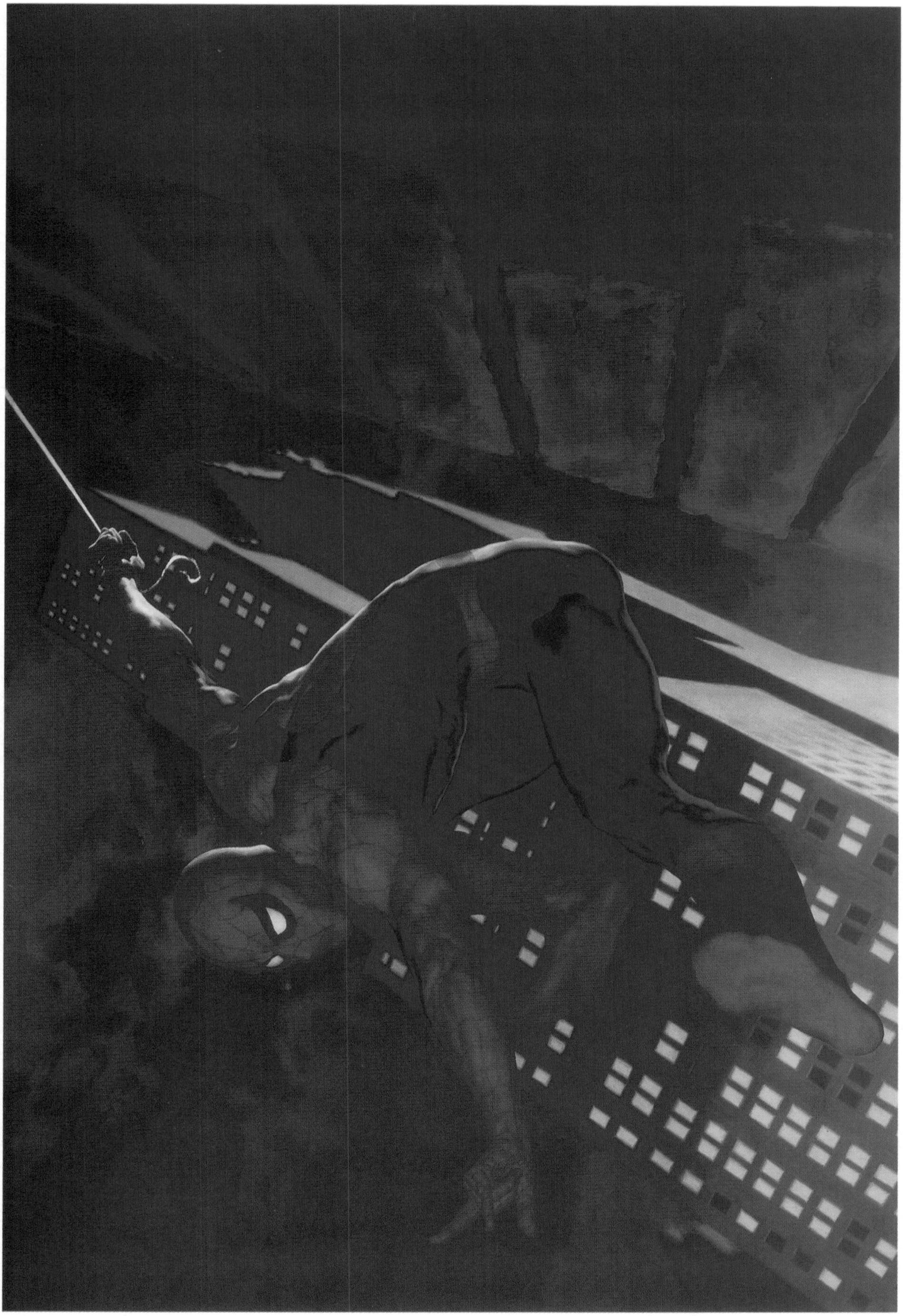
Art by Glen Orbik

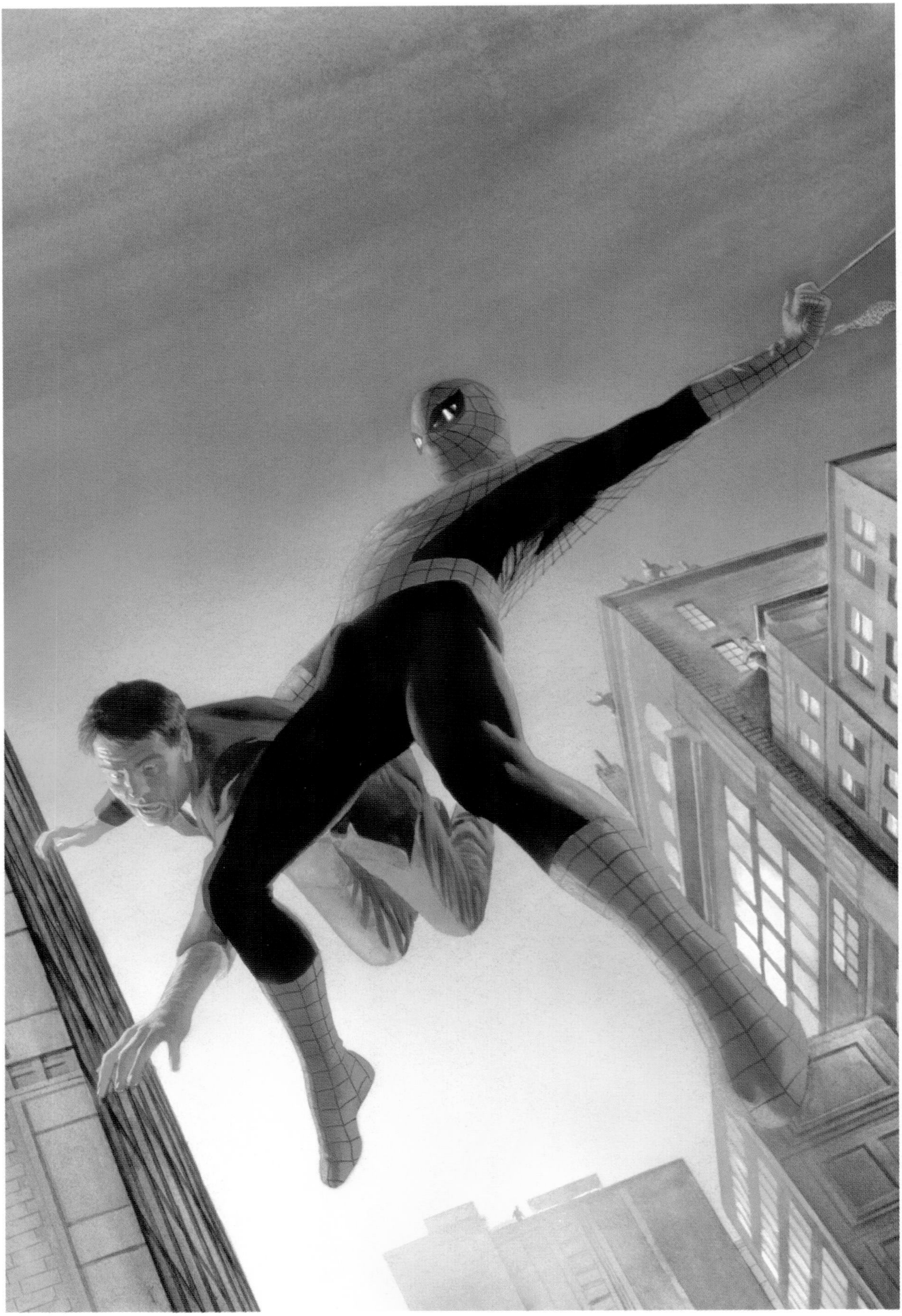

Art by Alex Ross

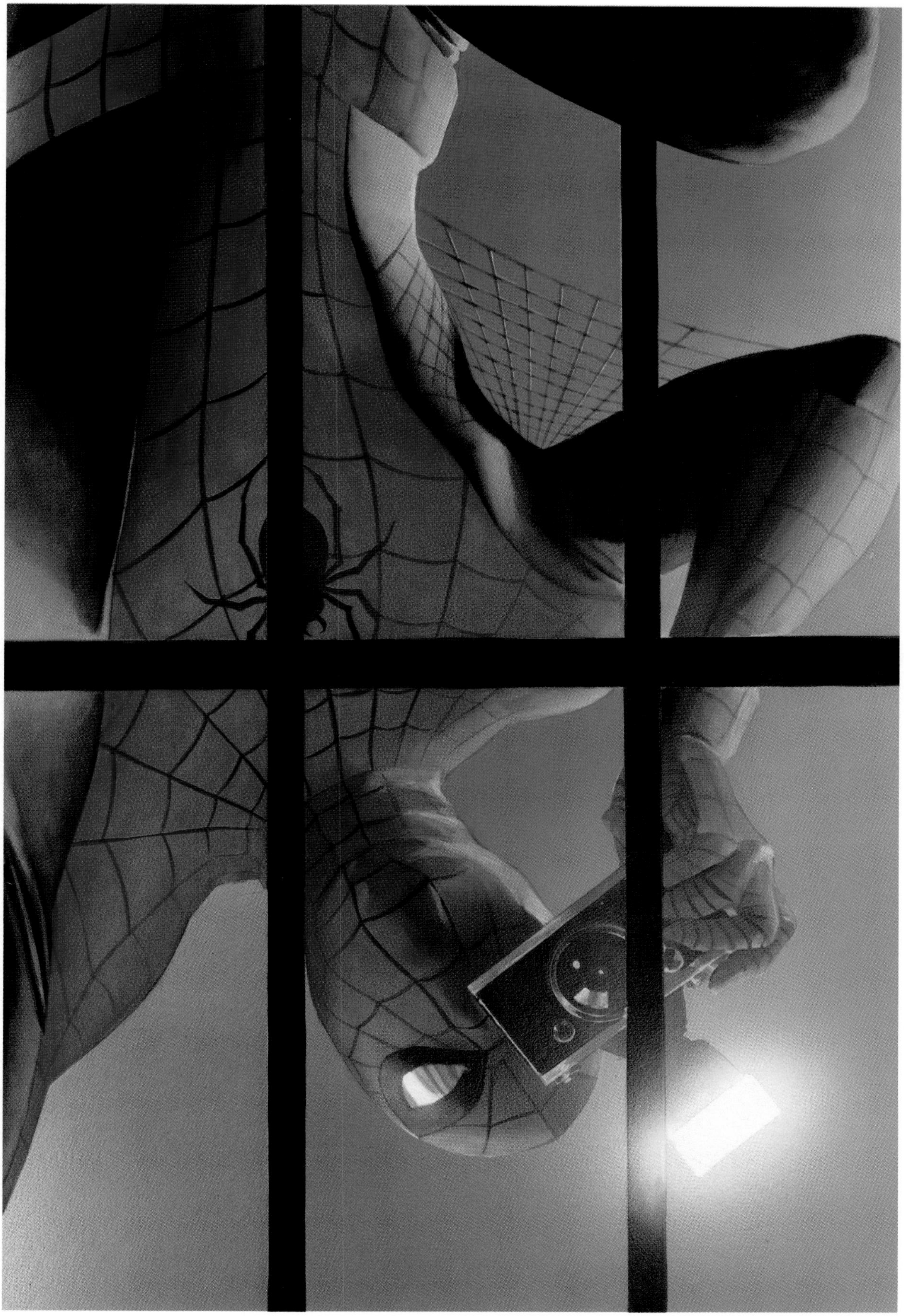

Art by Alex Ross

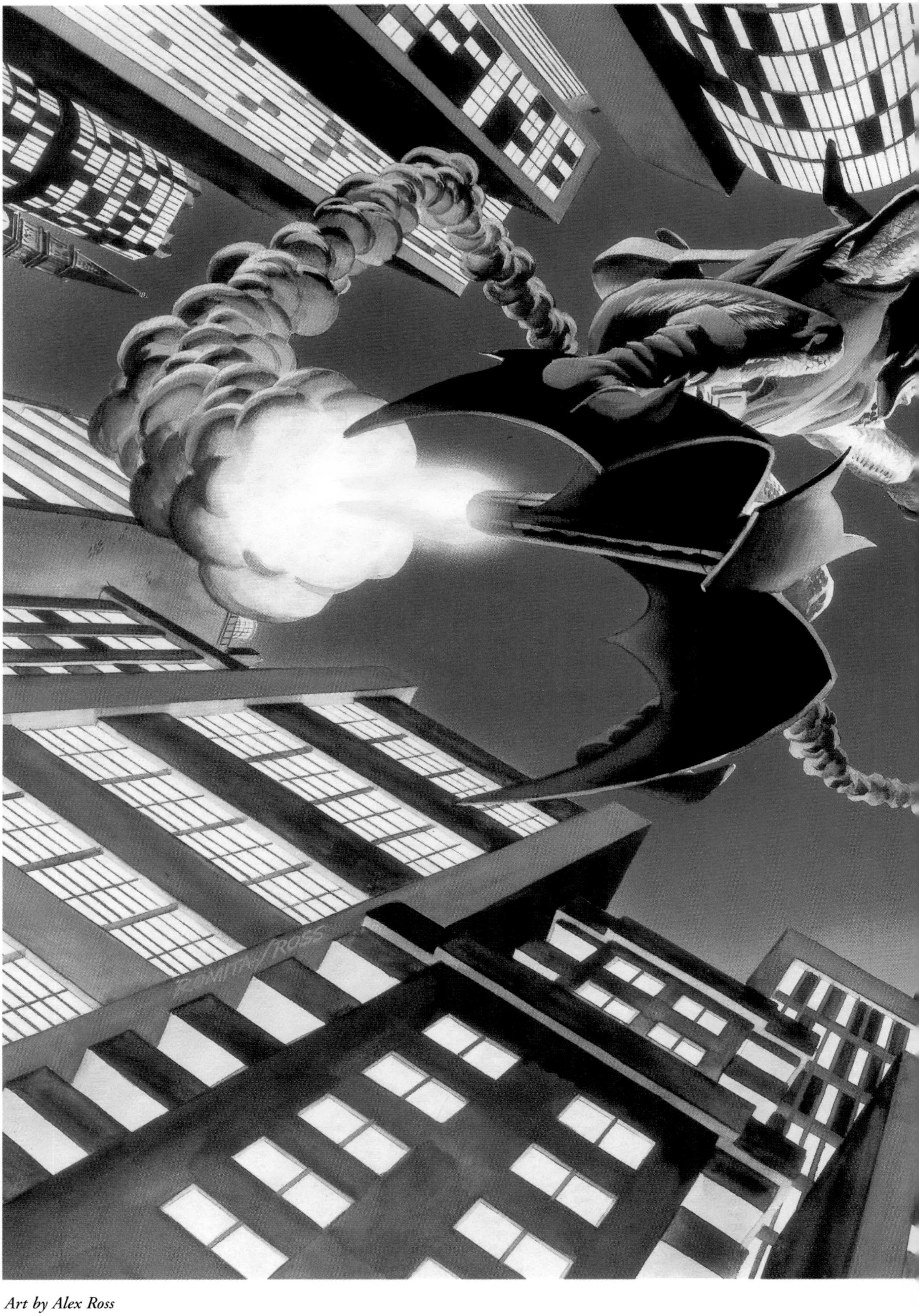
ROMITA/ROSS

Art by Alex Ross

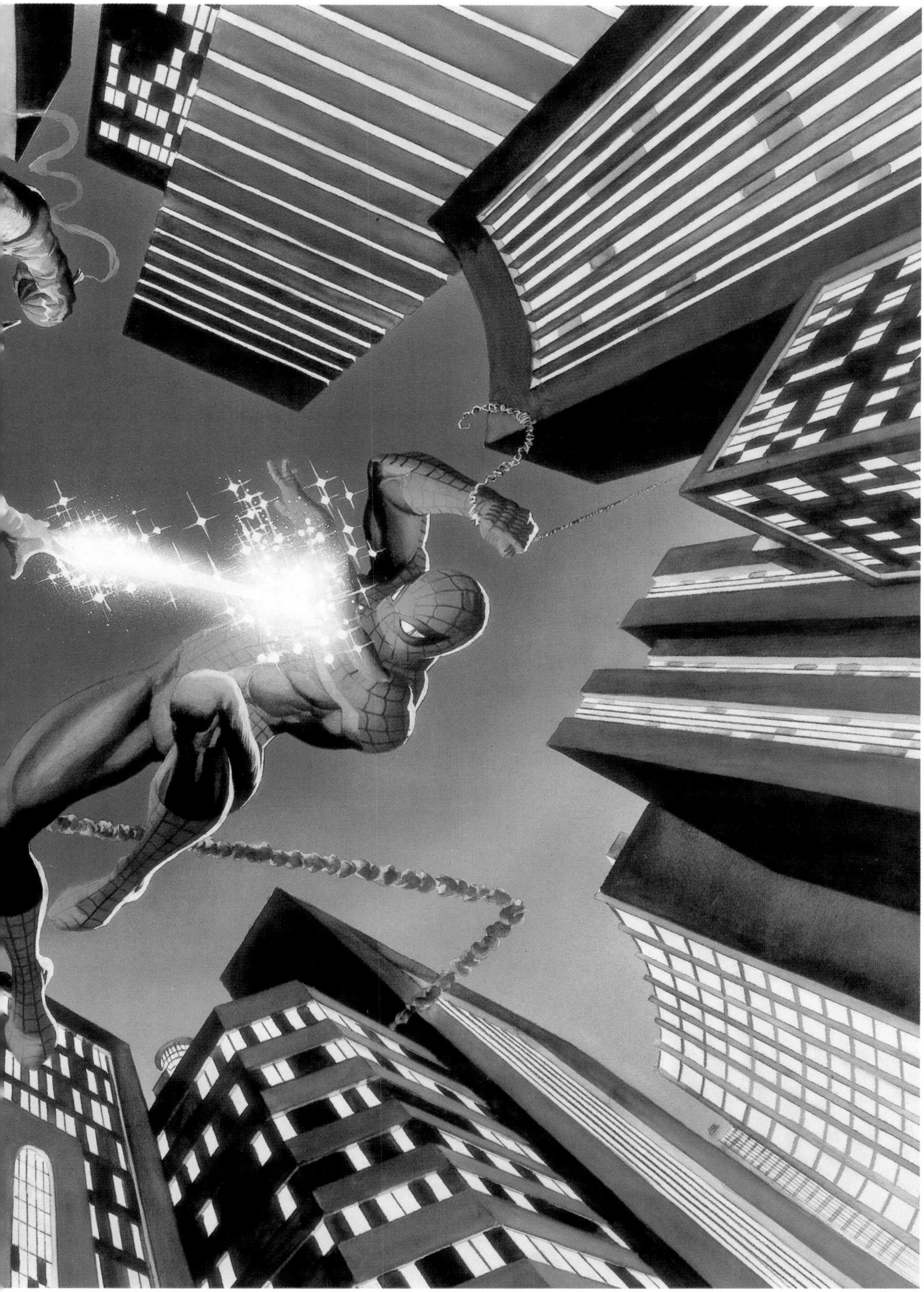

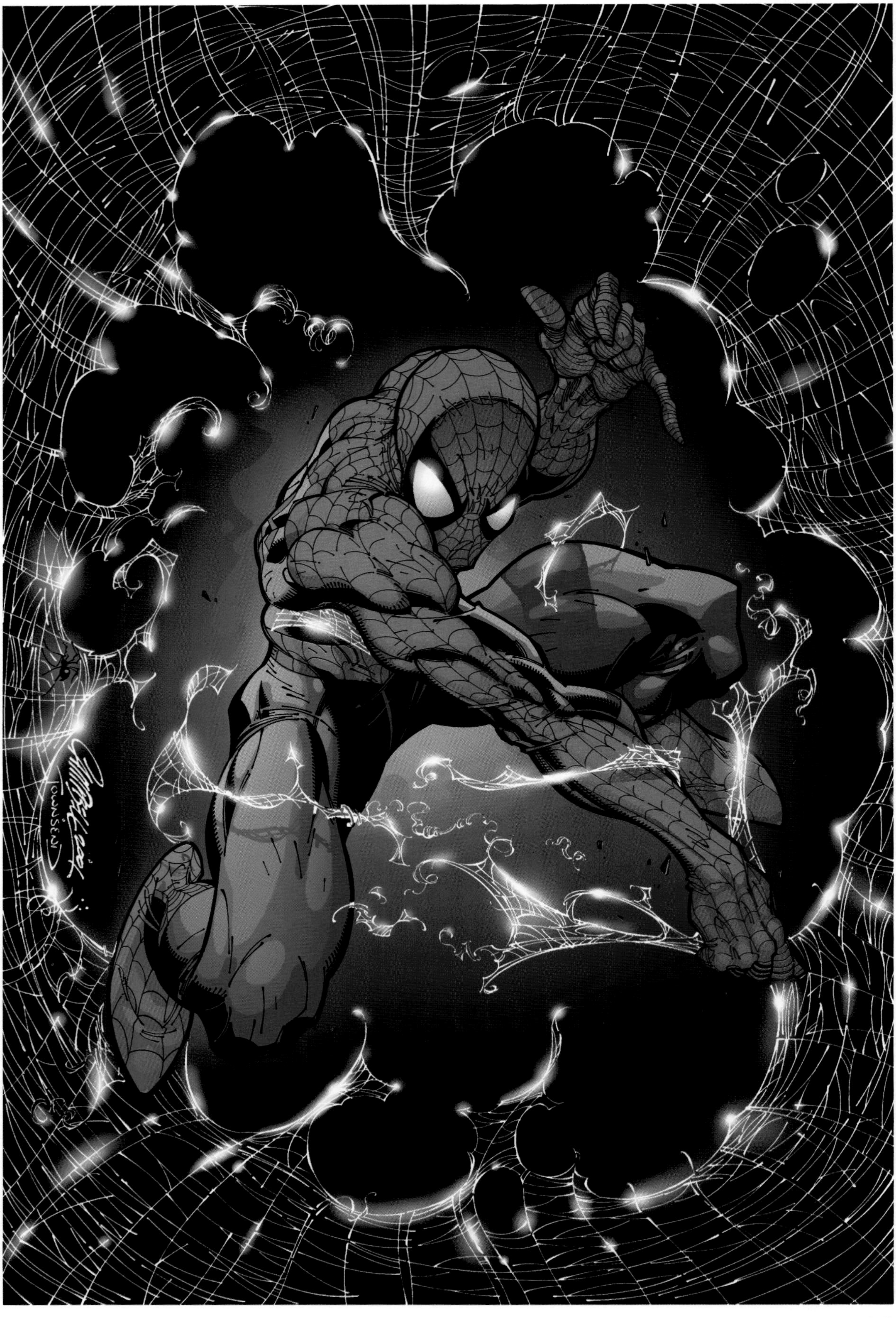

Art by J. Scott Campbell

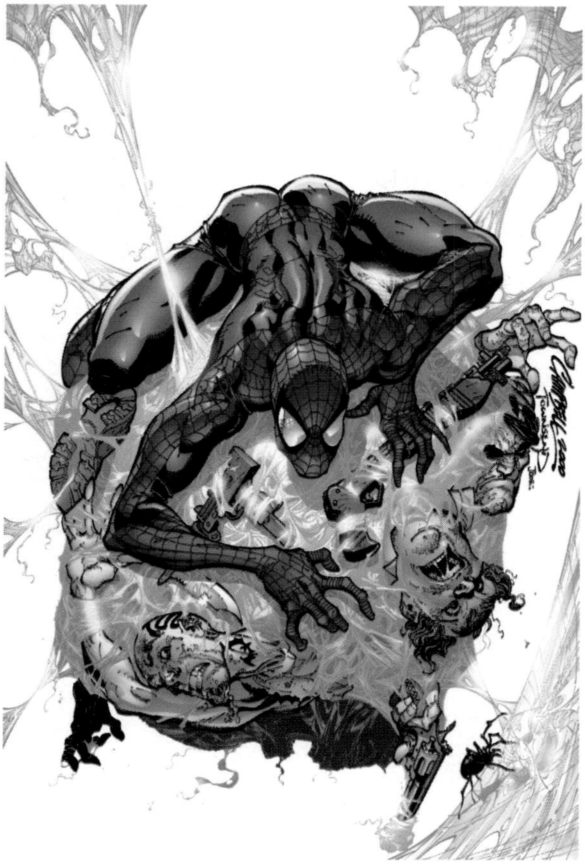

"The world's favorite wall-crawler, who violated every rule in comic-book publishing history, became the most popular super hero in all of comic-bookdom! And the more unique and more off-beat we made him, the more his popularity grew ... Not bad for a guy named after an insect that everyone hates!"

Stan Lee
Spider-Man co-creator

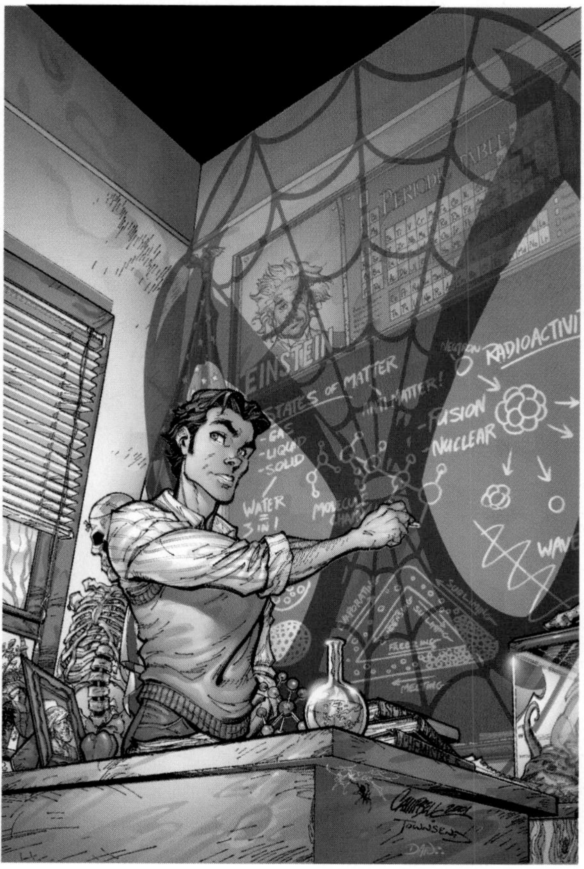
STATES OF MATTER
FUSION
NUCLEAR
WATER

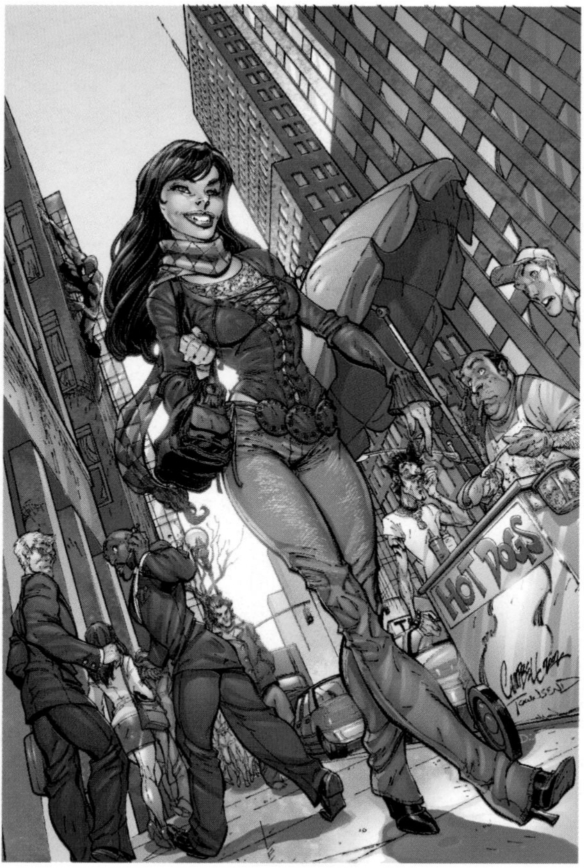
HOT DOGS

Art by J. Scott Campbell

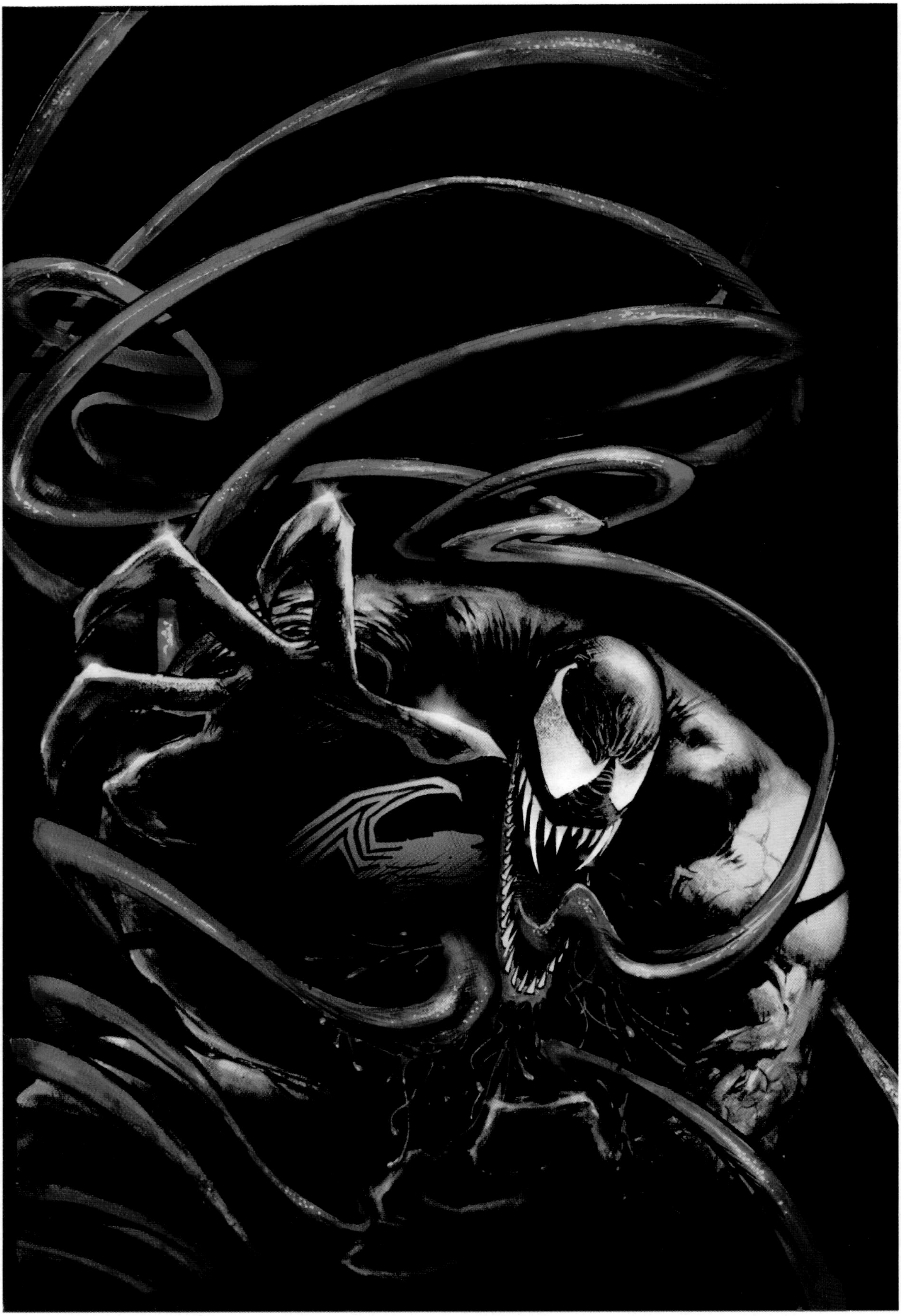

Art by Sam Kieth

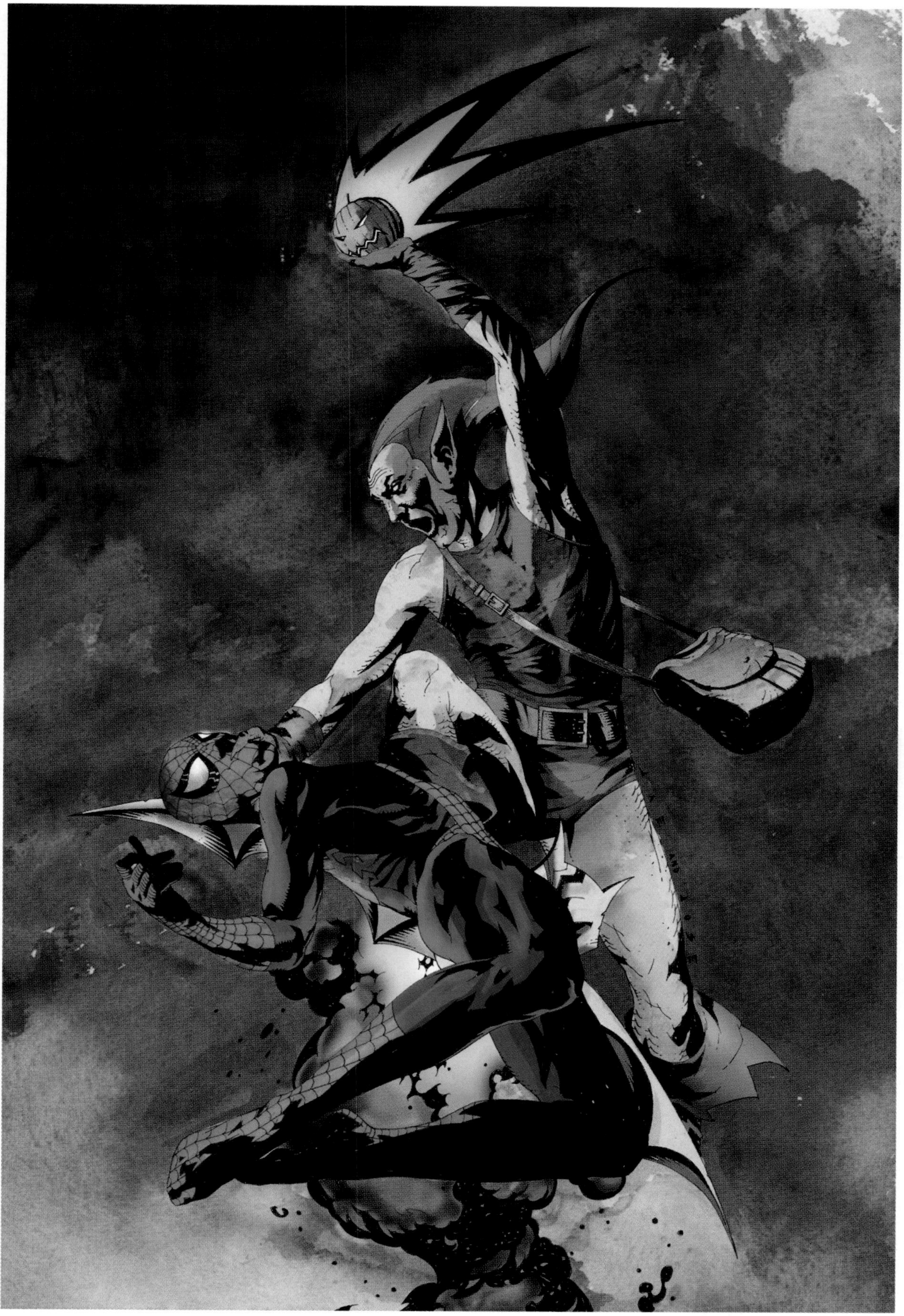

Art by Jae Lee

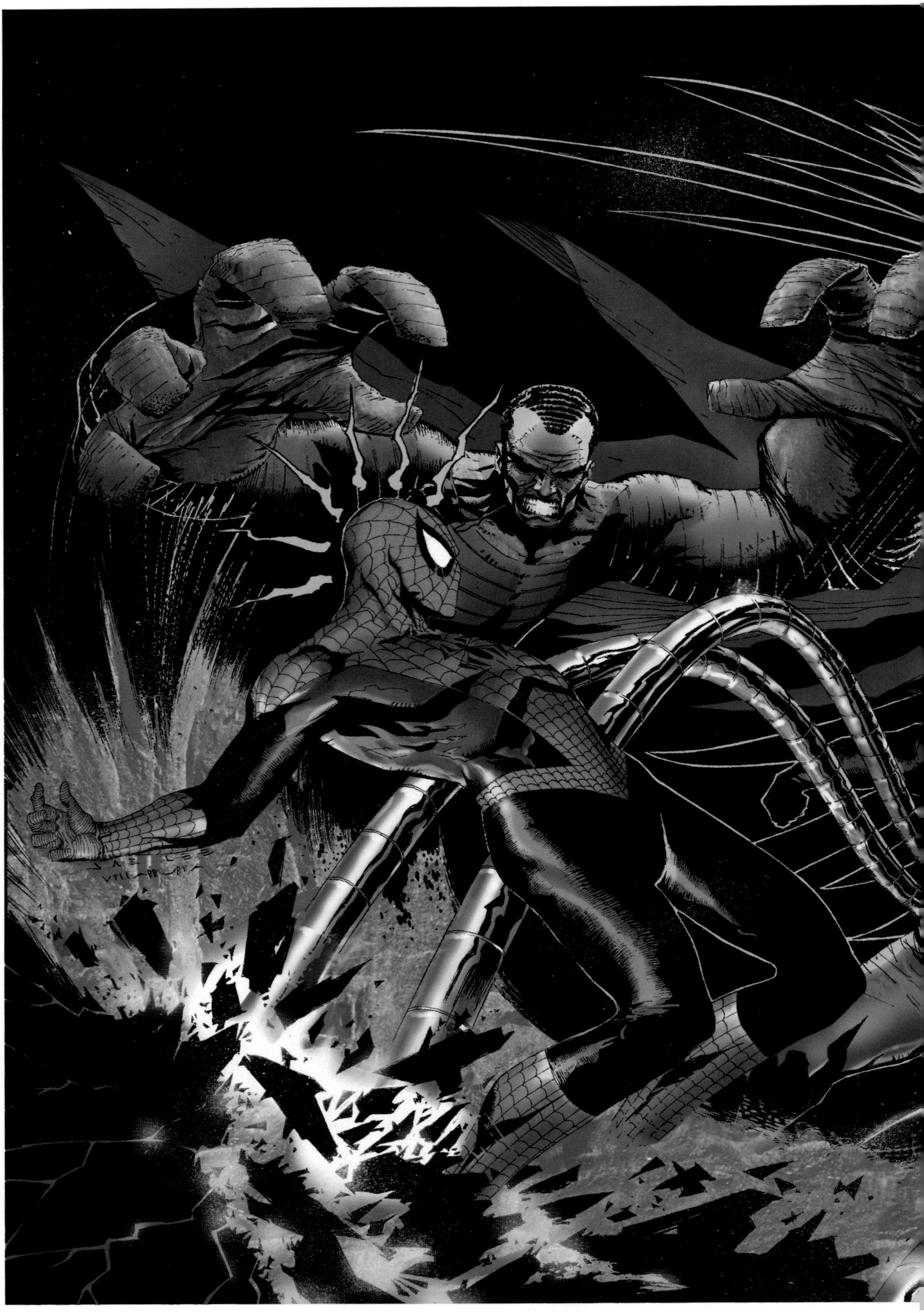

Art by Jae Lee

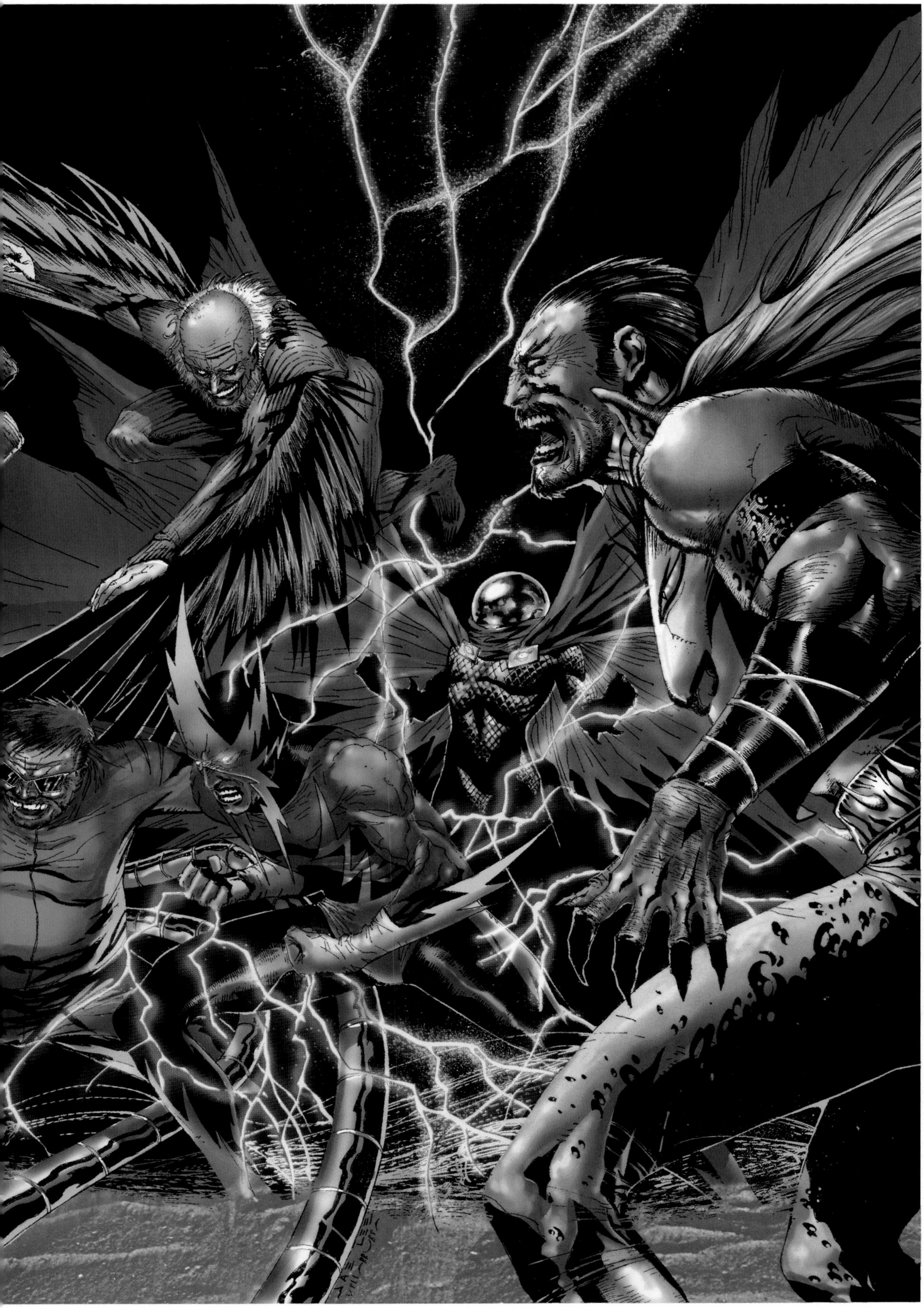

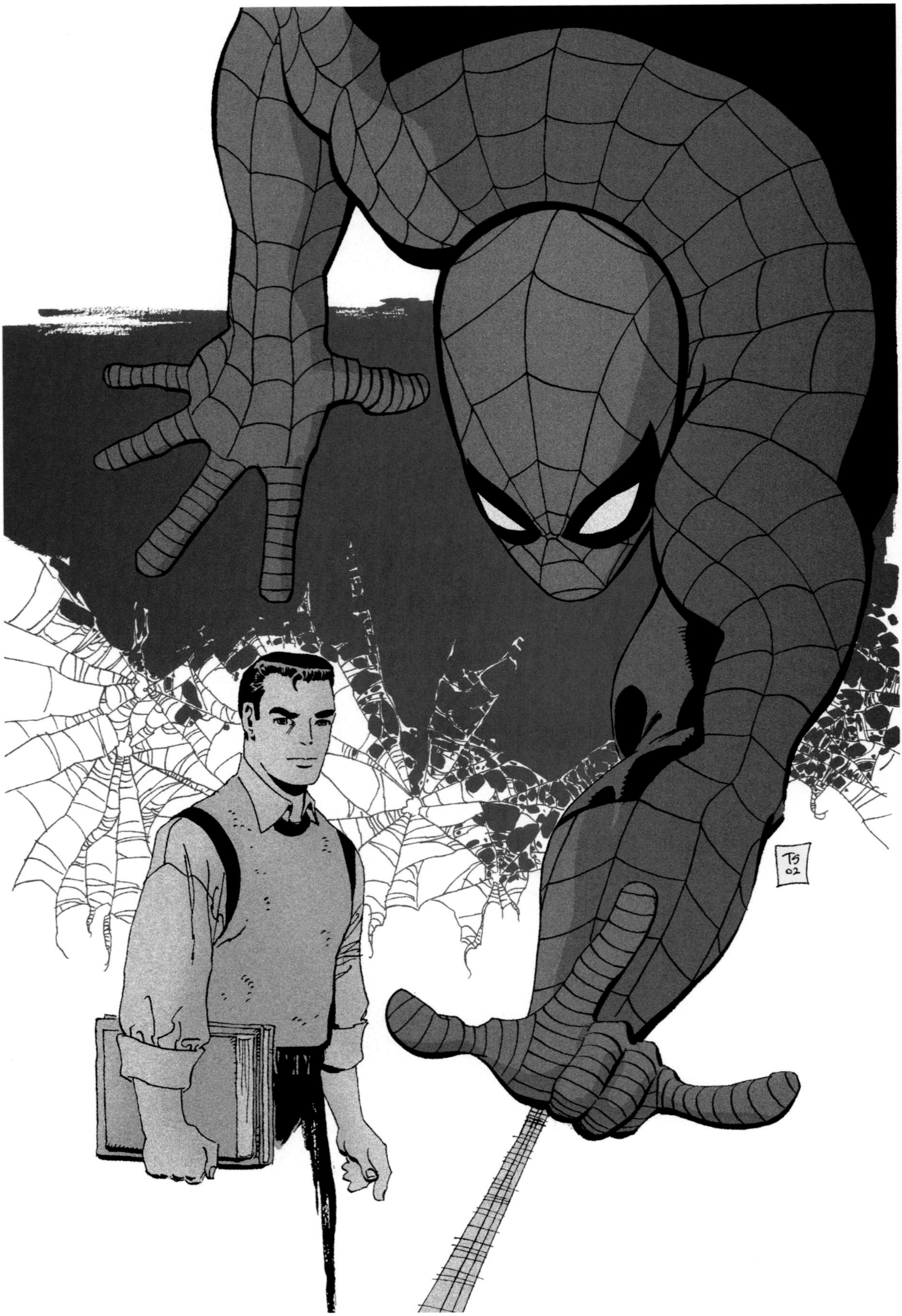
TS
02

Art by Tim Sale

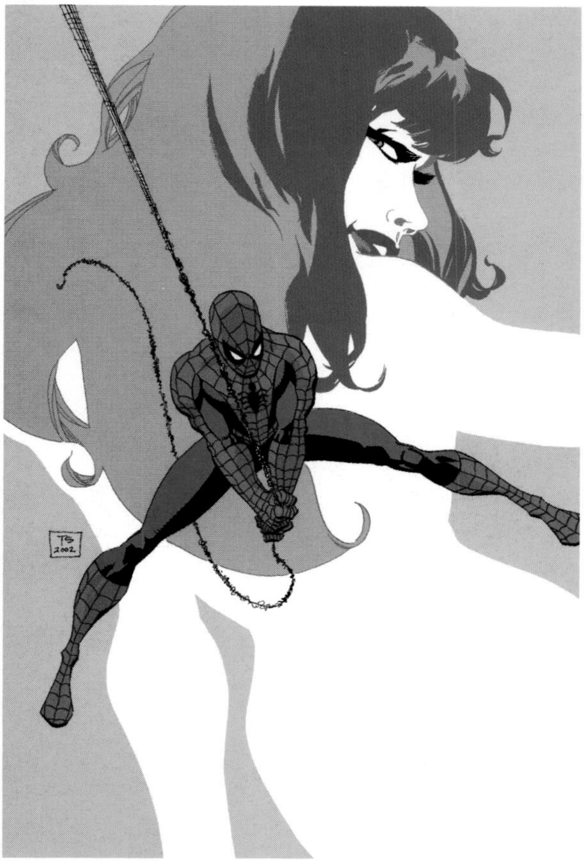

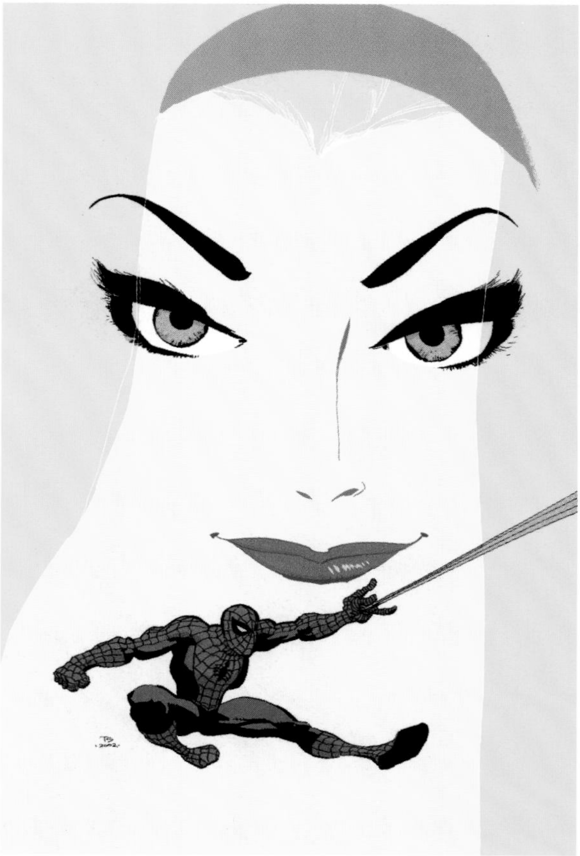

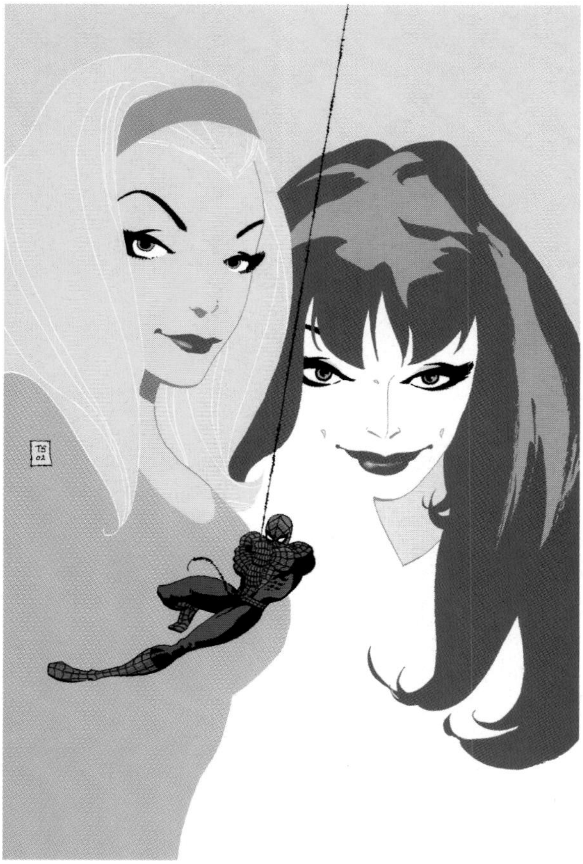

Art by Tim Sale

"I knew that Gwen and MJ were going to be the stars of this series, at least they *would* if I could just figure out how to give them even a tenth of the style and glamour contributed by the incredible John Romita Sr. in the original series. I also knew that there was no way I could ever draw girls as pretty as did Romita ... so I had to come up with a style inspired by the master, but still very much my own."

Tim Sale
Artist
Spider-Man: Blue

Art by Joe Quesada

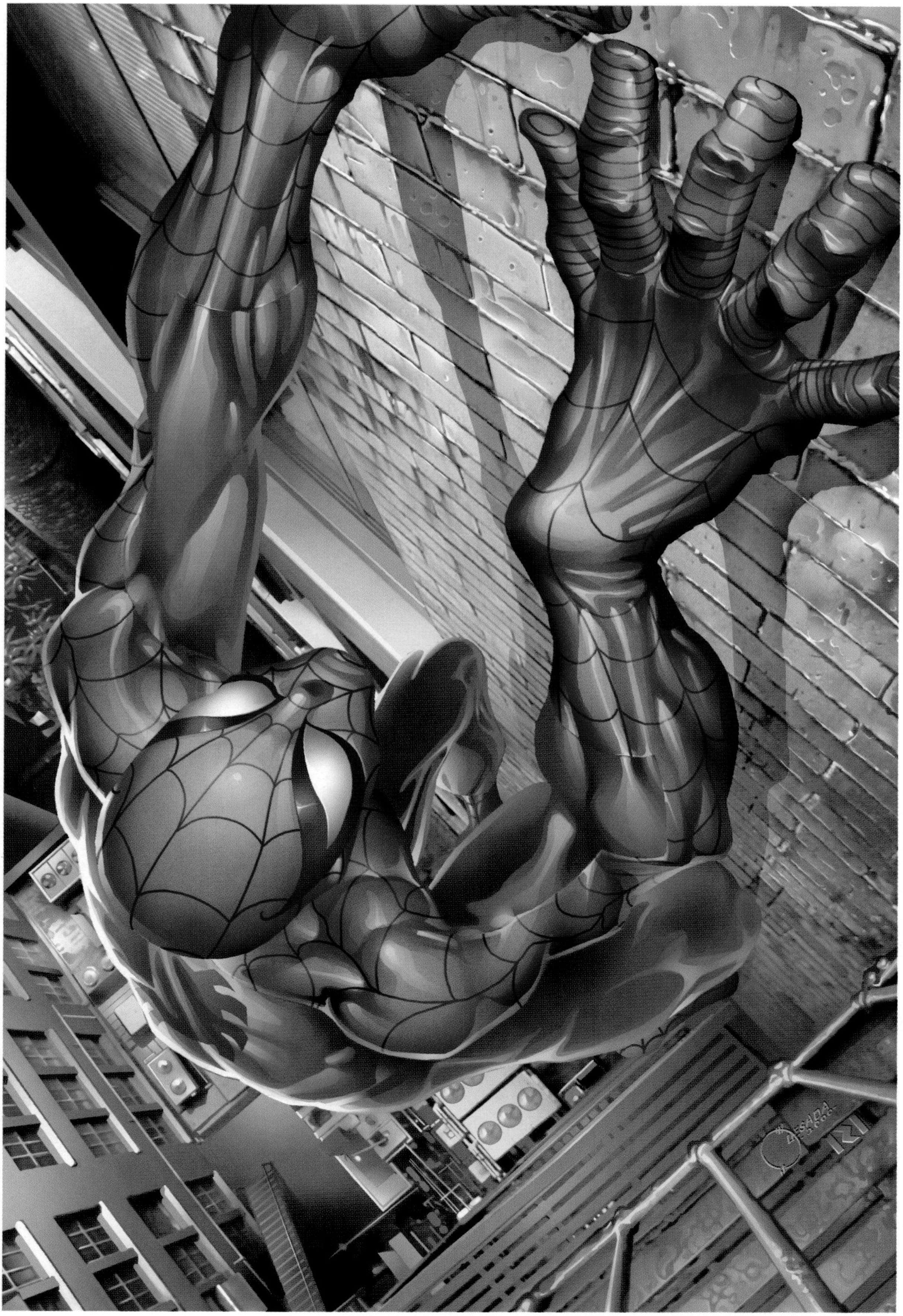
QUESADA

Art by Joe Quesada

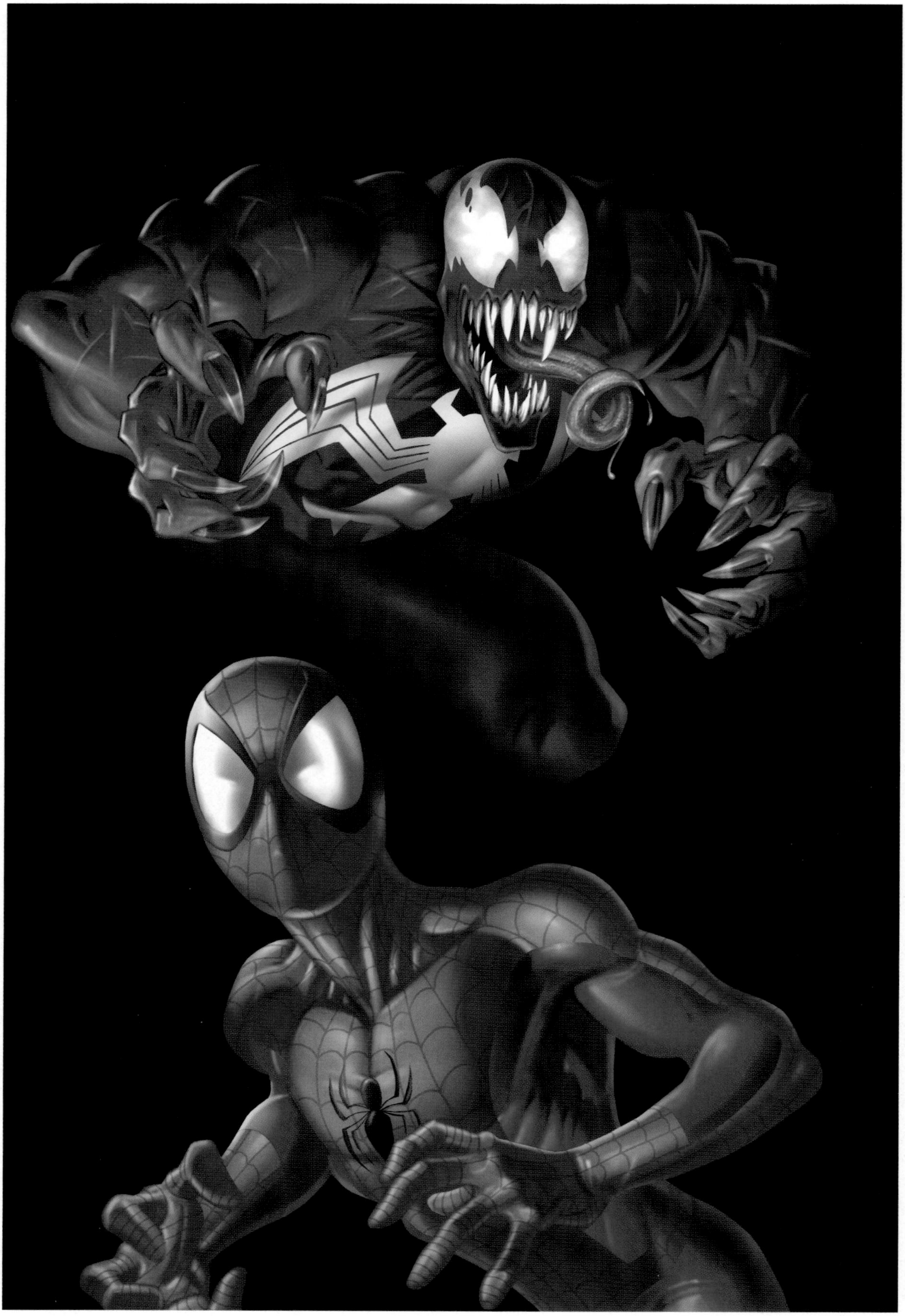

Art by Mark Bagley

"Doesn't matter how over the top I want the action to go. Doesn't matter how subtle or complex I want the emotions of the characters to run. Doesn't matter how fantastical, how realistic, how silly, how intense, how horrific, how charming I hope a page will be. No matter what, [*Ultimate Spider-Man* artist] Mark [Bagley] can do it."

Brian Michael Bendis
Writer
Ultimate Spider-Man

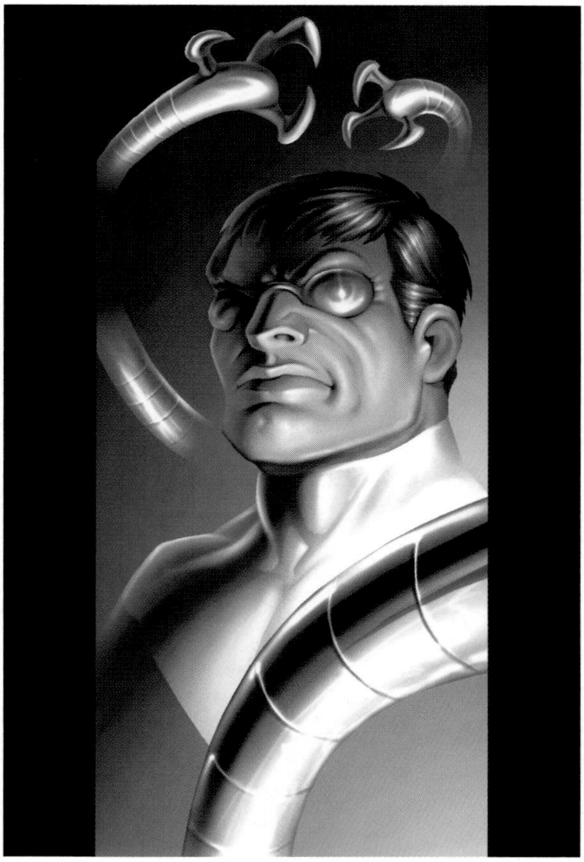

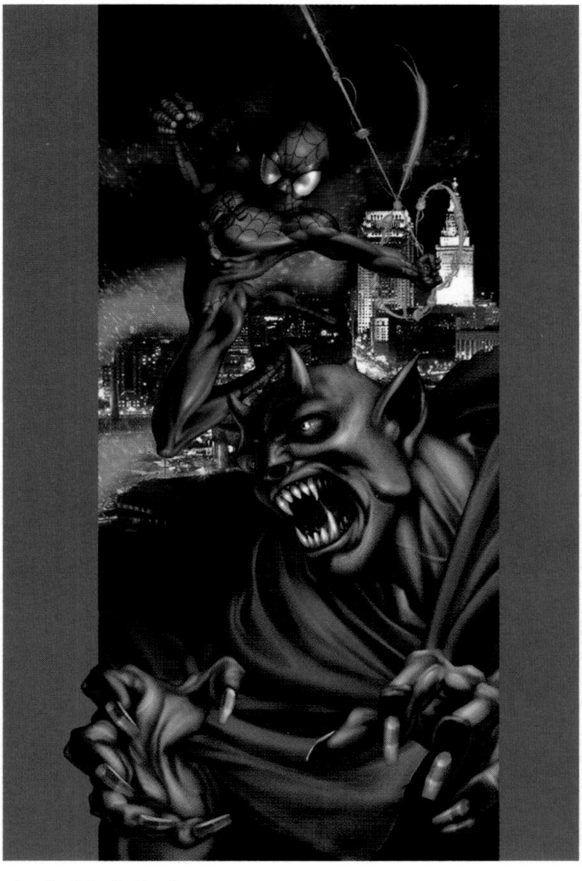

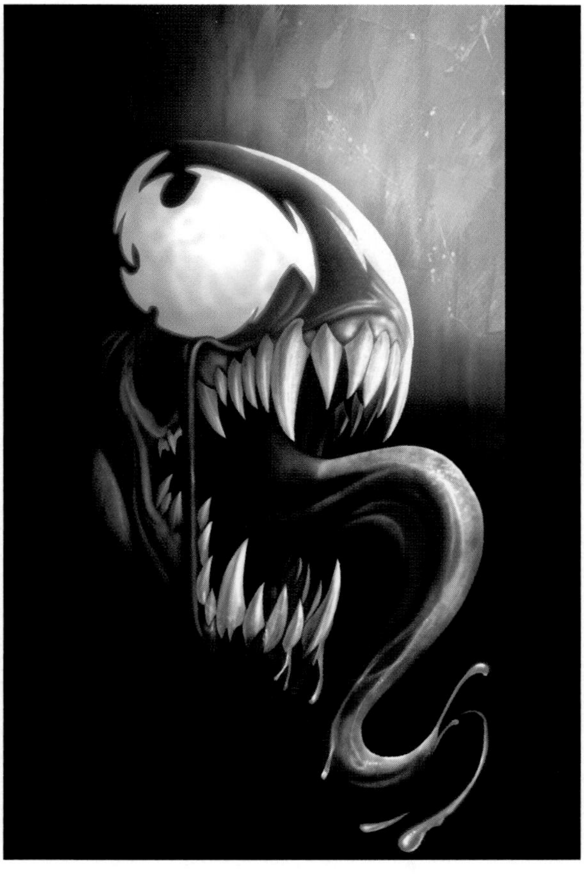

Art by Mark Bagley

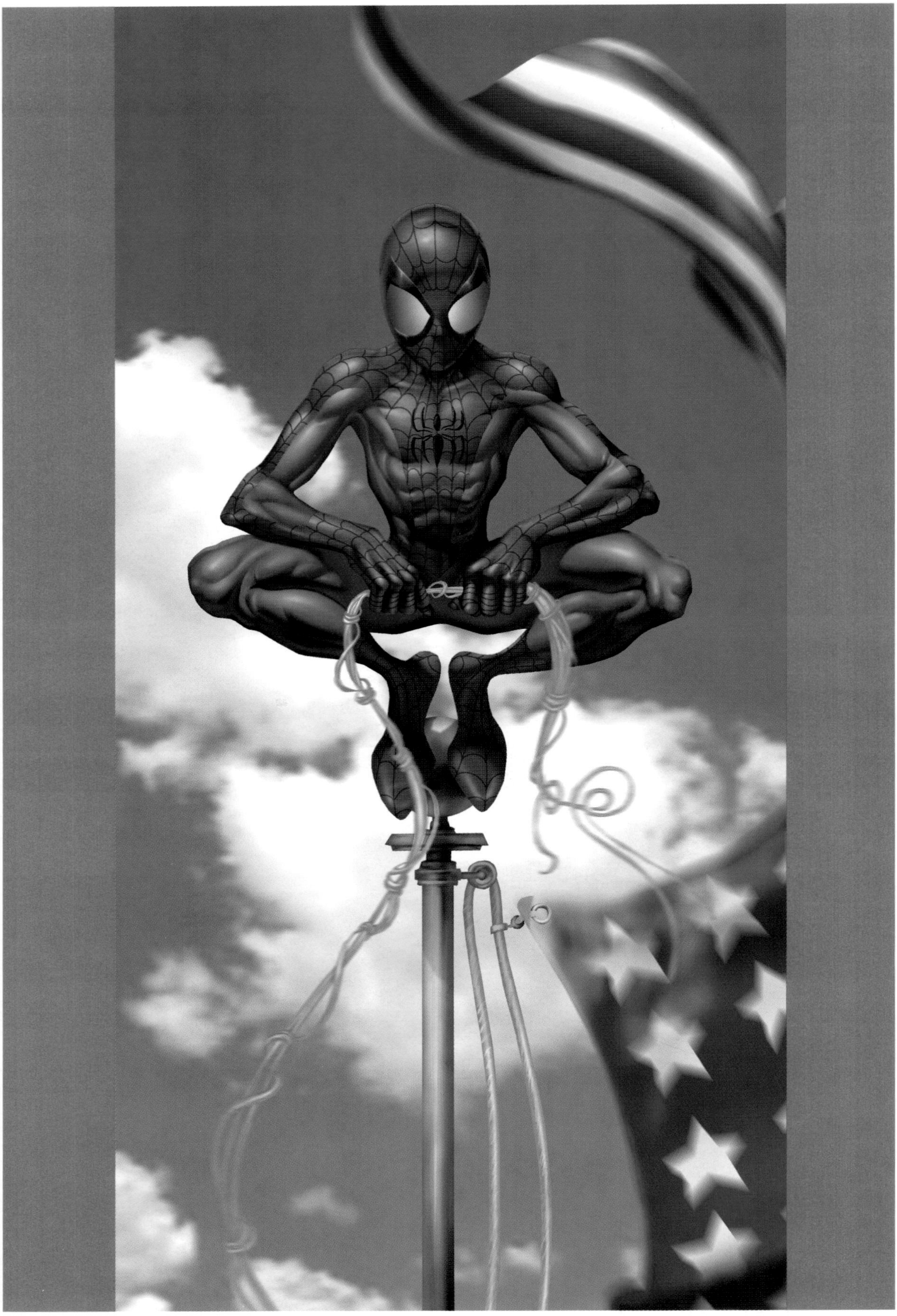

Art by Mark Bagley

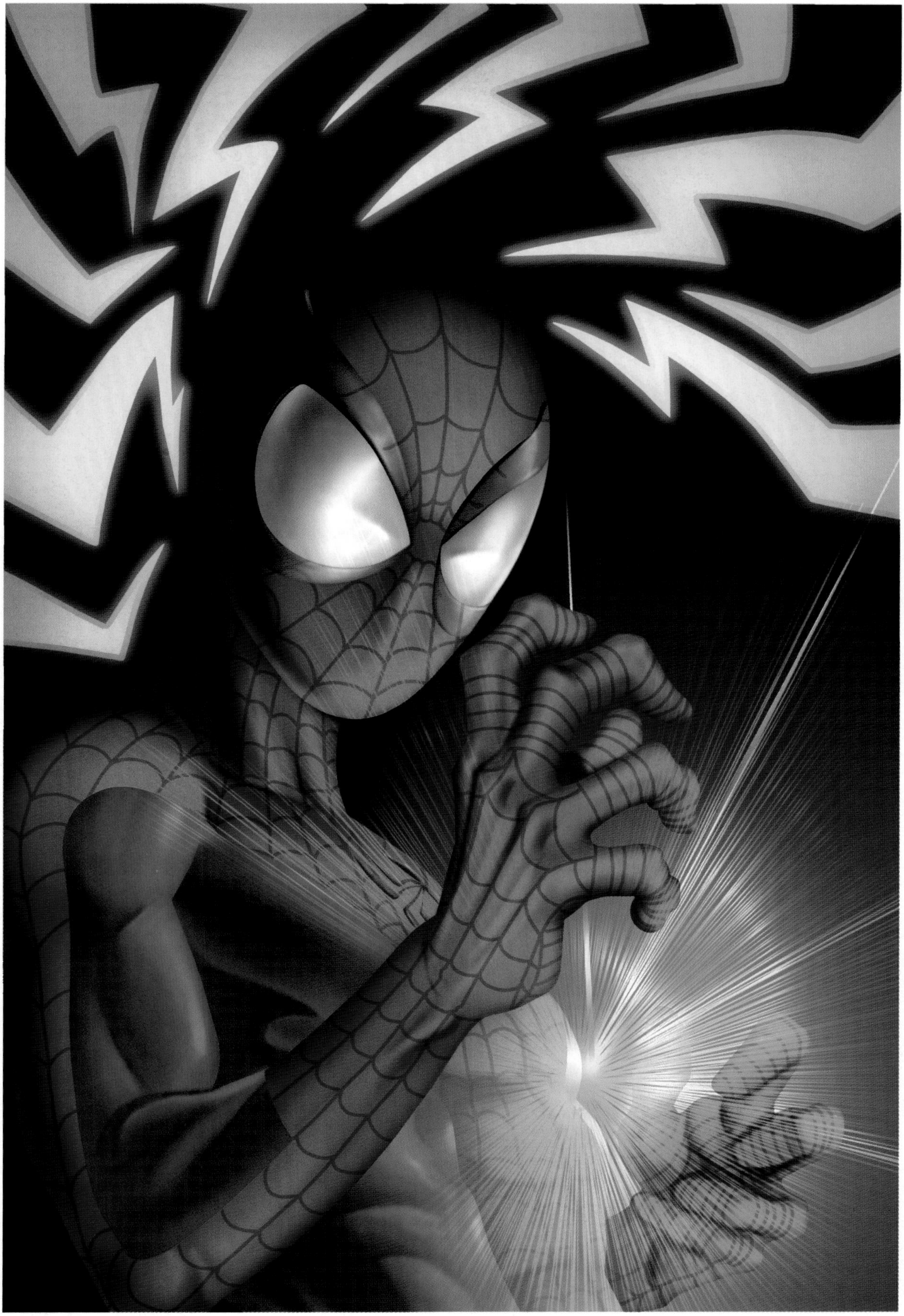

Art by Mark Bagley

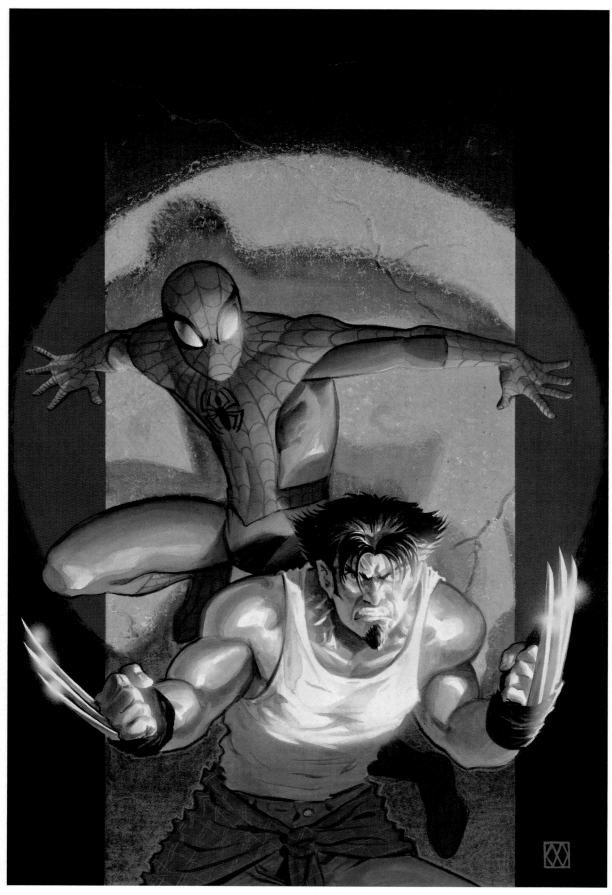

Art by Matt Wagner

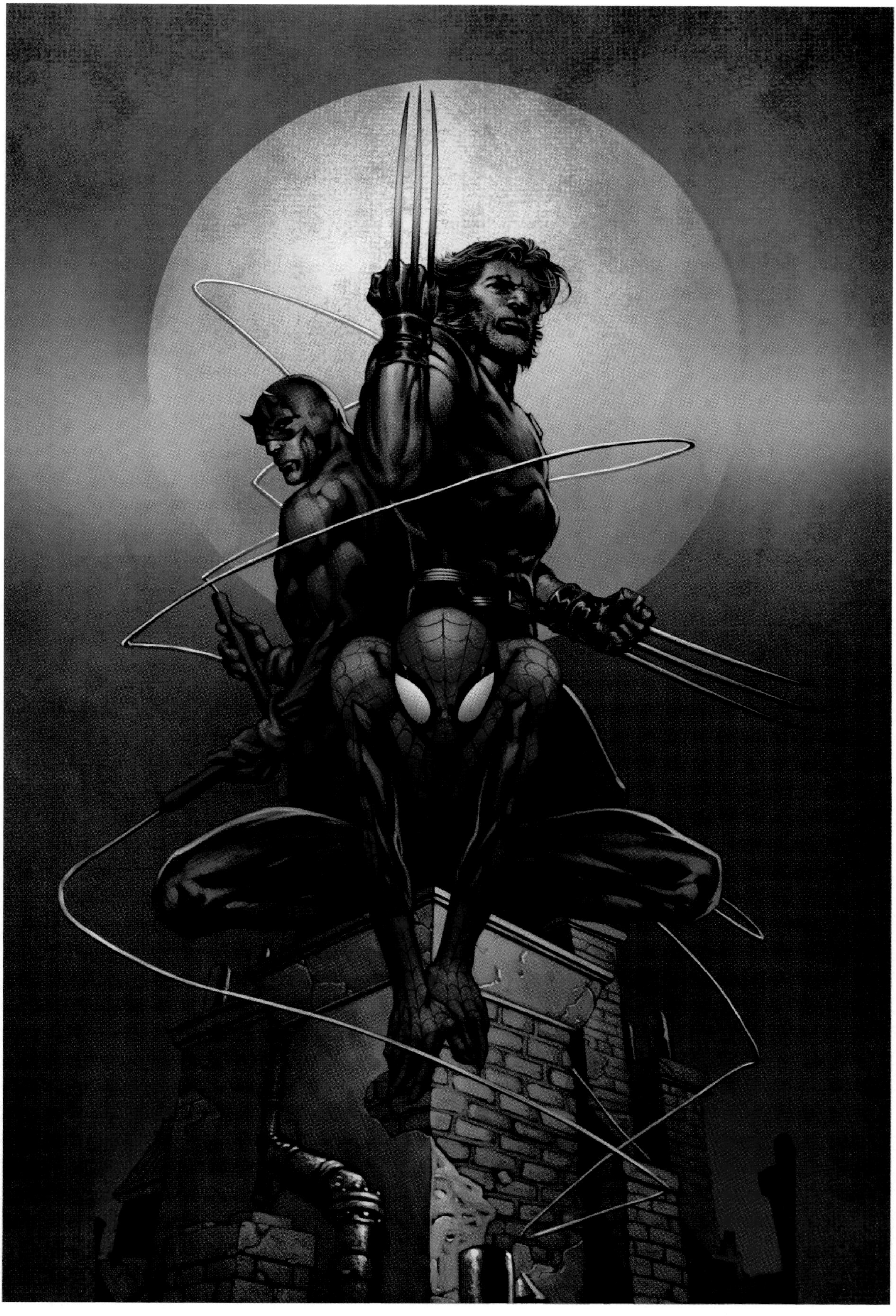

Art by David Finch

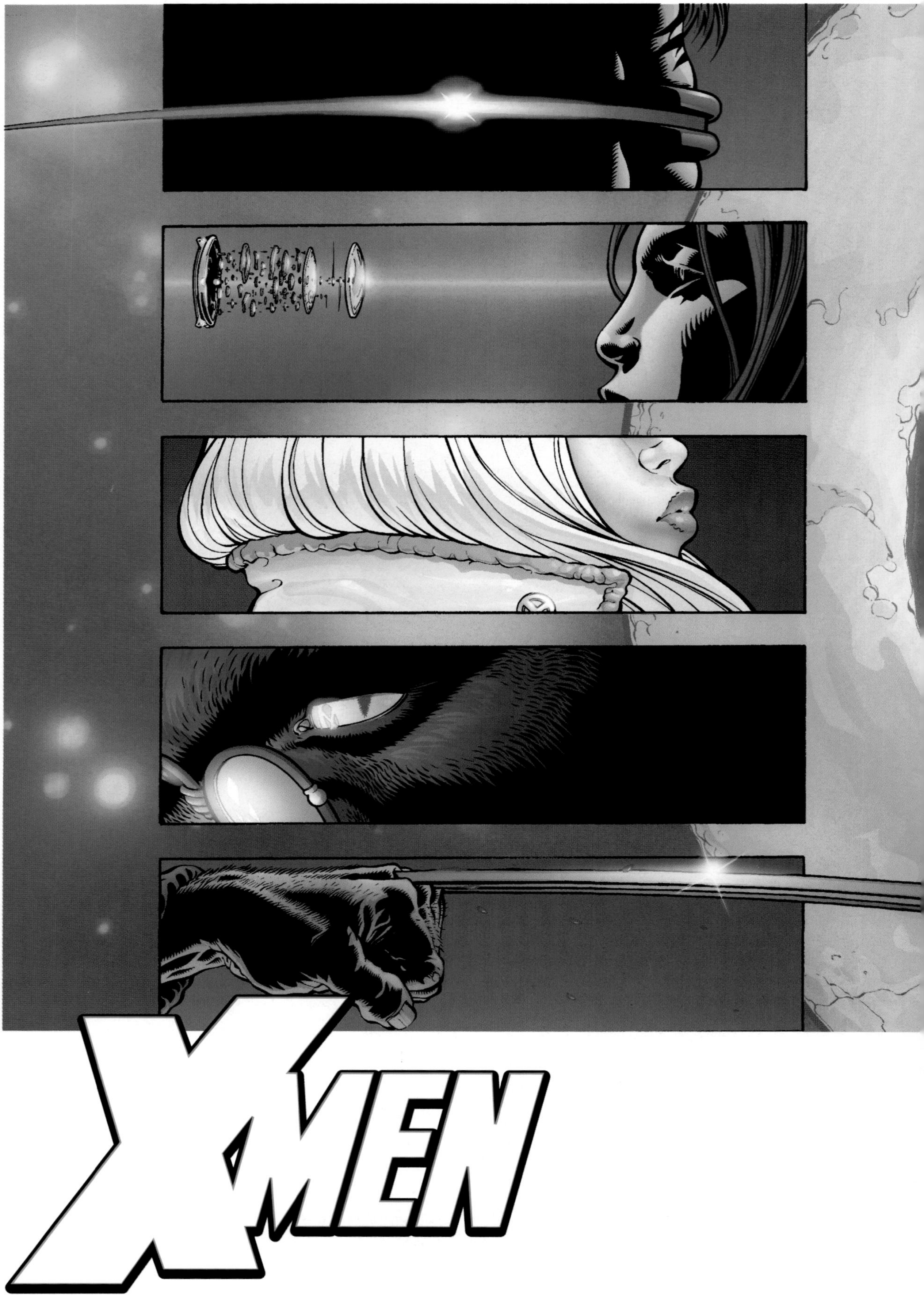
X-MEN

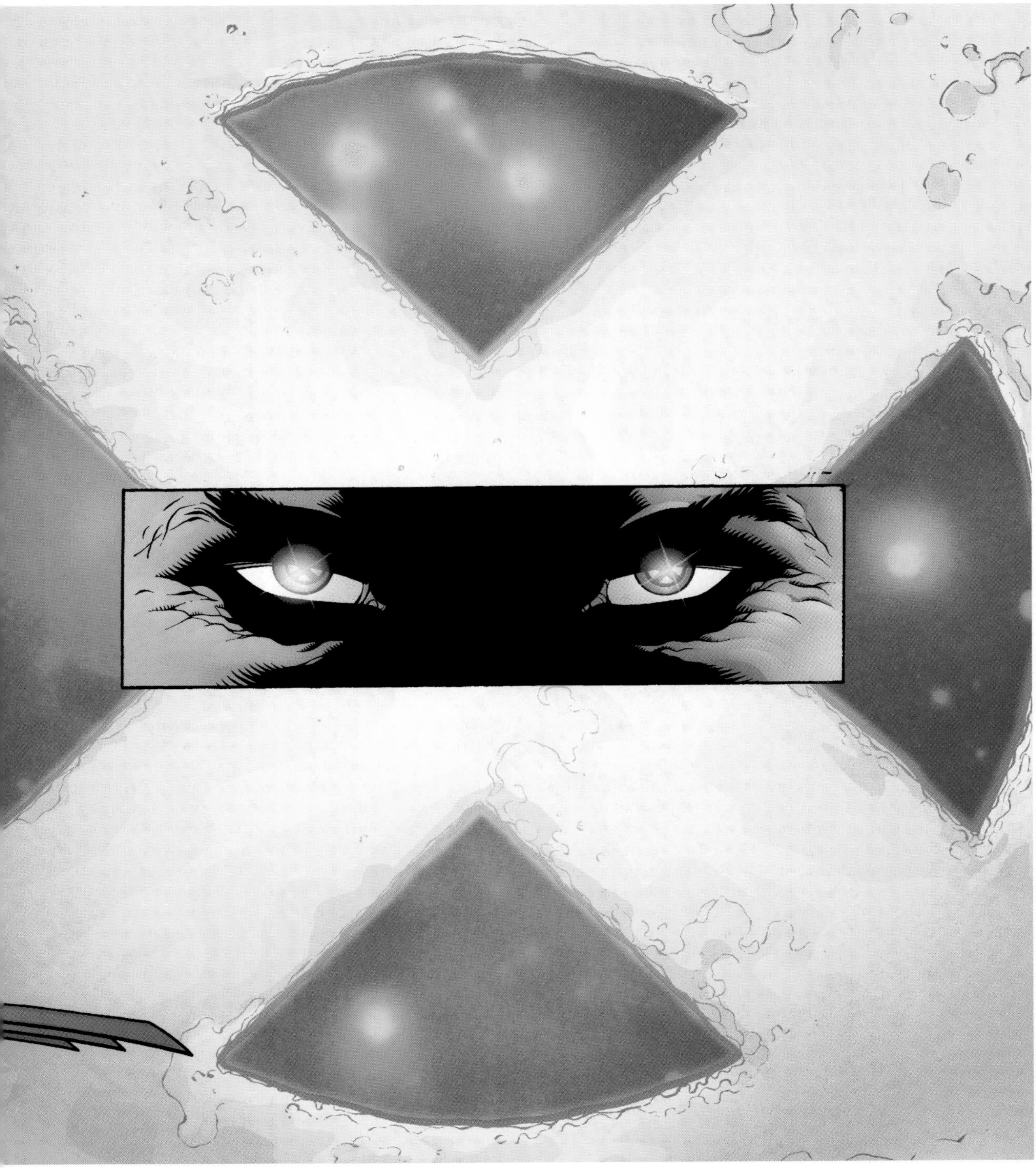

Art by Frank Quitely

The X-Men are a worldwide team of mutant volunteer workers gifted with new evolutionary talents. They are a rescue and emergency force on the front lines of the genetic battlefield of the 21st century. Founded and financed by the brilliant telepath Professor Charles Xavier, the X-Men are forever sworn to protect a world that hates and fears them.

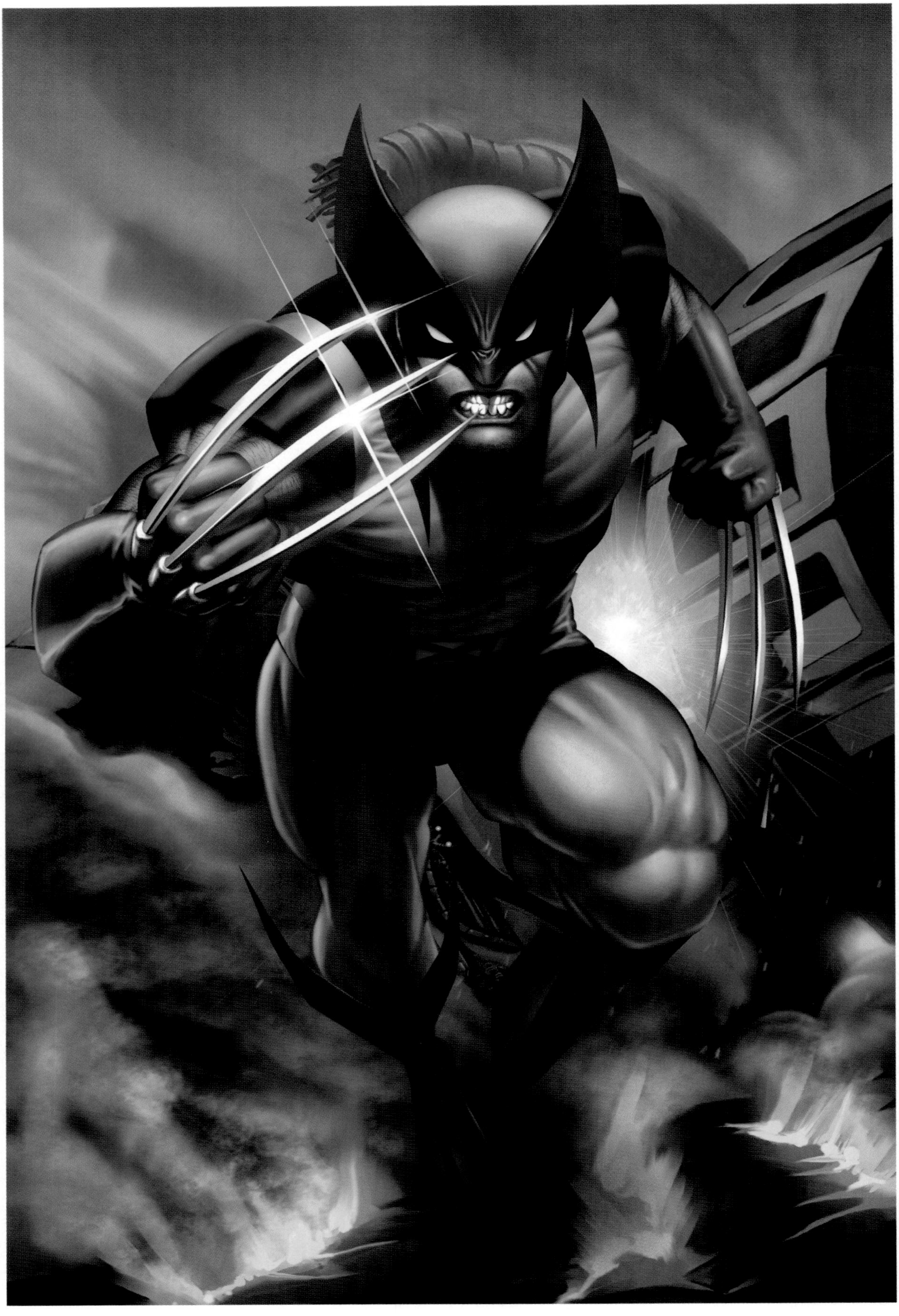

Art by Dale Keown

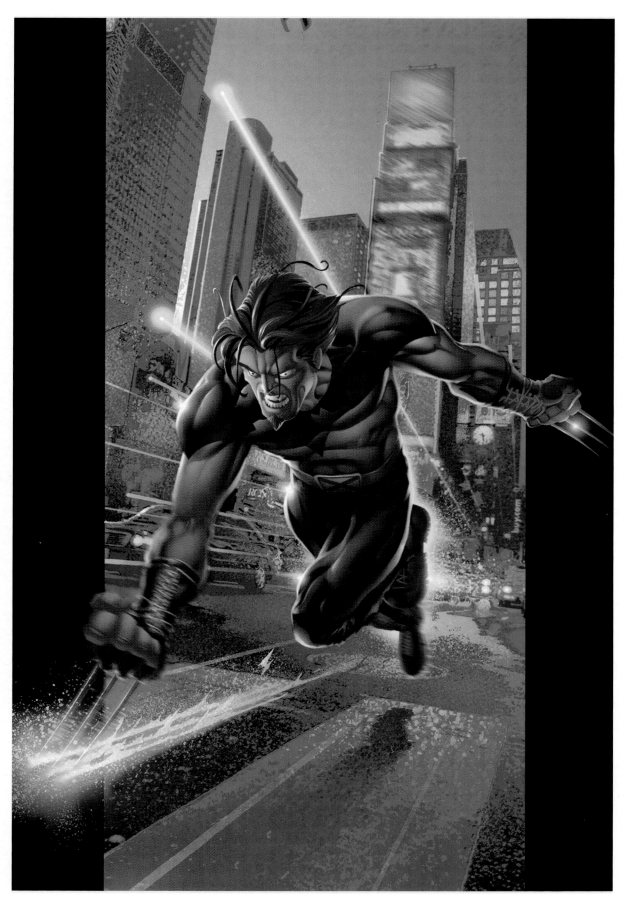

Art by Joe Quesada

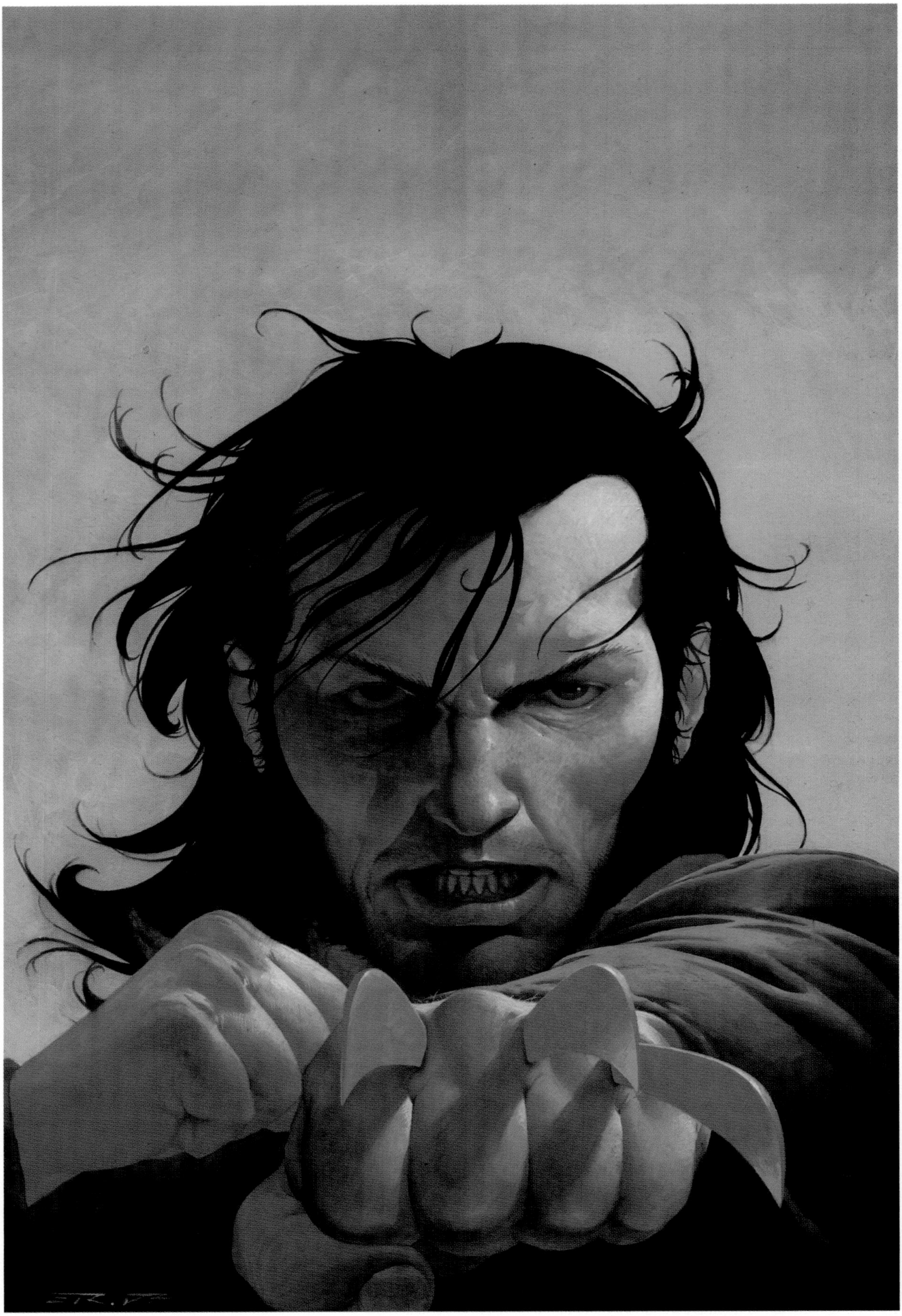

Art by Esad Ribic

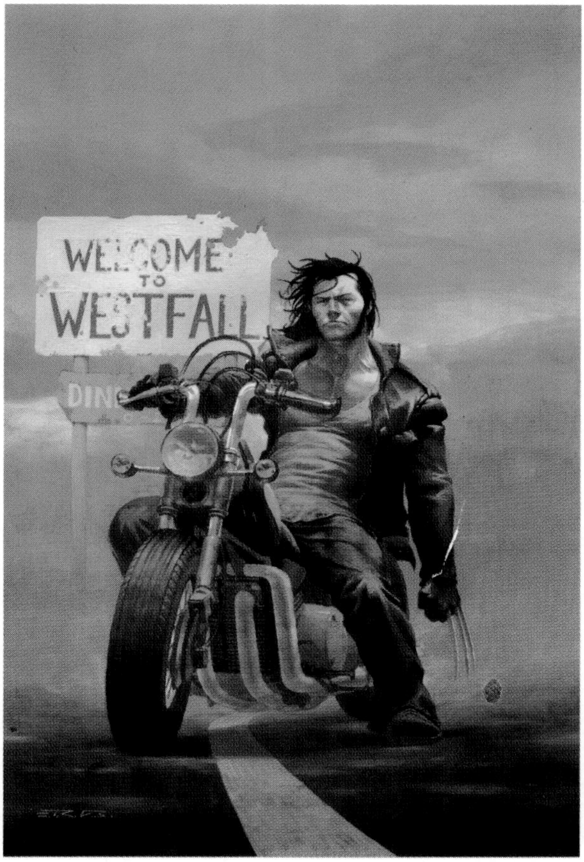
WELCOME
TO
WESTFALL

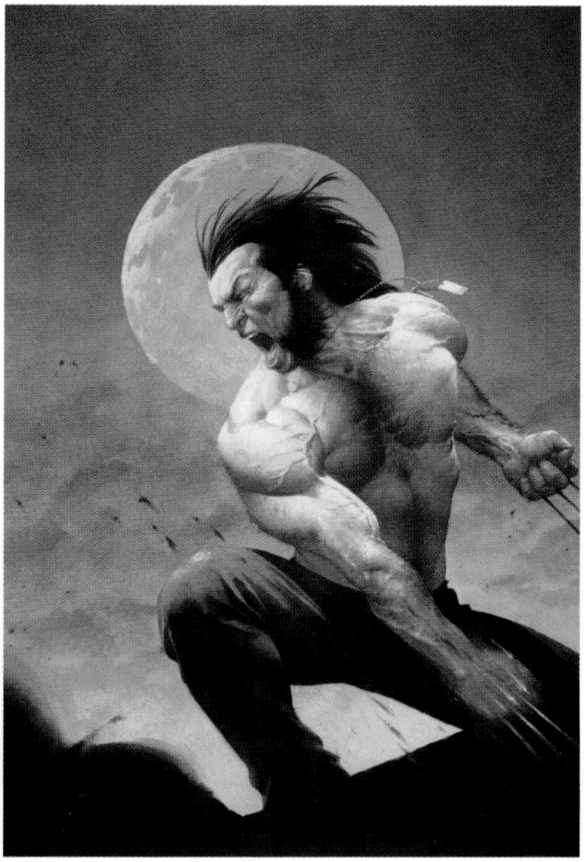

"Wolverine is a highly moral, highly ethical warrior. But the morals, the ethics, they're his, and they don't necessarily jibe with what's going on around him. That sense of right and wrong, and a pragmatic view of how the world works, are what motivate him, for the most part. I like his warrior ethic. I like the fact that he wastes nothing, that he has no time for ********, or games. I also think he's very, very smart."

Greg Rucka
Writer
Wolverine

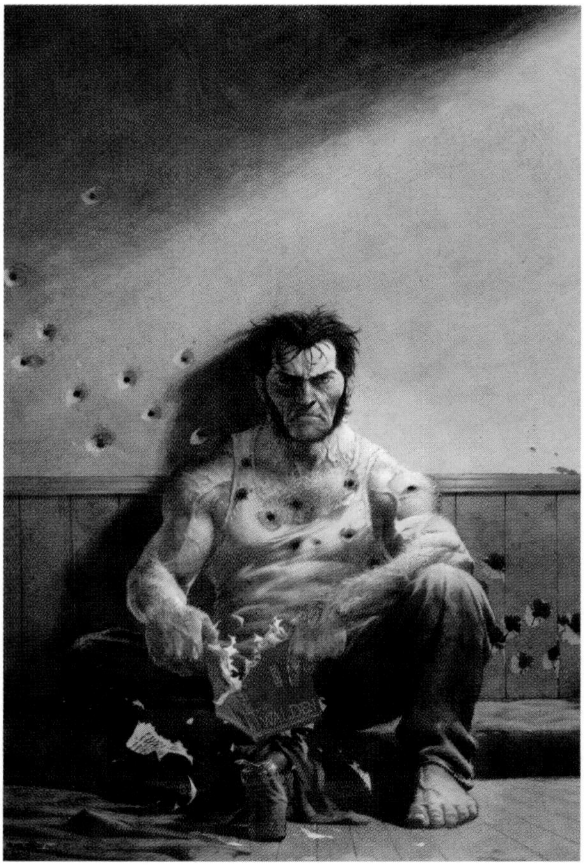

Art by Esad Ribic

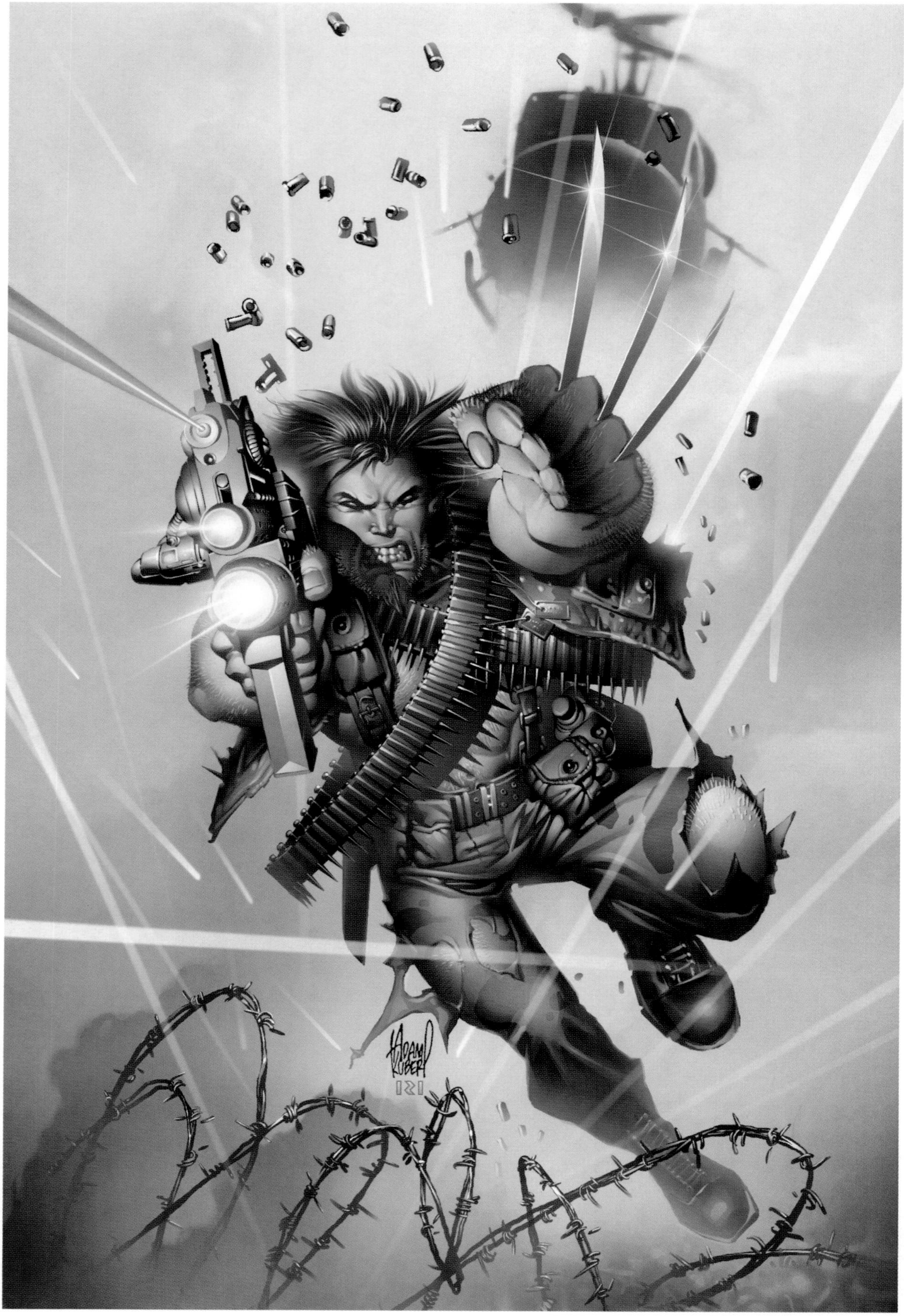
ADAM KUBERT

Art by Adam Kubert

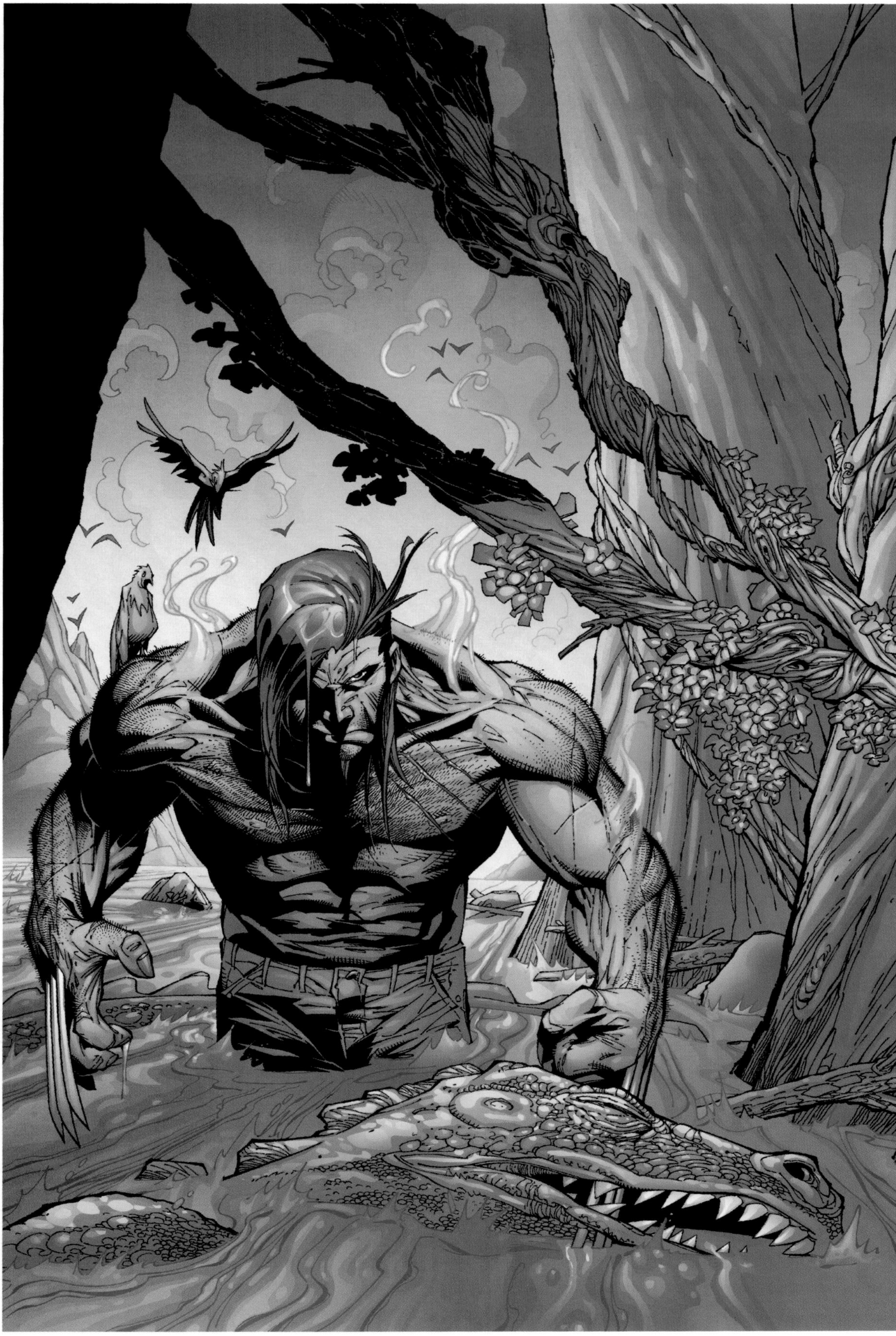

Art by Adam Kubert

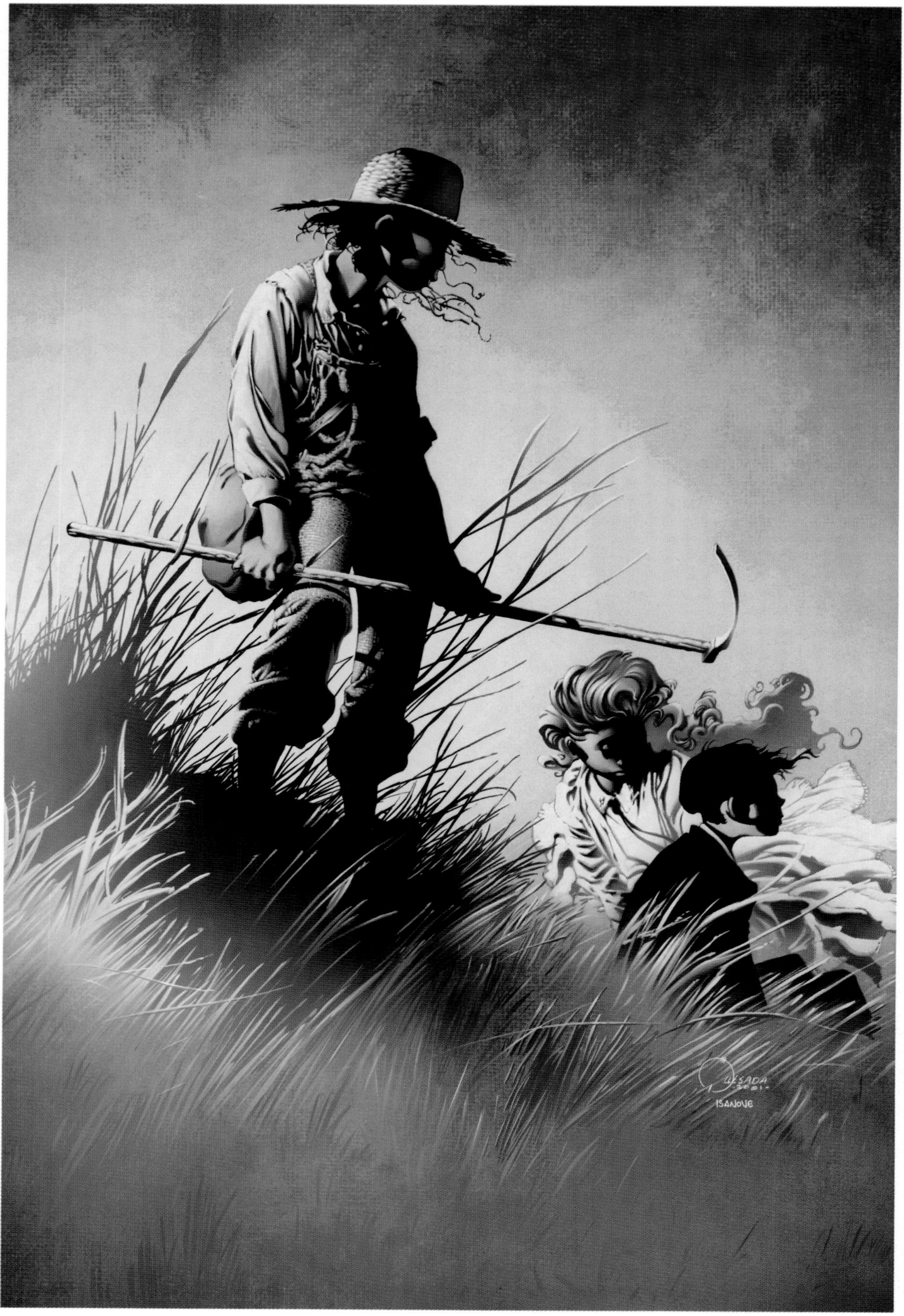
QUESADA
ISANOVE

Art by Joe Quesada

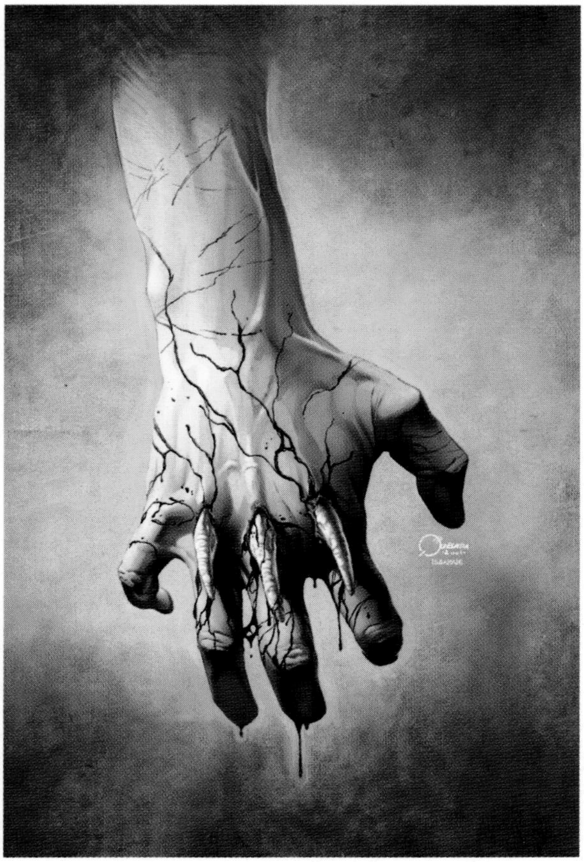

"It's funny, the one thing that it took for us at Marvel to even consider attempting to write Wolverine's origin is the one ingredient that ol' Wolvie and all our heroes have in spades ... *fearlessness*! It's something that we were really lacking at Marvel at the time, yet it was fearlessness that was the cornerstone upon which Stan Lee, Jack Kirby, Steve Ditko and so many others built the Marvel Universe."

Joe Quesada
Cover artist/co-plotter
Origin

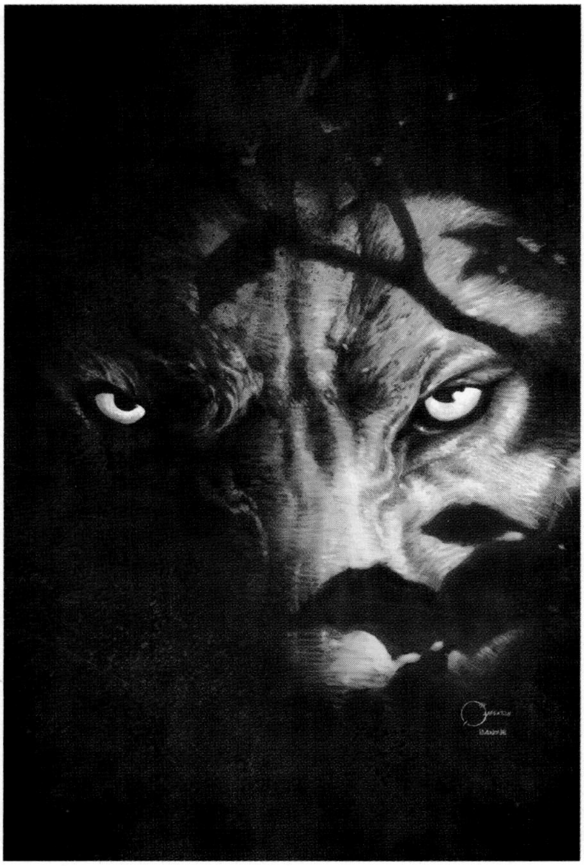

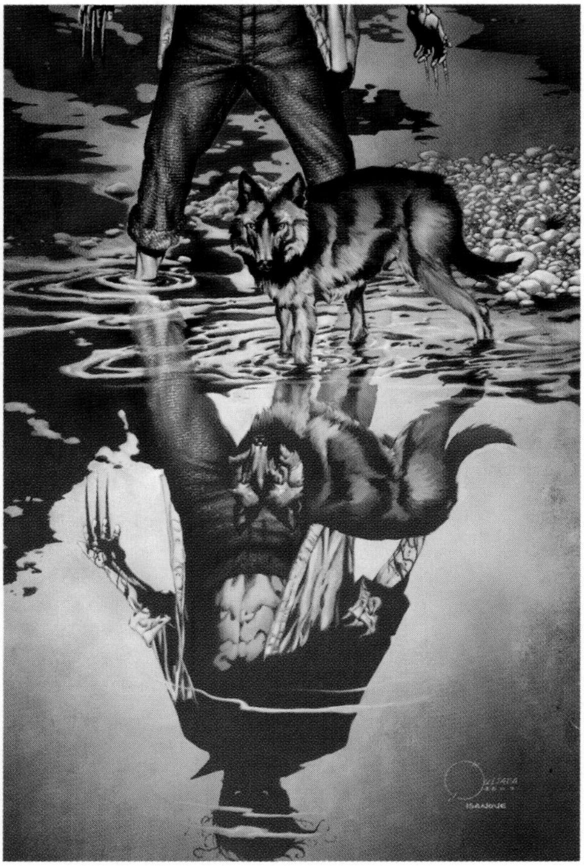

Art by Joe Quesada

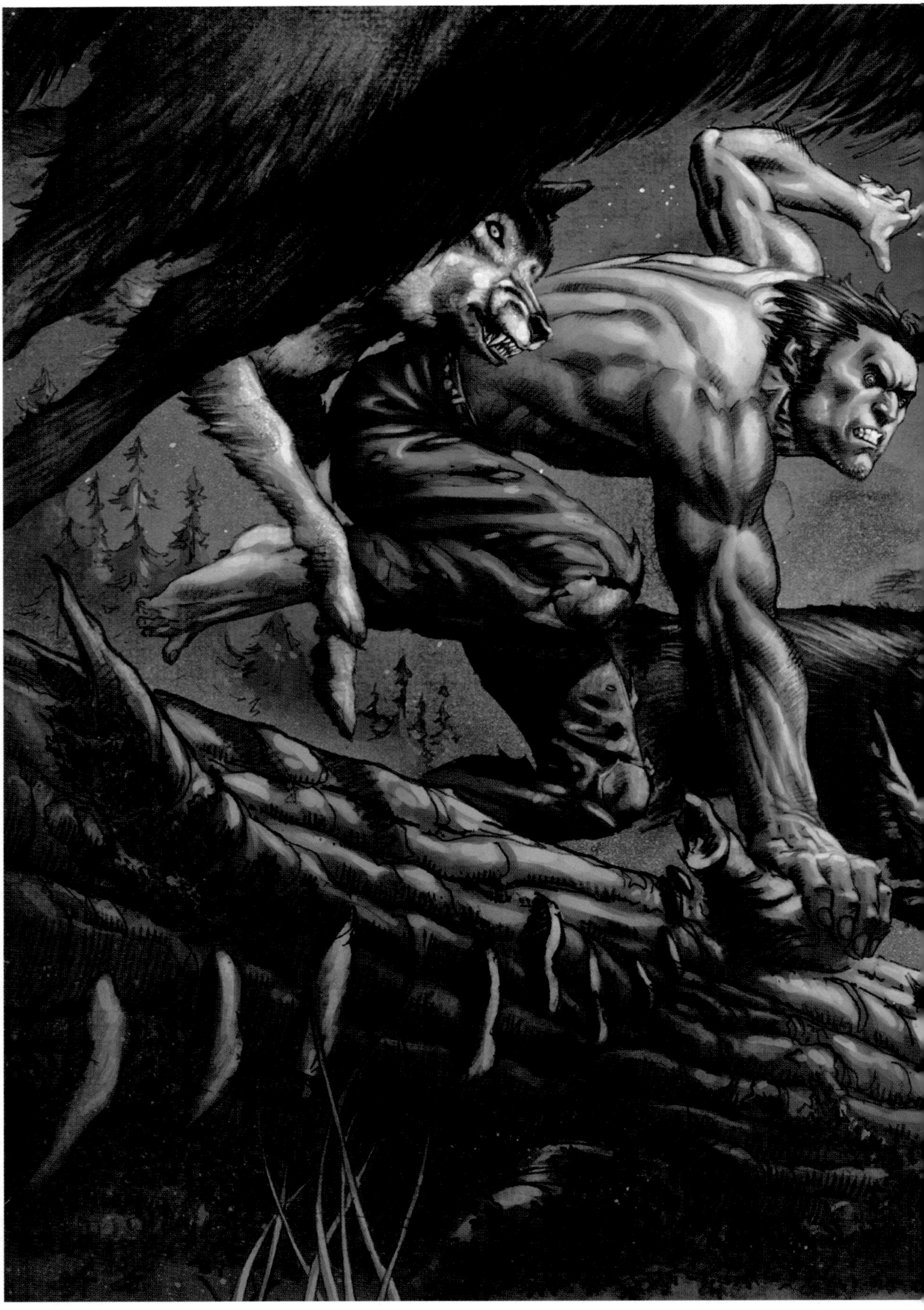

Art by Andy Kubert

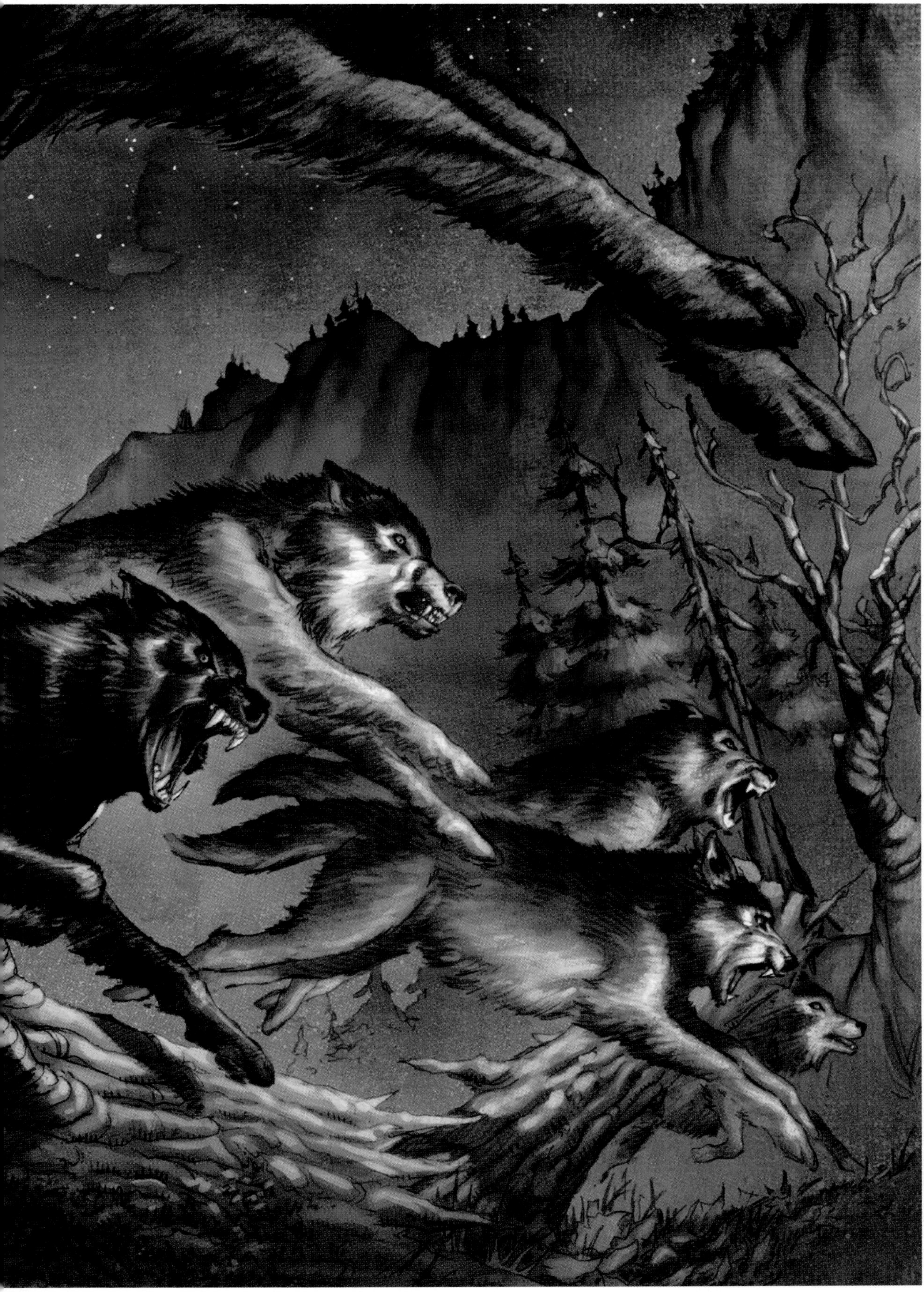

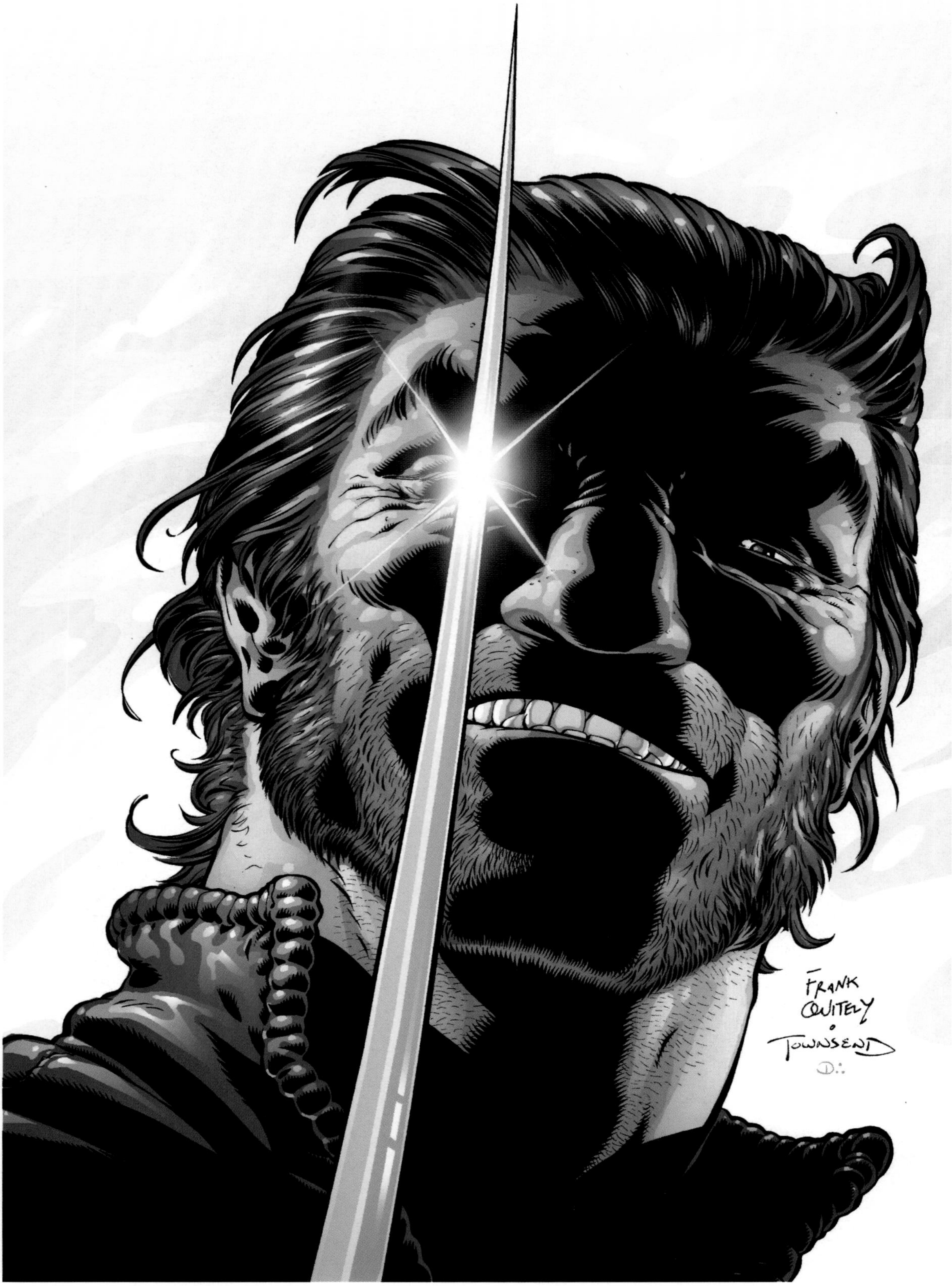
FRANK QUITELY
TOWNSEND

Art by Frank Quitely

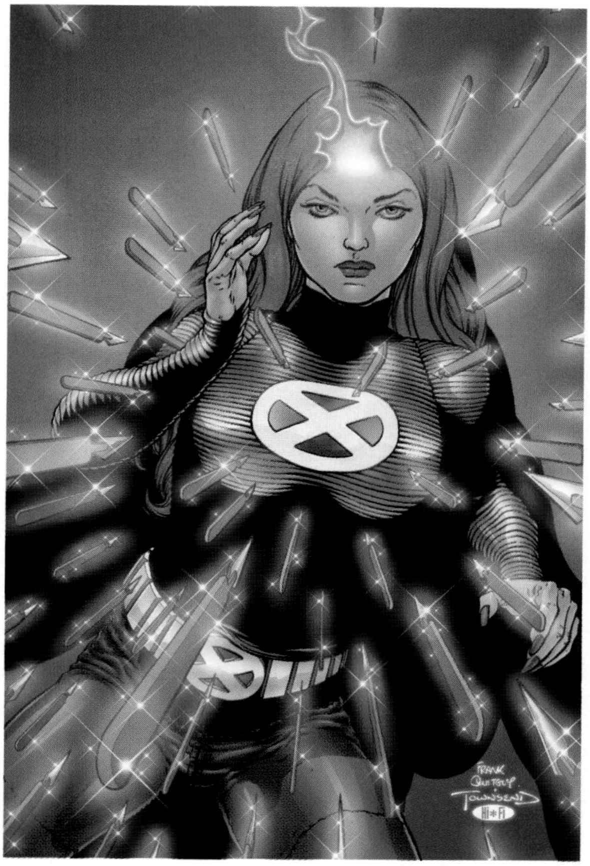

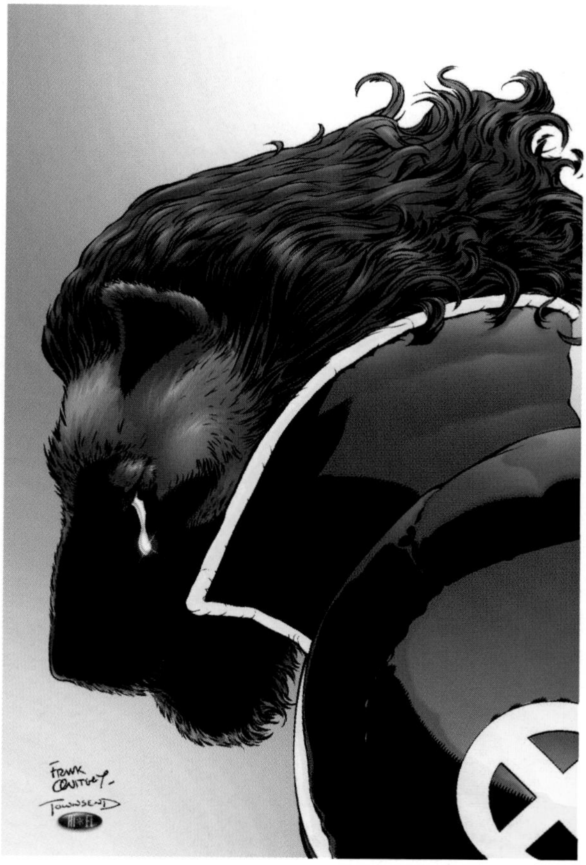

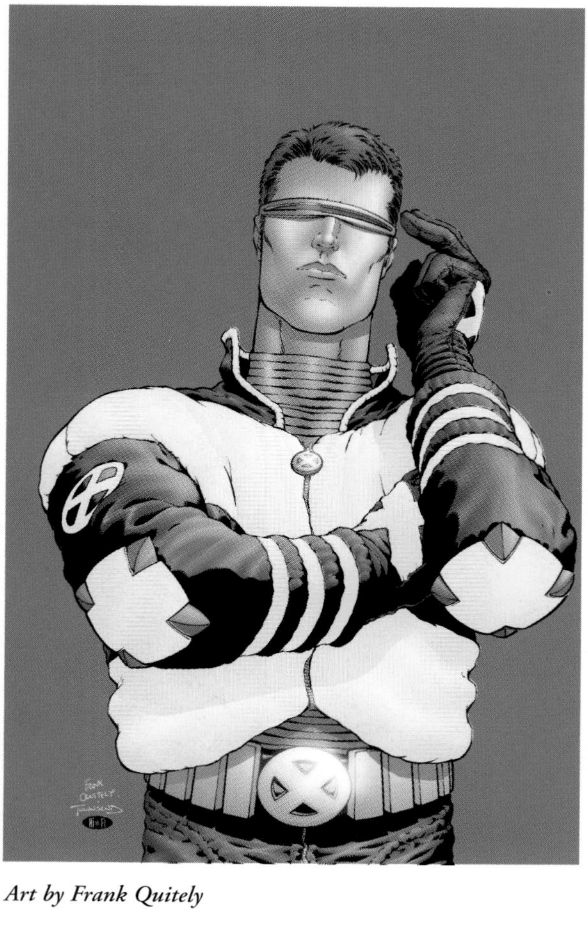

Art by Frank Quitely

"The X-Men are every rebel teenager wanting to change the world and make it better. Humanity is every adult, clinging to the past, trying to destroy the future even as he places all his hopes there. The super-hero element should be seen as only a small element in the vast potential of this franchise."

Grant Morrison
Writer
New X-Men

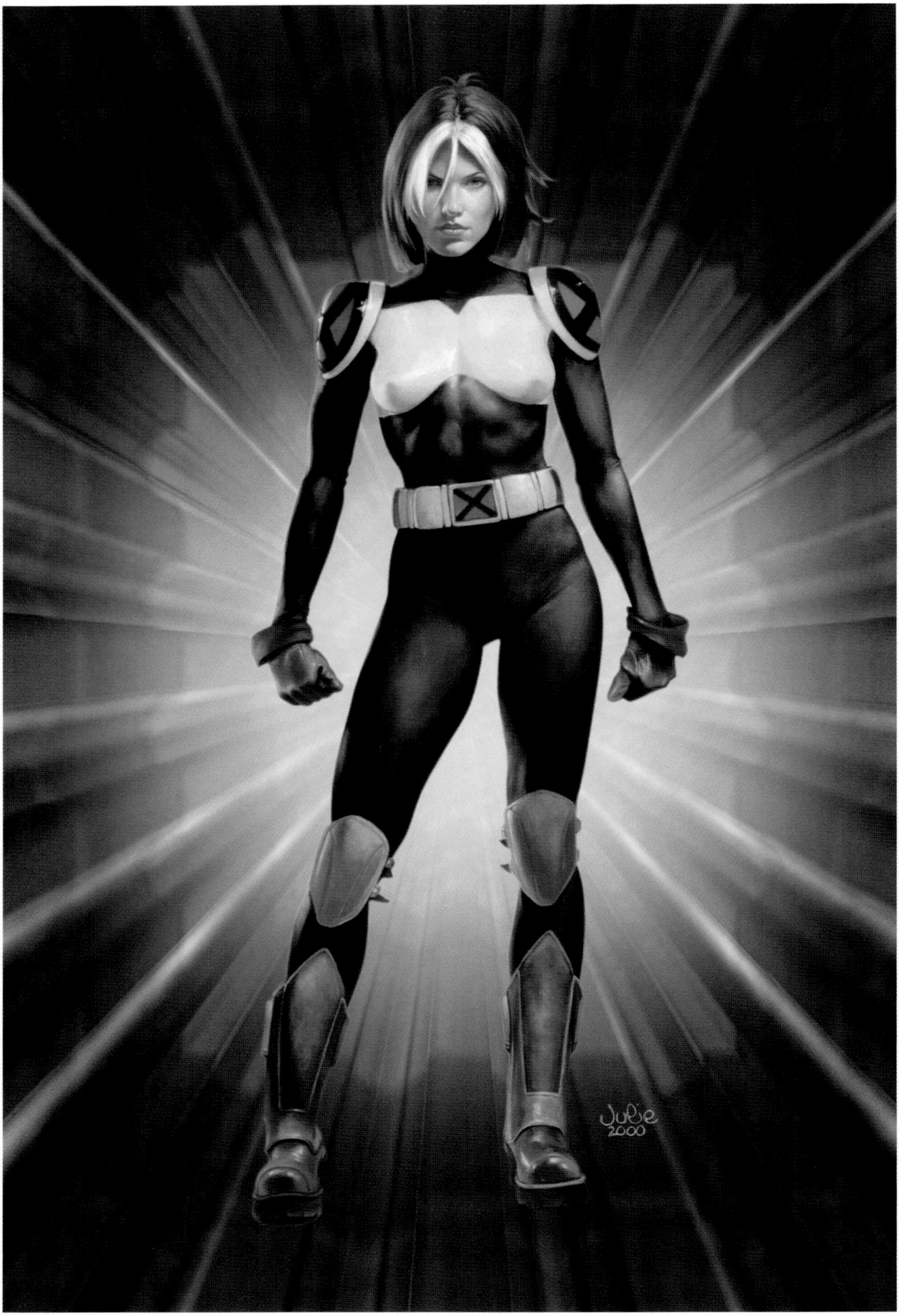
Julie
2000

Art by Julie Bell

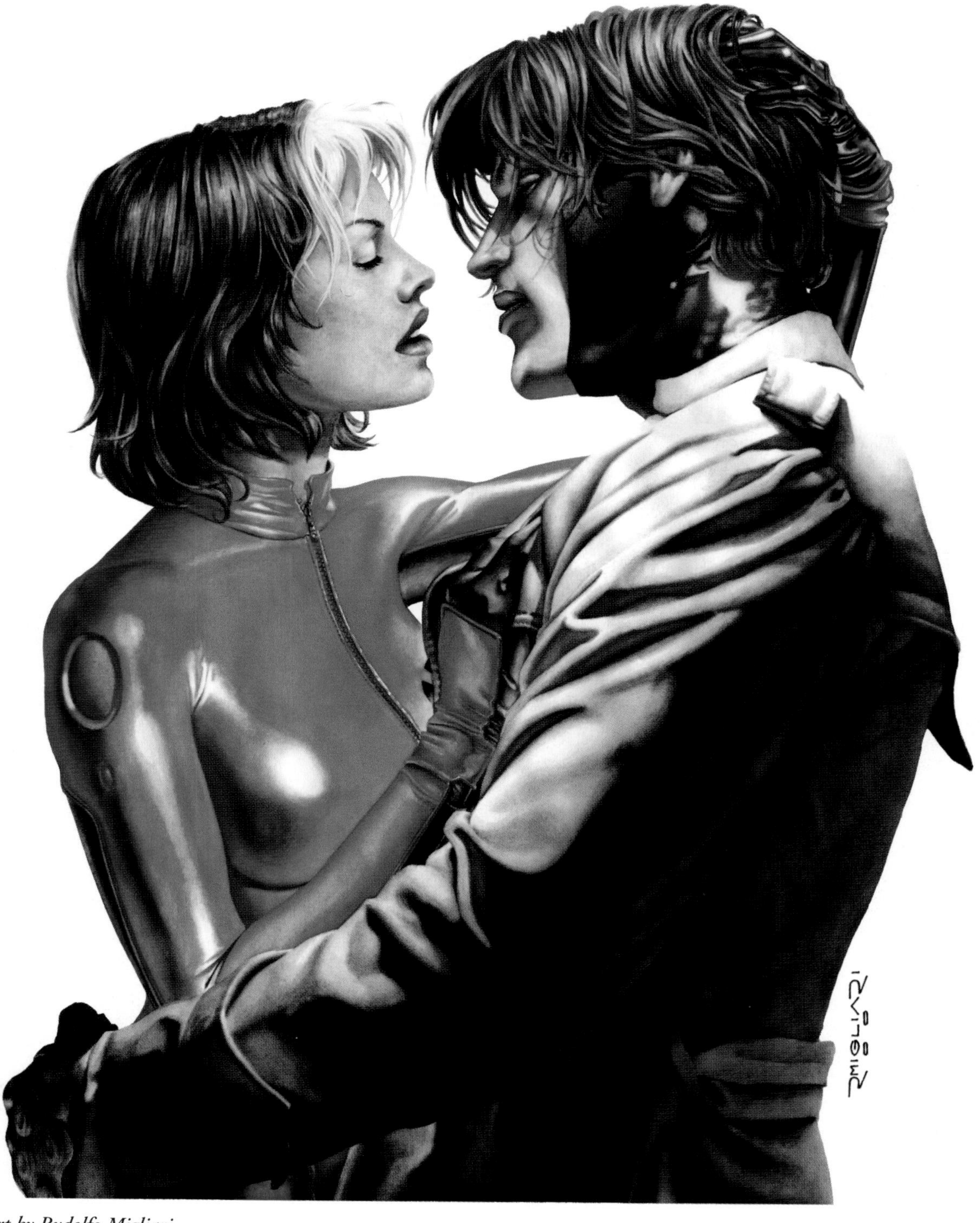
MIGLIARI
Art by Rudolfo Migliari

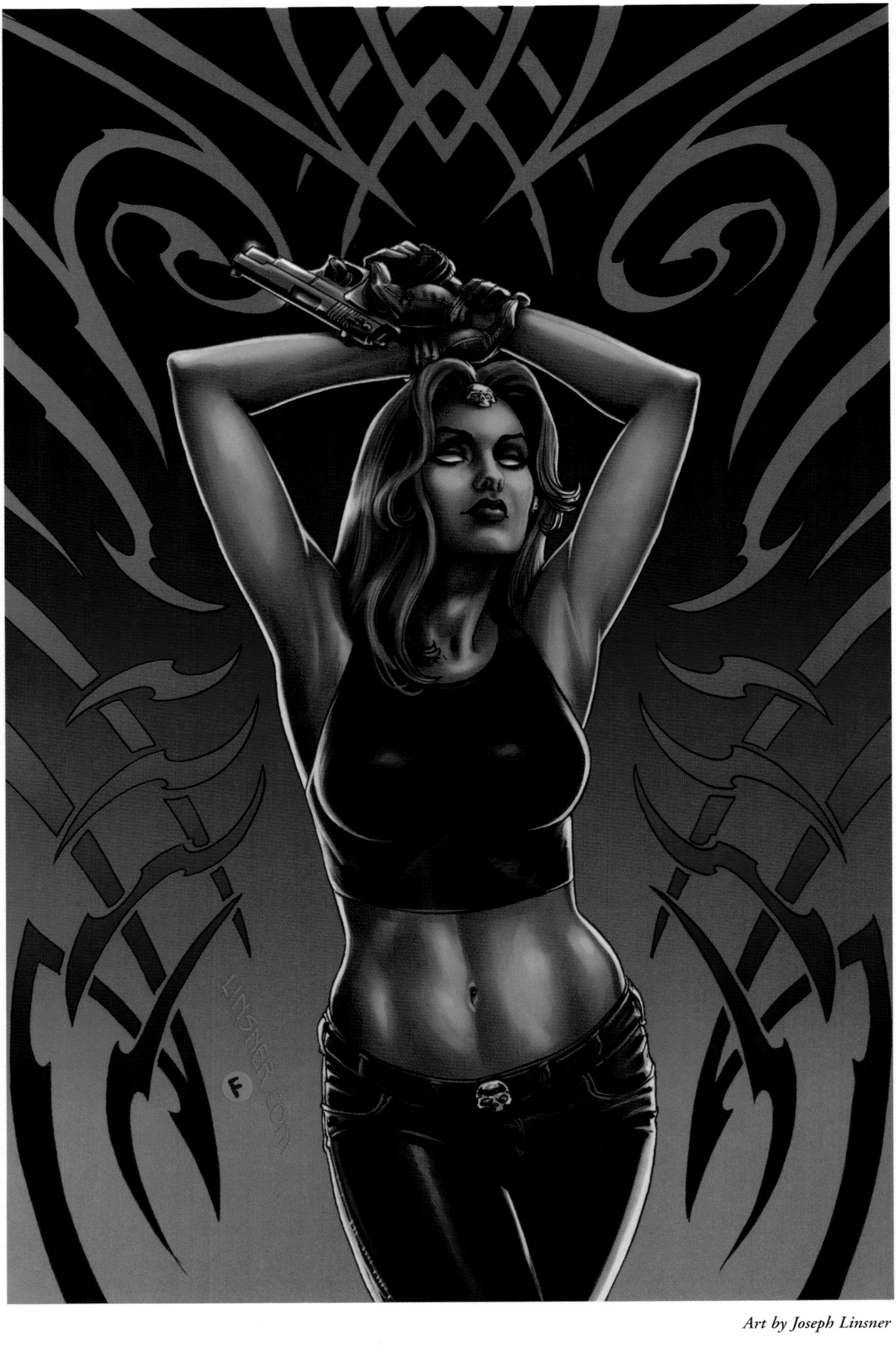
LINSNER.COM

Art by Joseph Linsner

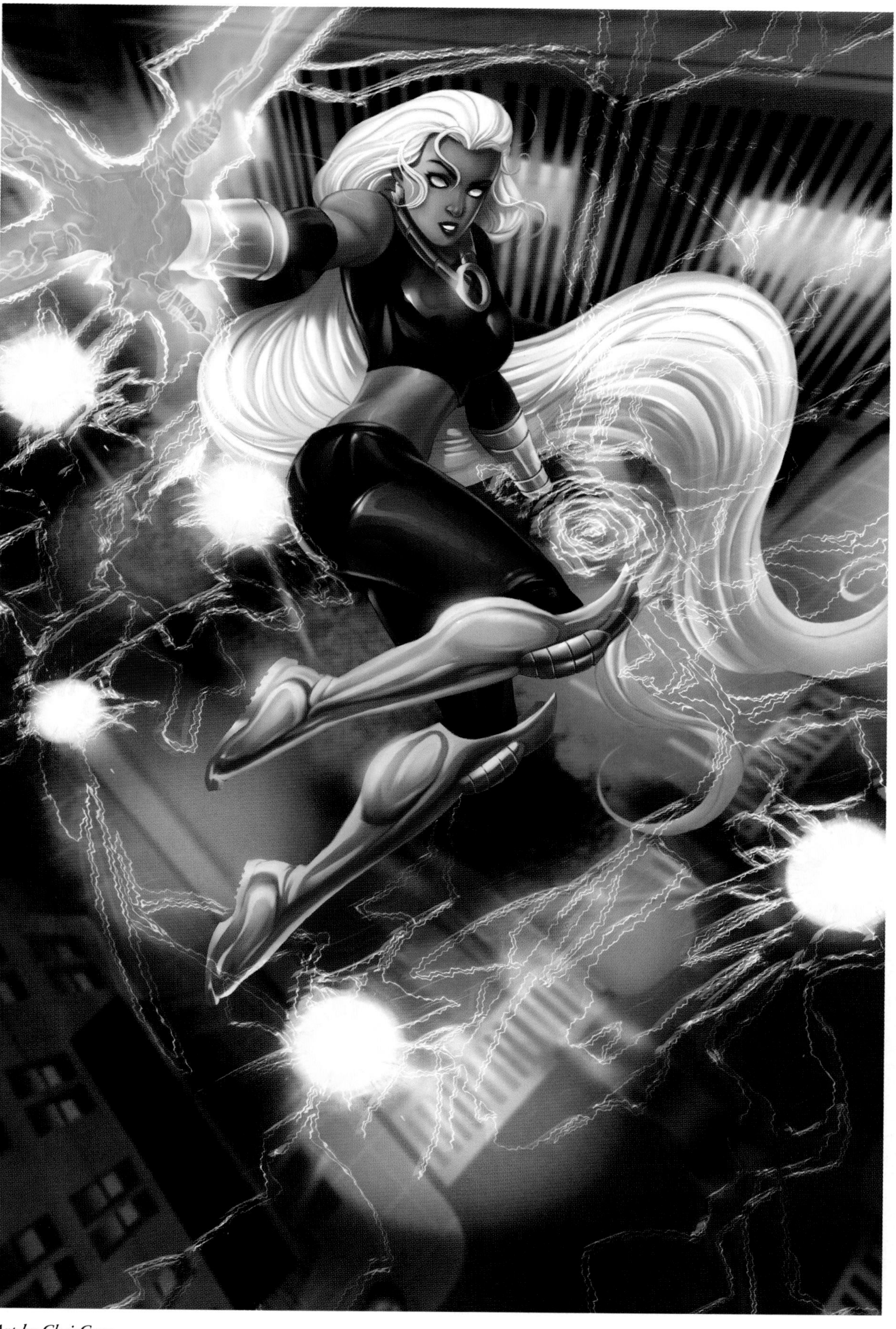

Art by ChrisCross

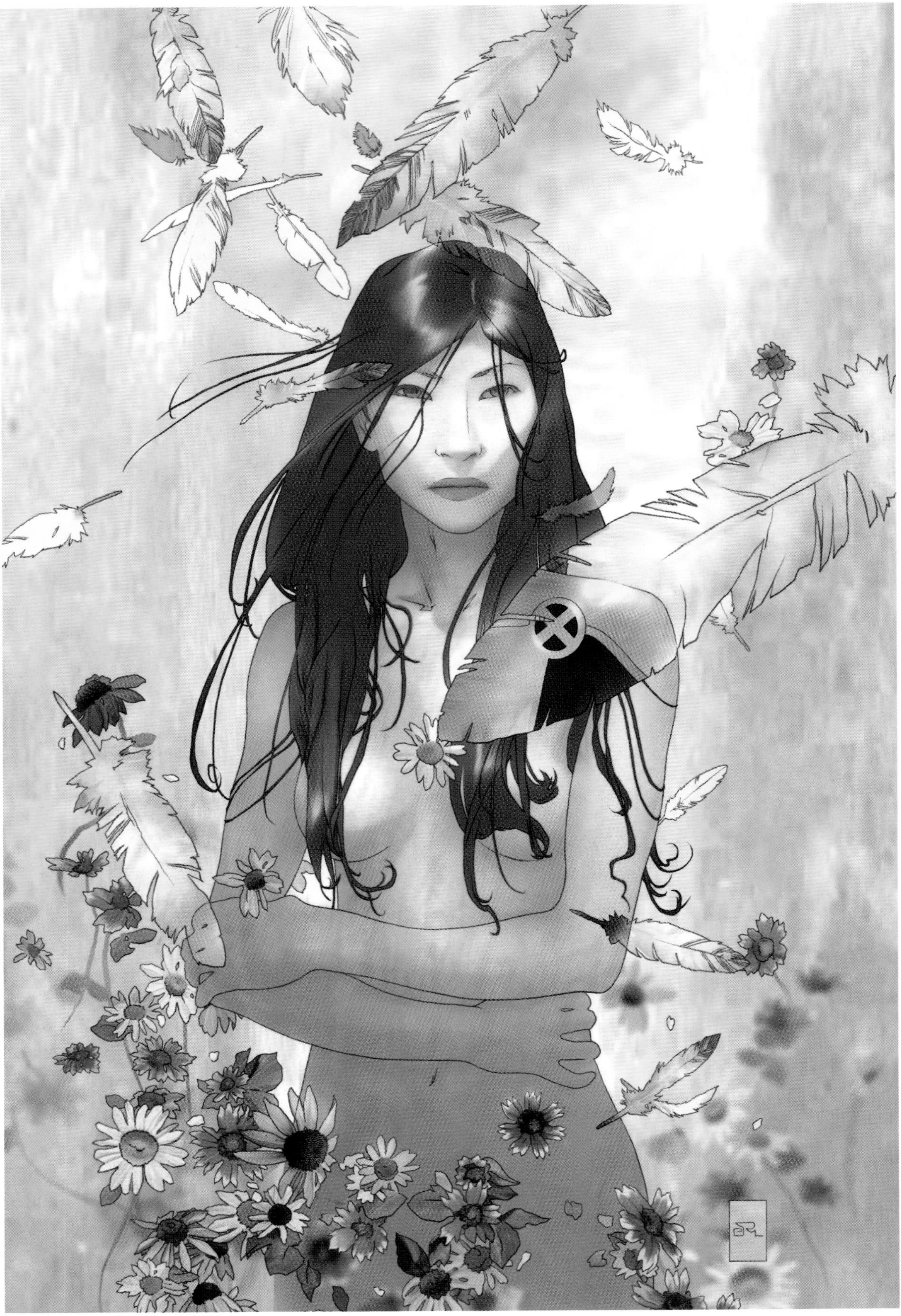

Art by Josh Middleton

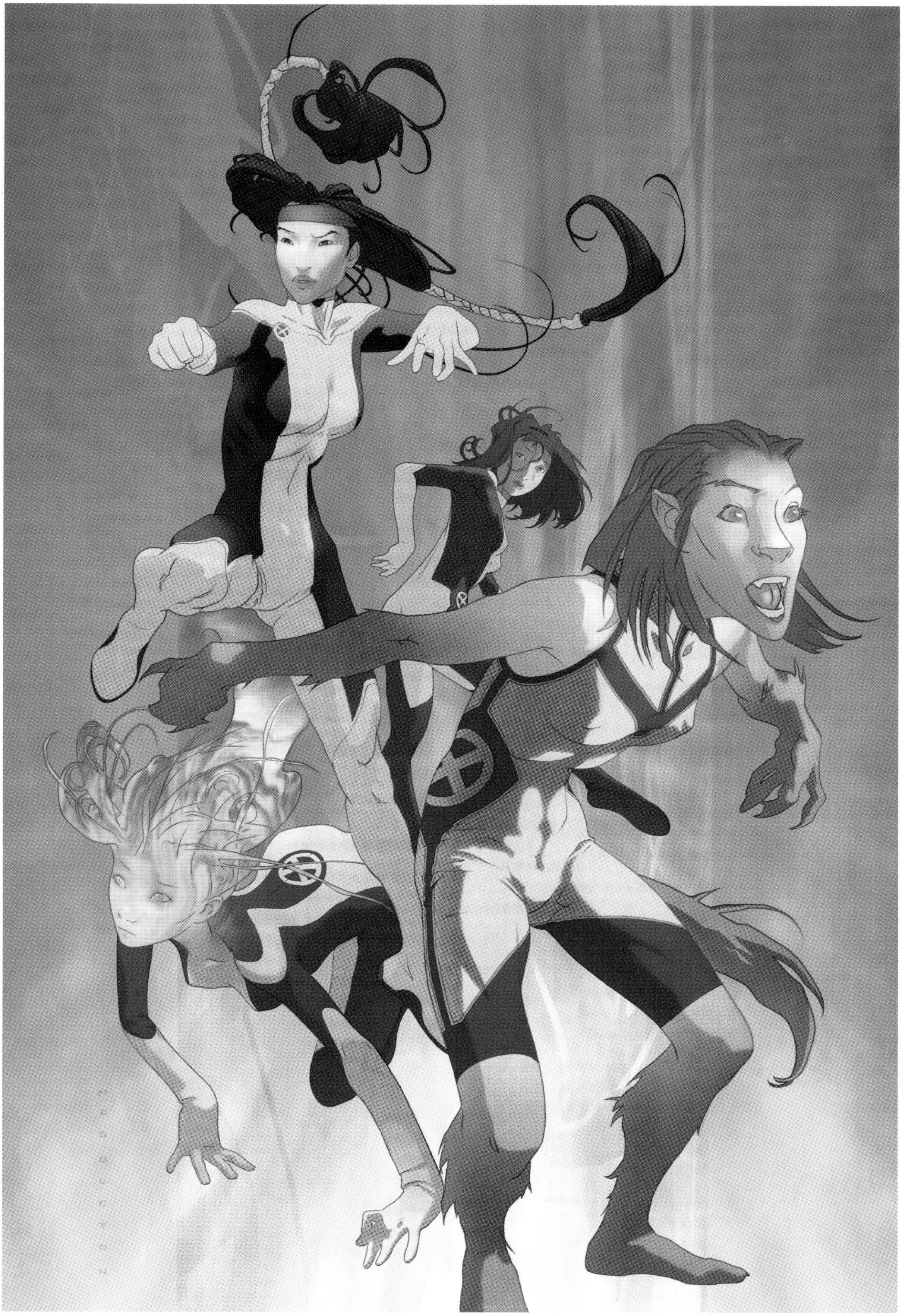
MIDDLETON

Art by Josh Middleton

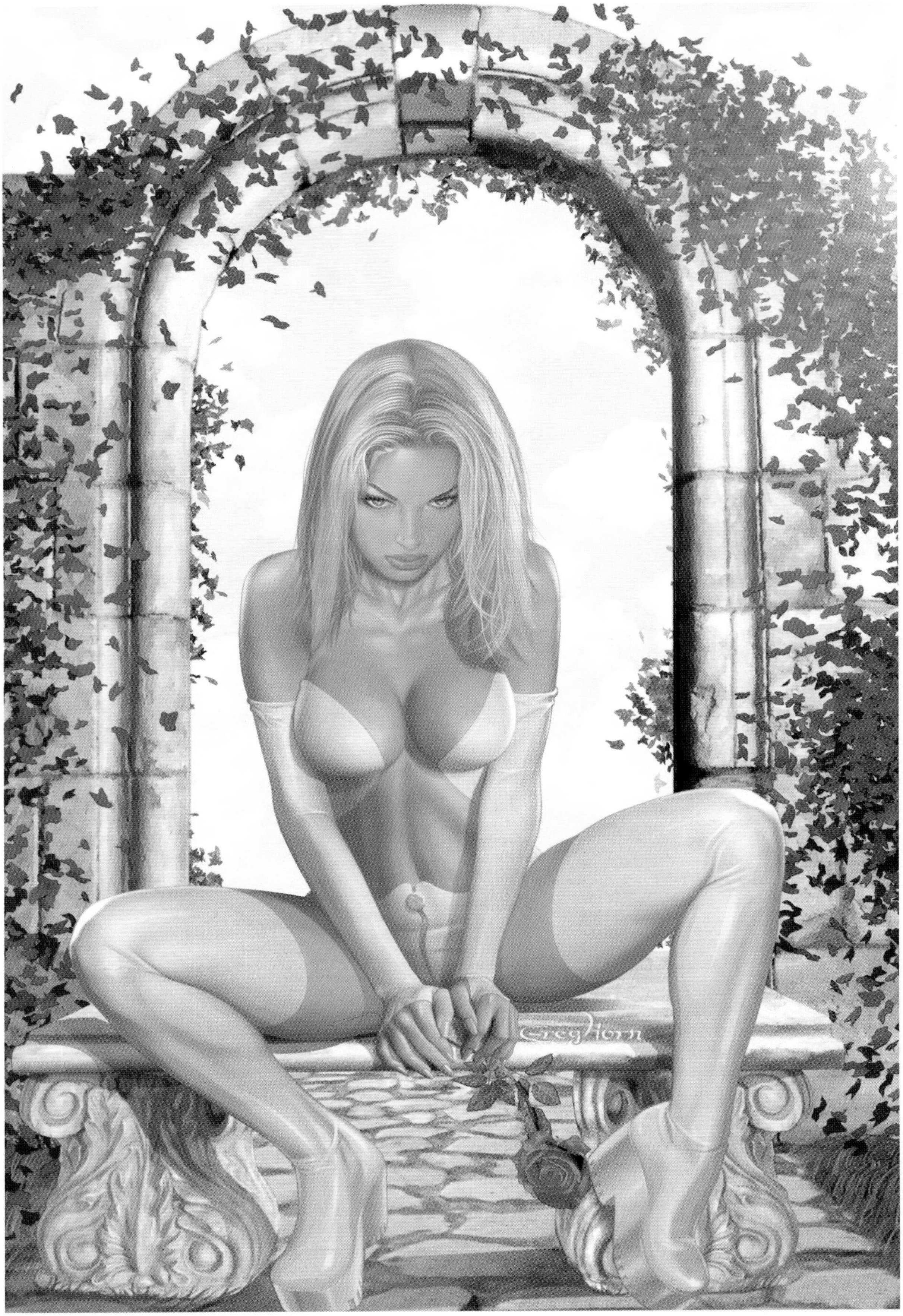
Greg Horn

Art by Greg Horn

"Unlike previous Marvel 'bad guys-turned-good guys' who either weren't really all that bad in the first place (Hawkeye, Scarlet Witch et al.) or were *so* evil that their conversion never seemed entirely plausible (Rogue, Magneto), the delightful Ms. Frost fights the good fight while retaining every iota of her nasty edge ... and *then* some. You get the feeling she could revert to super-villainy in a heartbeat."

Bruce Timm
Emmy Award-winning producer/designer
Batman: The Animated Series, Superman, Batman Beyond, Justice League

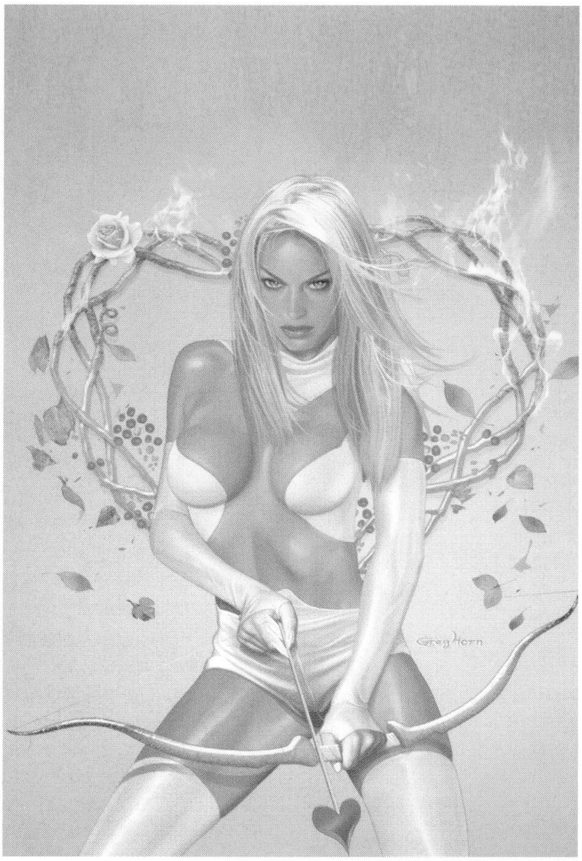

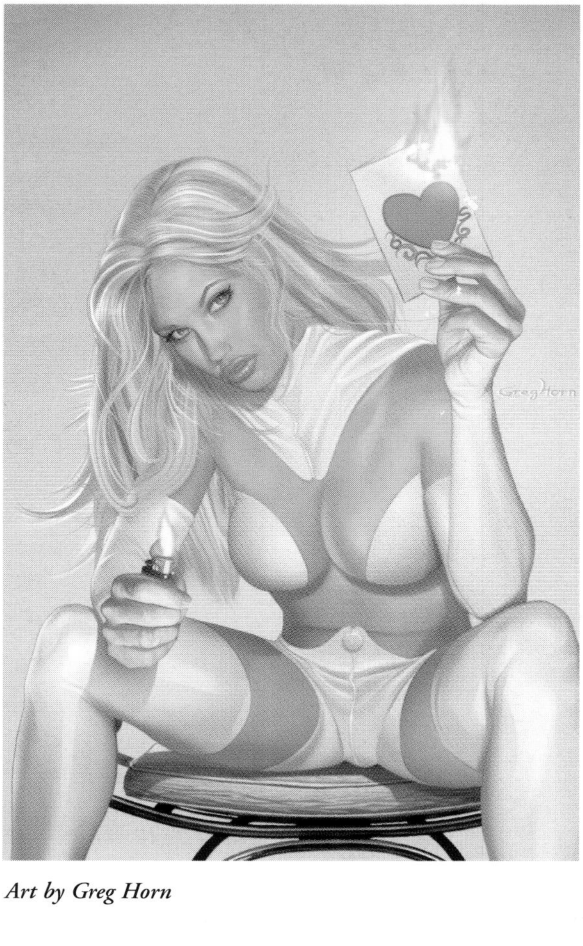

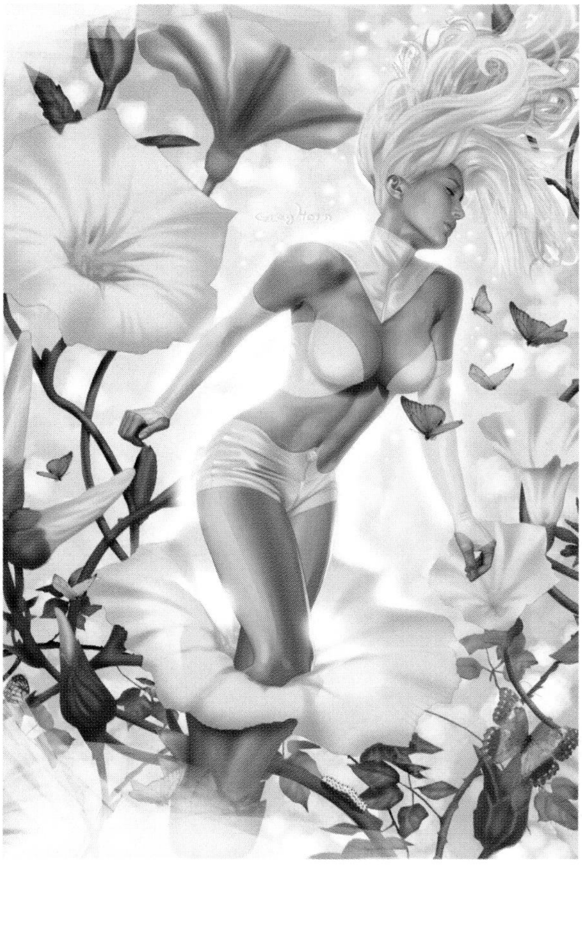

Art by Greg Horn

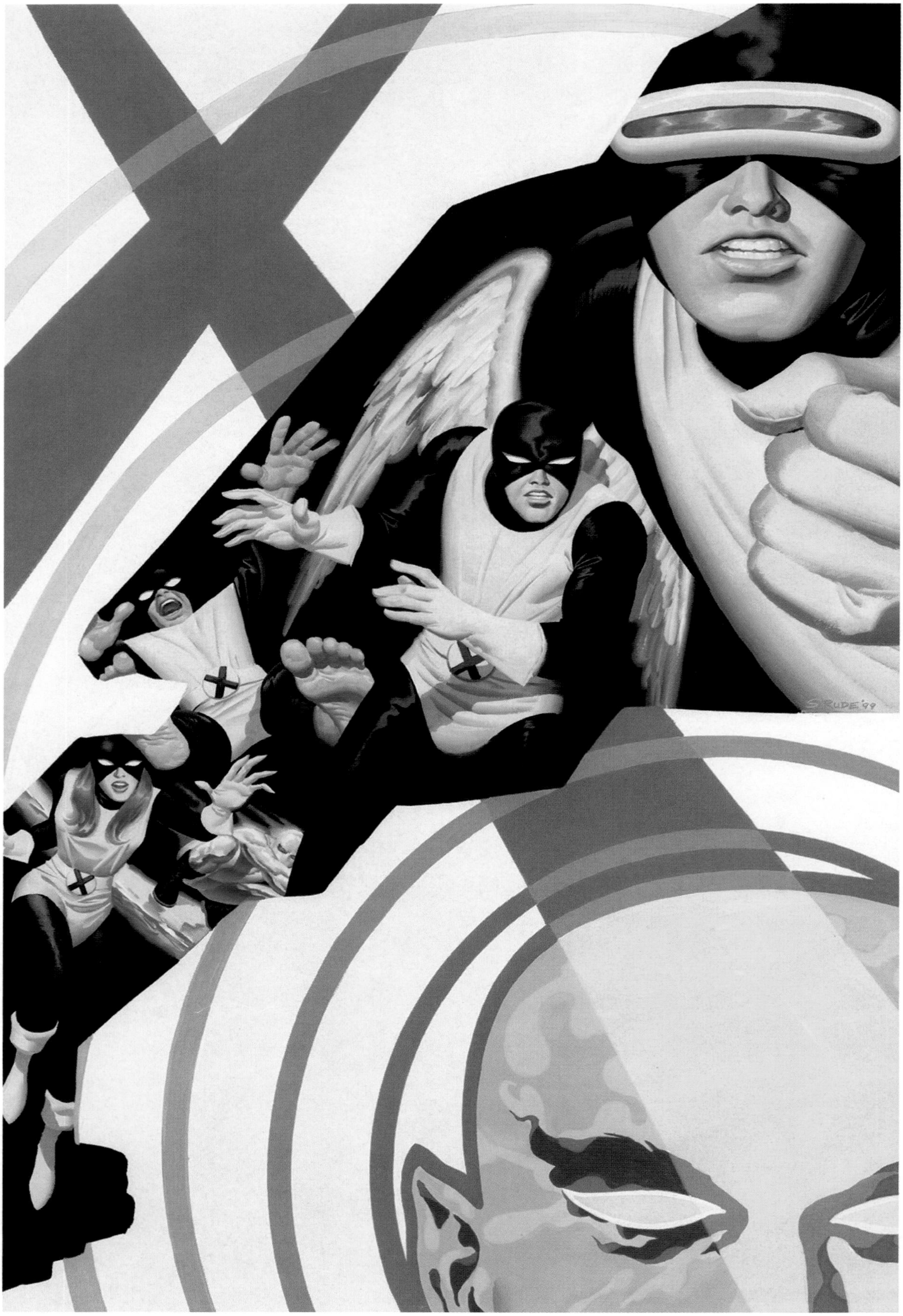
S RUDE '99

Art by Steve Rude

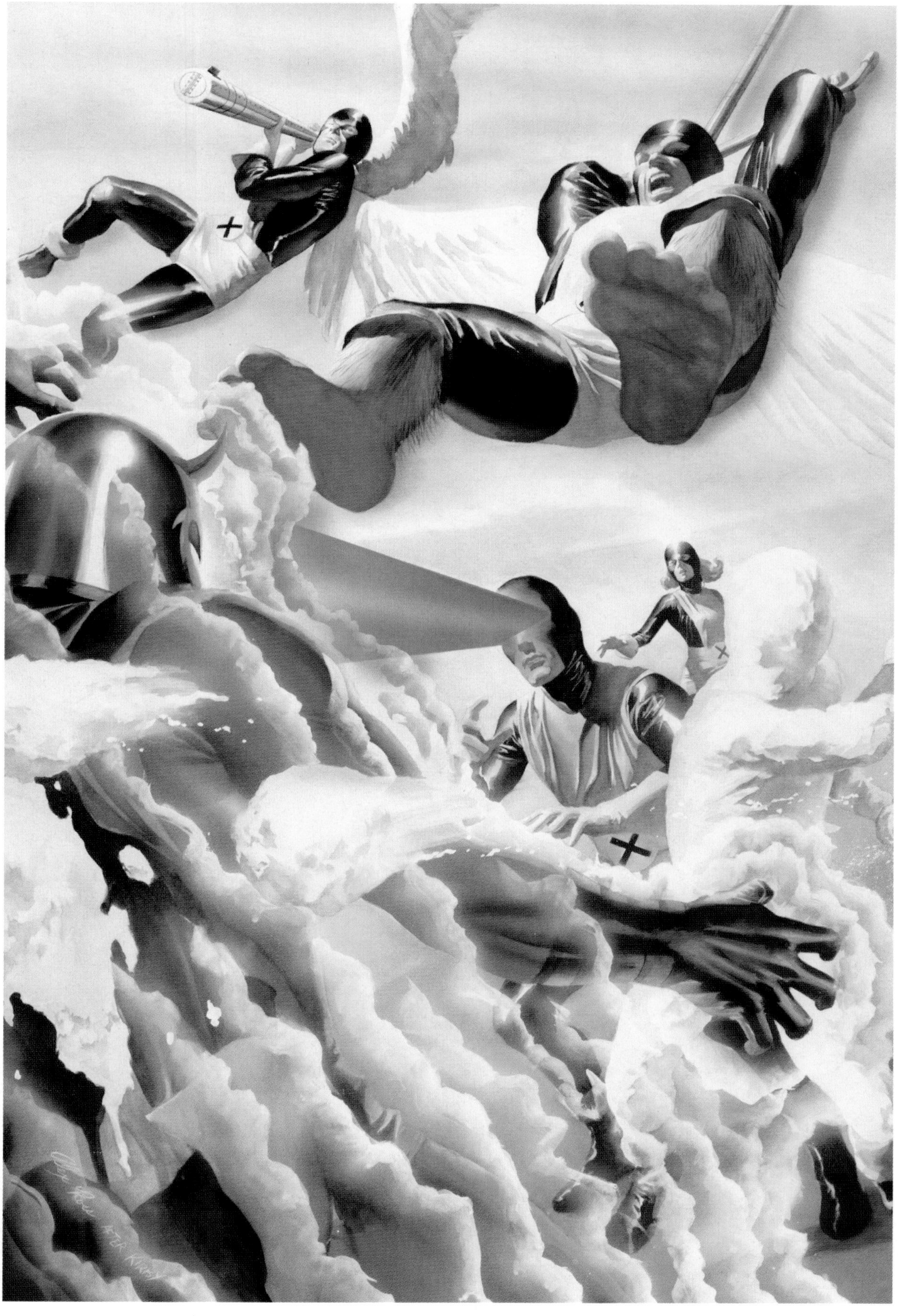

Art by Alex Ross

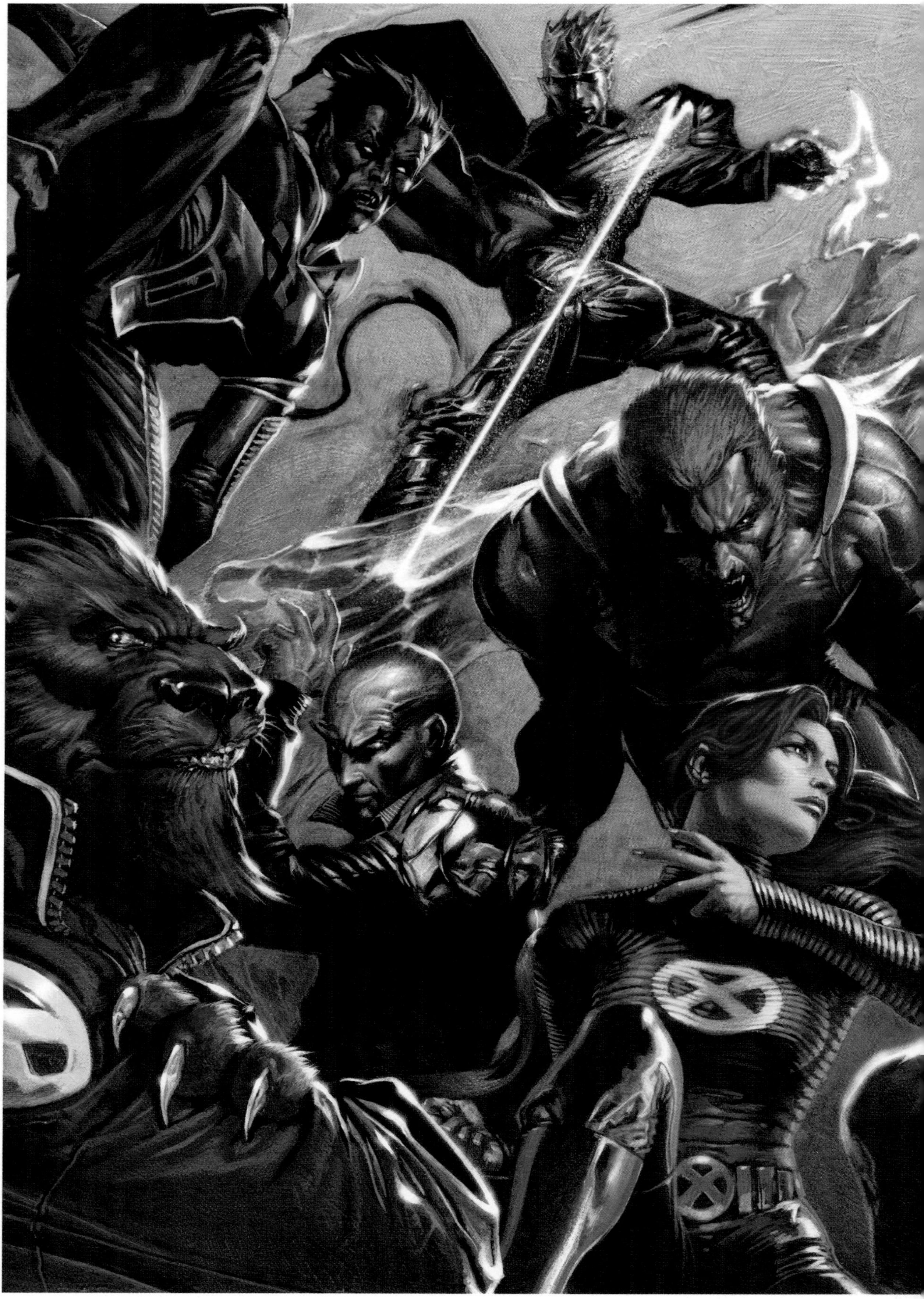

Art by Gabriele Dell'Otto

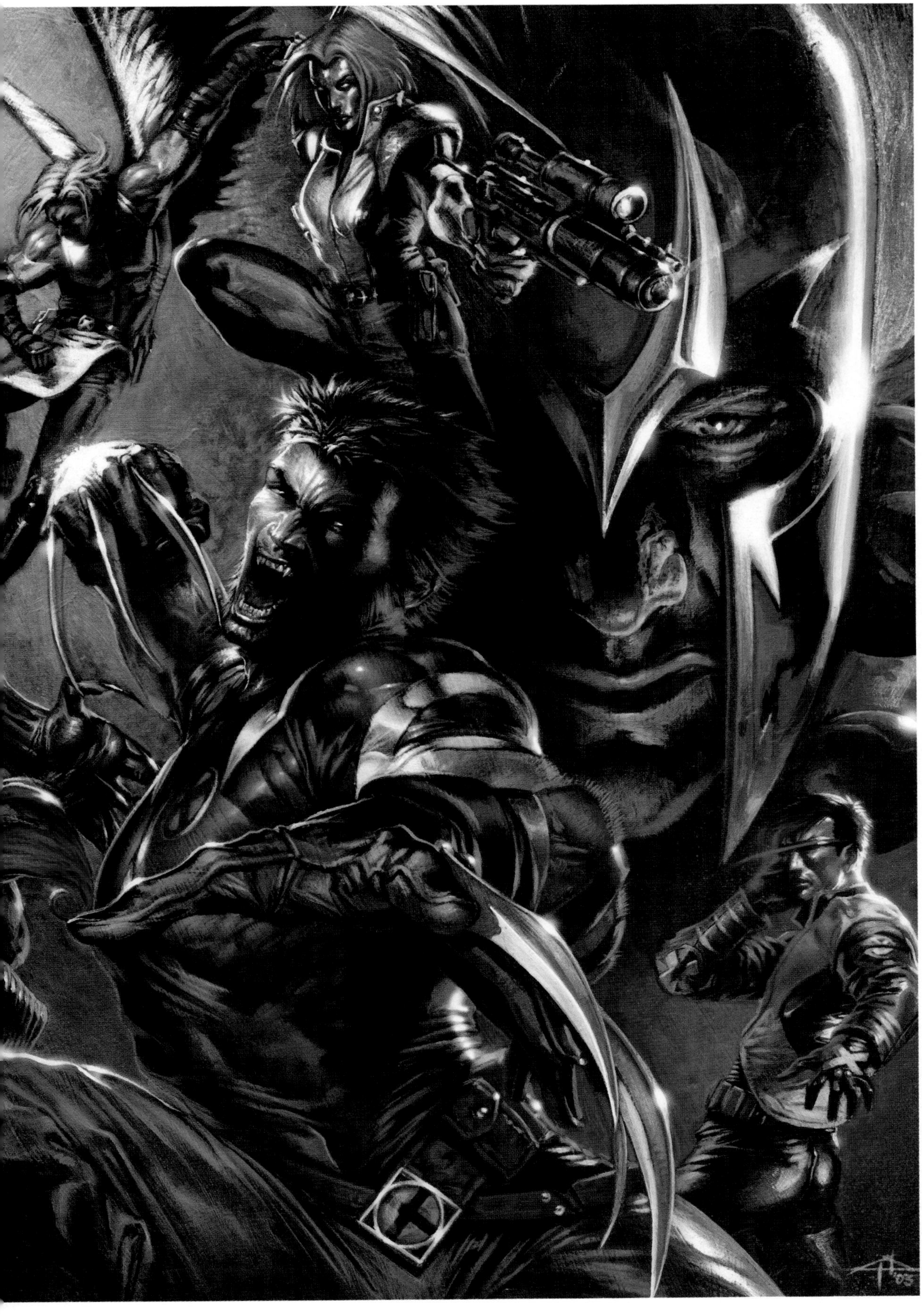

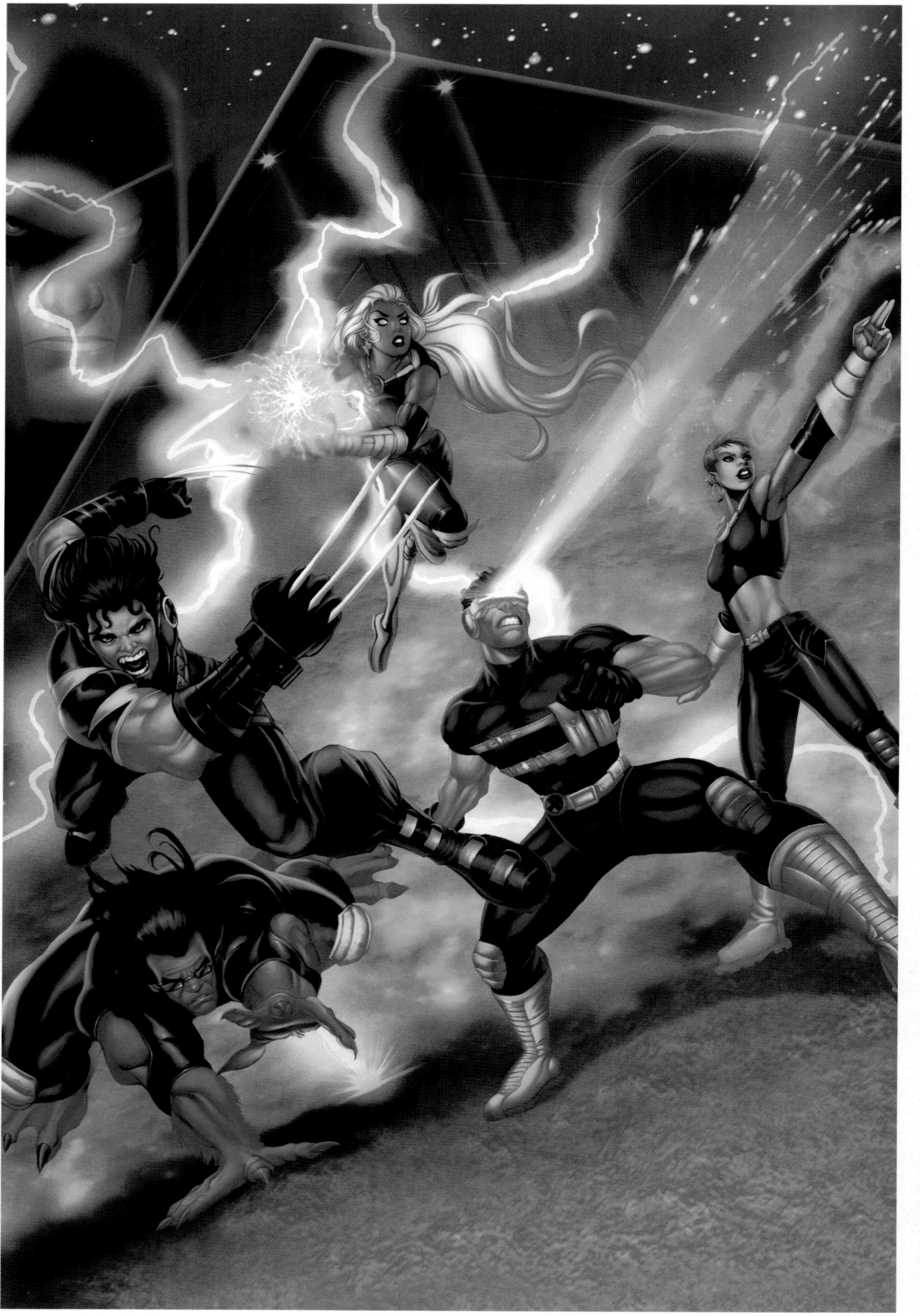

Art by ChrisCross

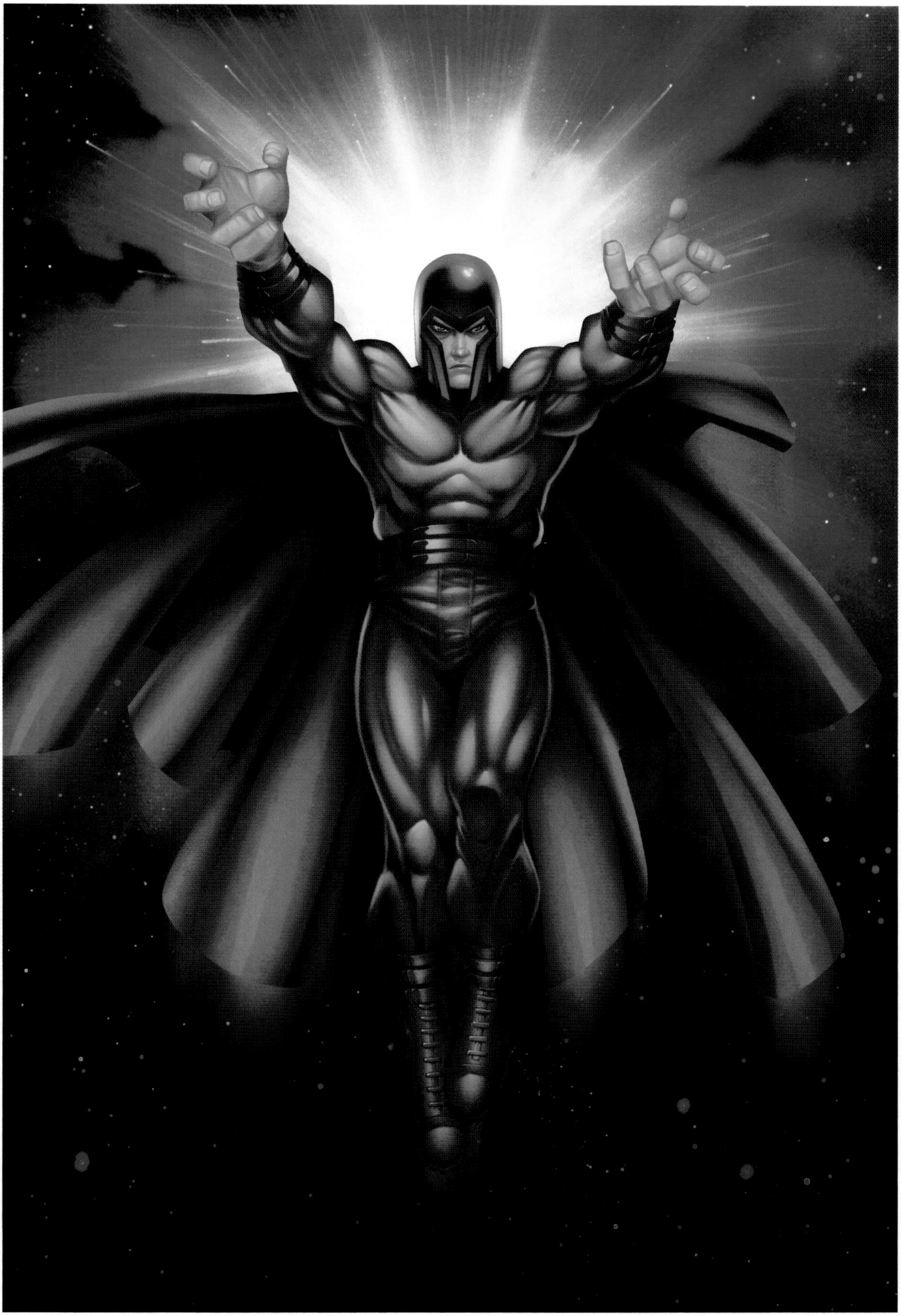

Art by Salvador Larroca

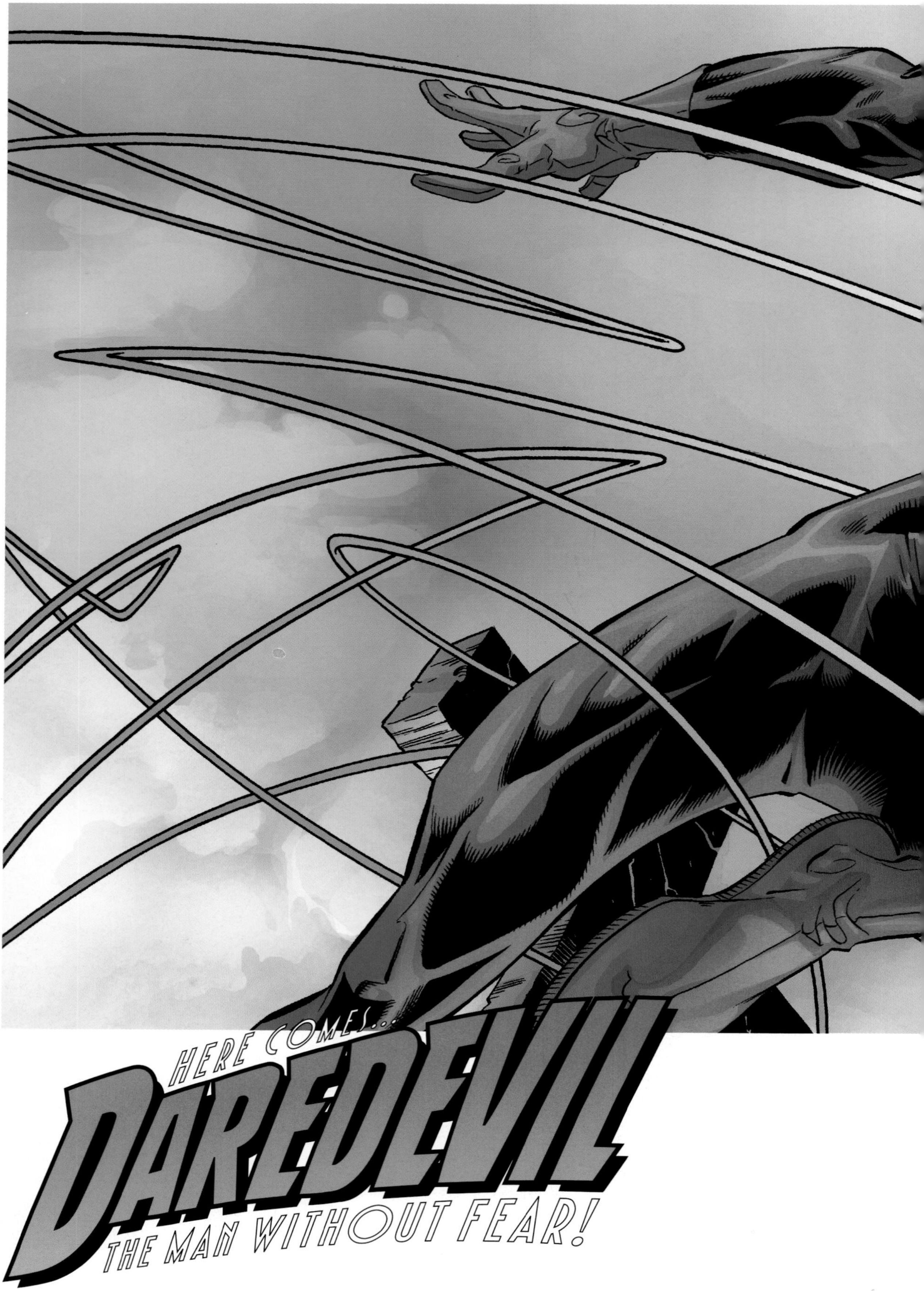
HERE COMES...
DAREDEVIL
THE MAN WITHOUT FEAR!

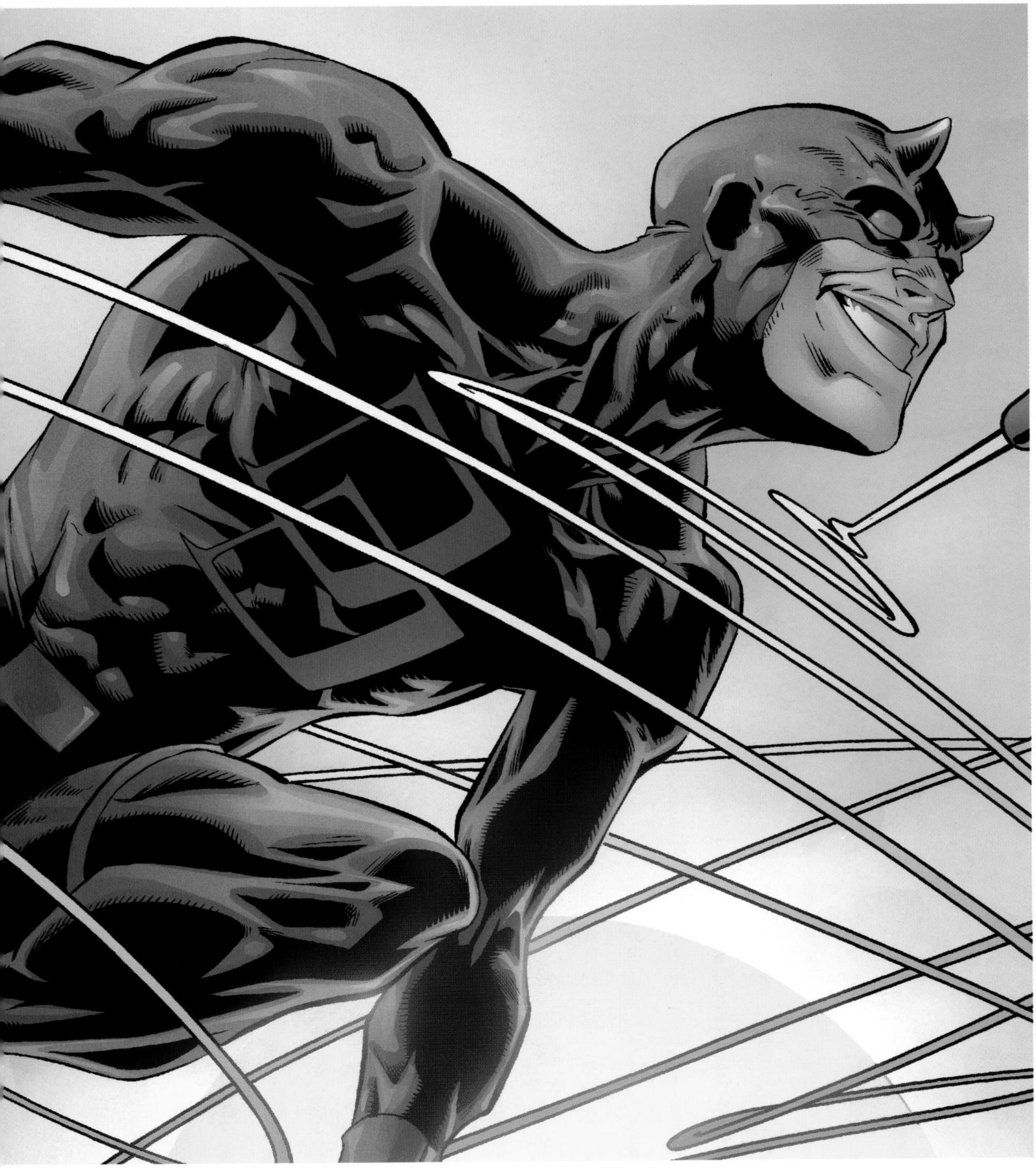

Art by Joe Quesada

Attorney Matt Murdock is blind, but his other four senses function with superhuman sharpness. With amazing fighting skills and a radar sense, he stalks the streets at night, a relentless avenger of justice: Daredevil, the Man Without Fear.

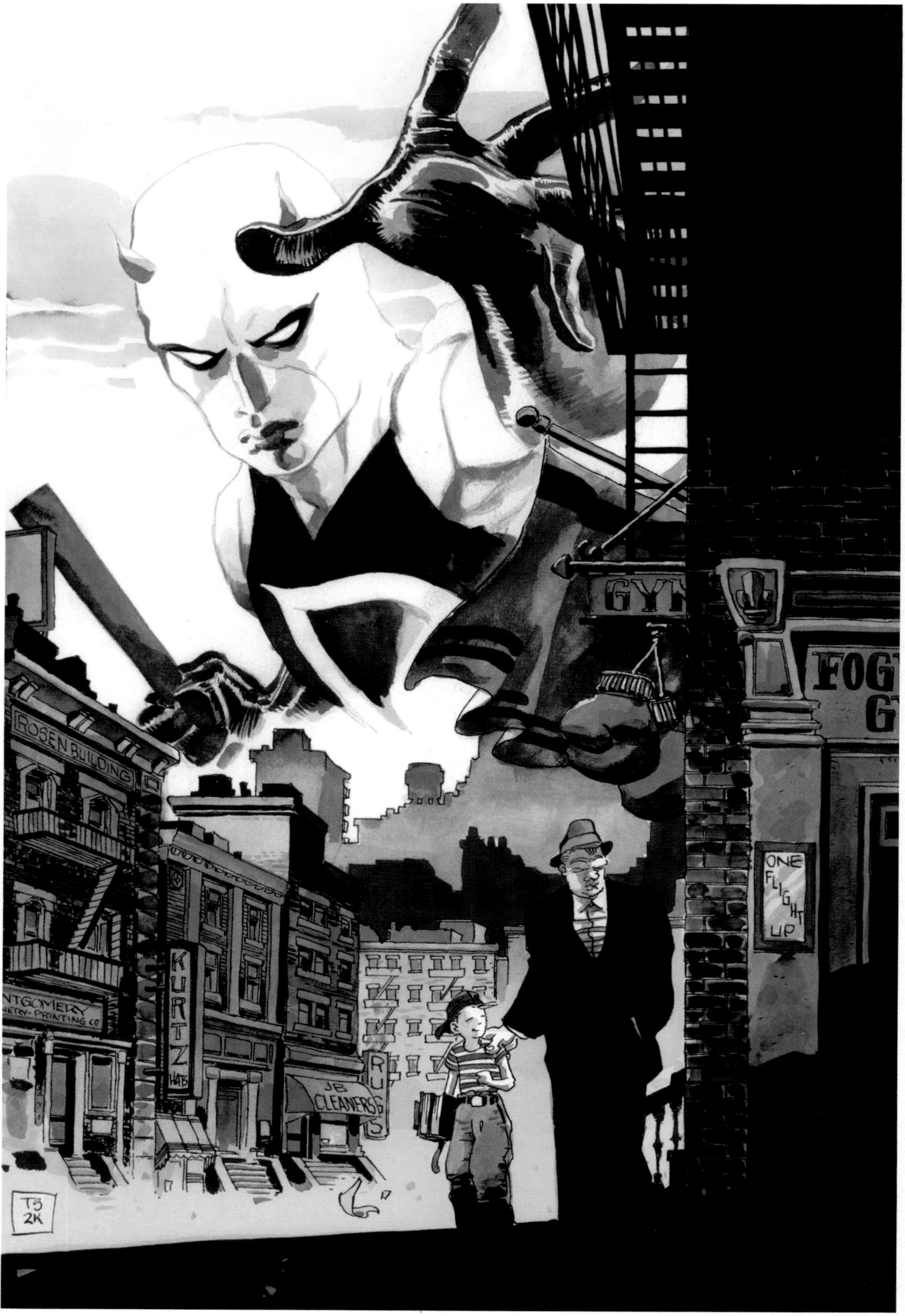
GYM
FOG
ROSEN BUILDING
NTGOMERY
PRINTING CO
KURTZ
HATS
JB CLEANERS
RUSS
ONE FLIGHT UP
TS 2K

Art by Tim Sale

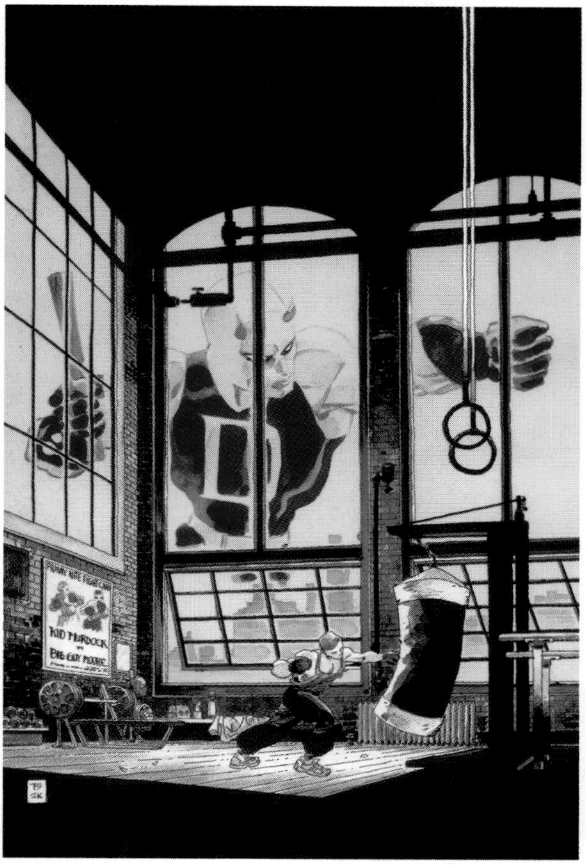
FRIDAY NITE FIGHT CARD
KID MURDOCK
vs
BIG GUY MOORE

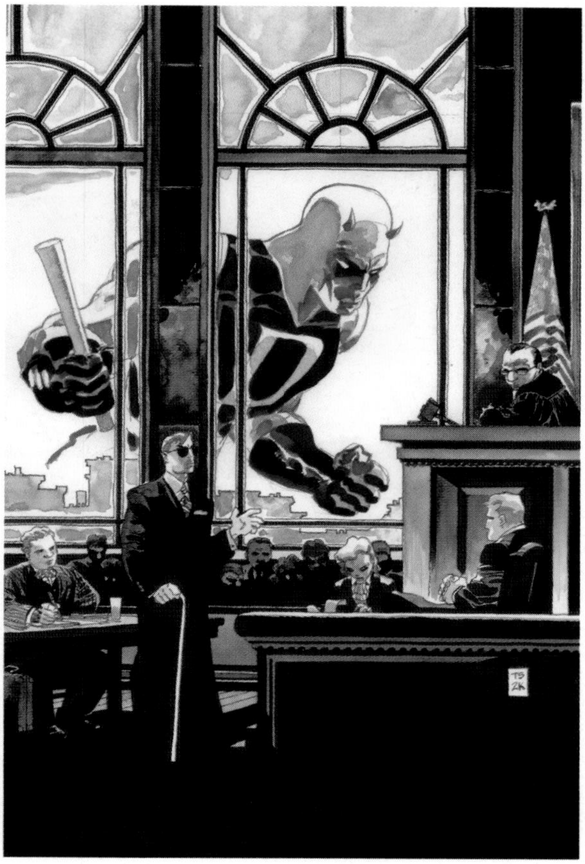

“Daredevil has long been high on my list of favorite super heroes. His sightlessness, his courage, his ability to bounce back from some of the most tragic events to have befallen any costumed cavorter, have always made his stories seem incredibly dramatic to me—and man, do I like drama!”

Stan Lee
Co-creator
Daredevil

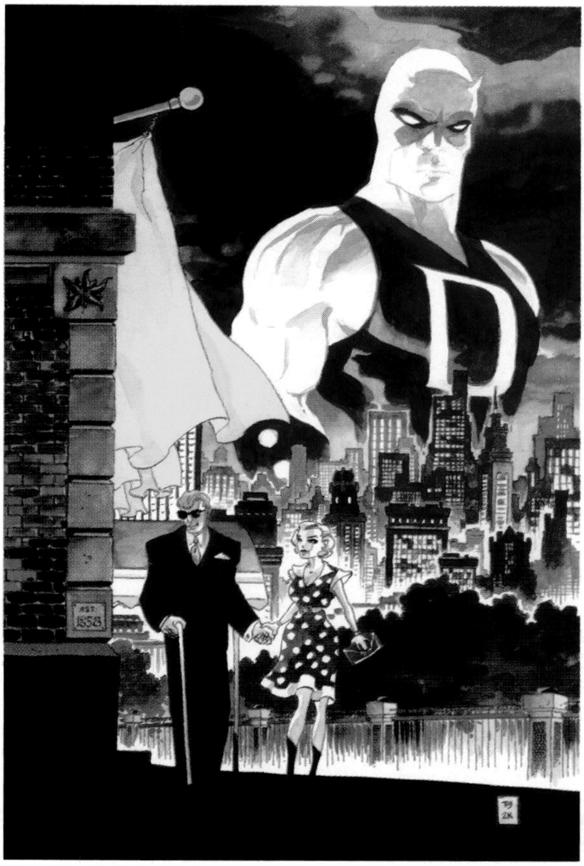

Art by Tim Sale

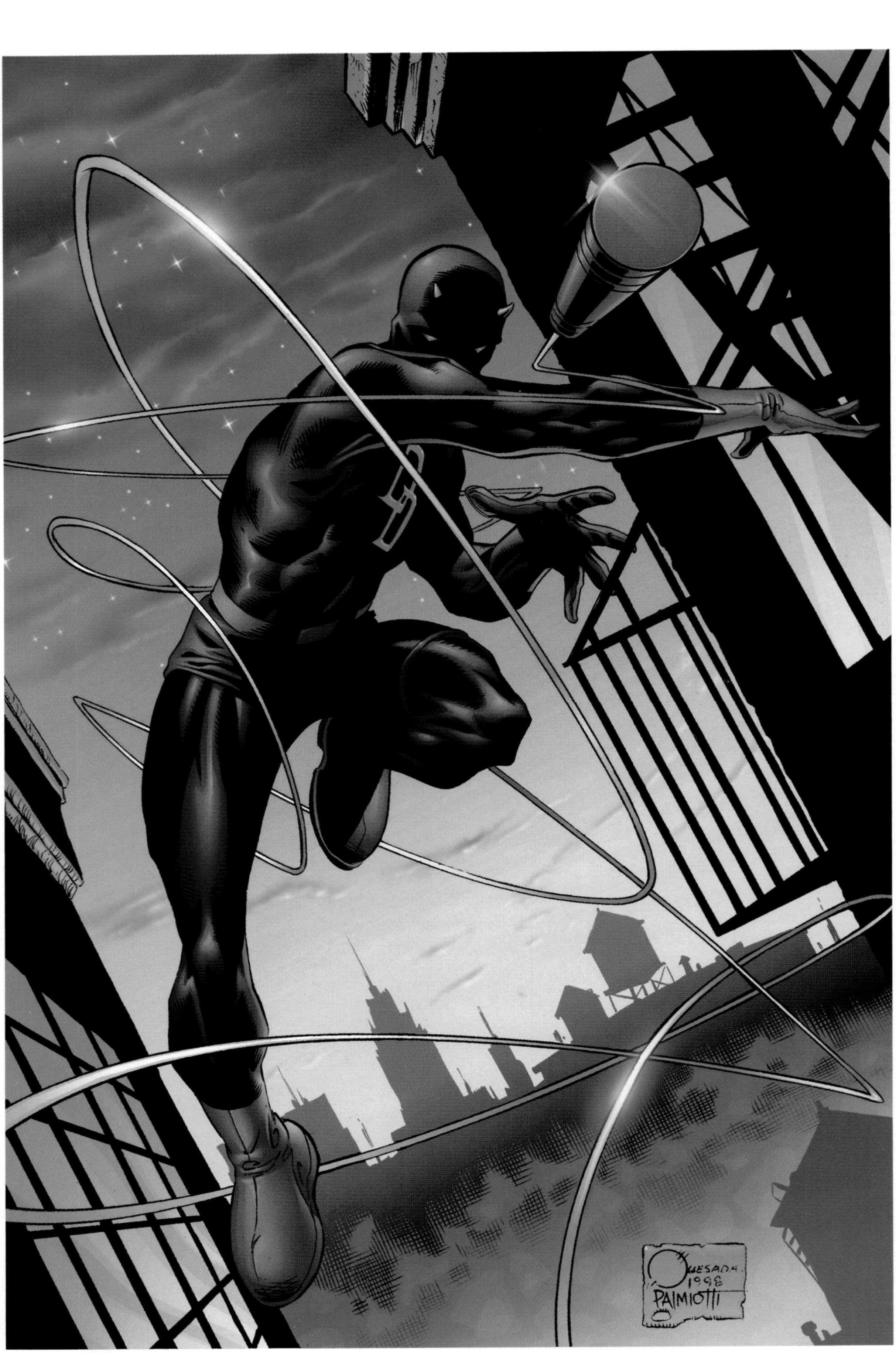
QUESADA
1998
PALMIOTTI

Art by Joe Quesada

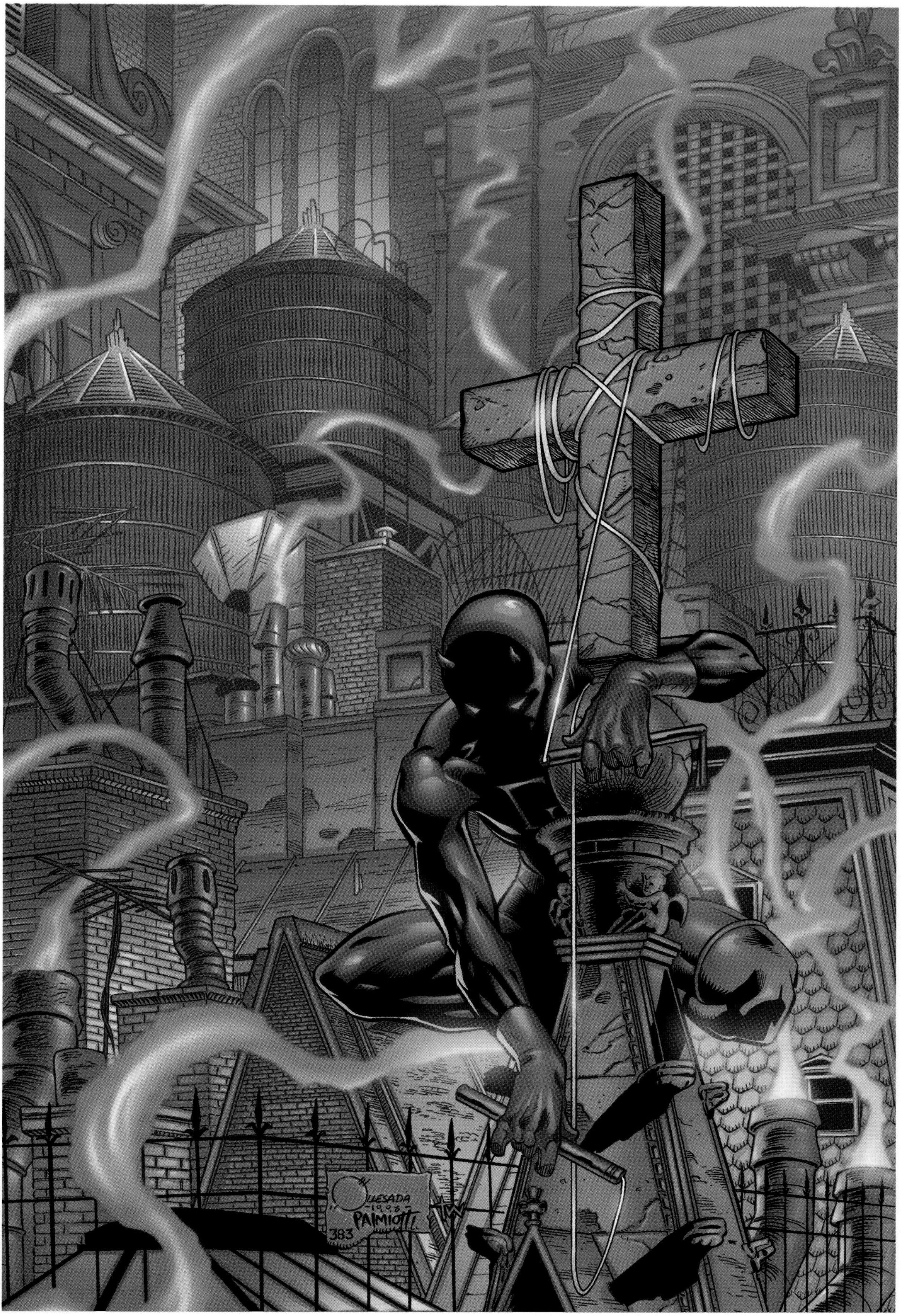

Art by Joe Quesada

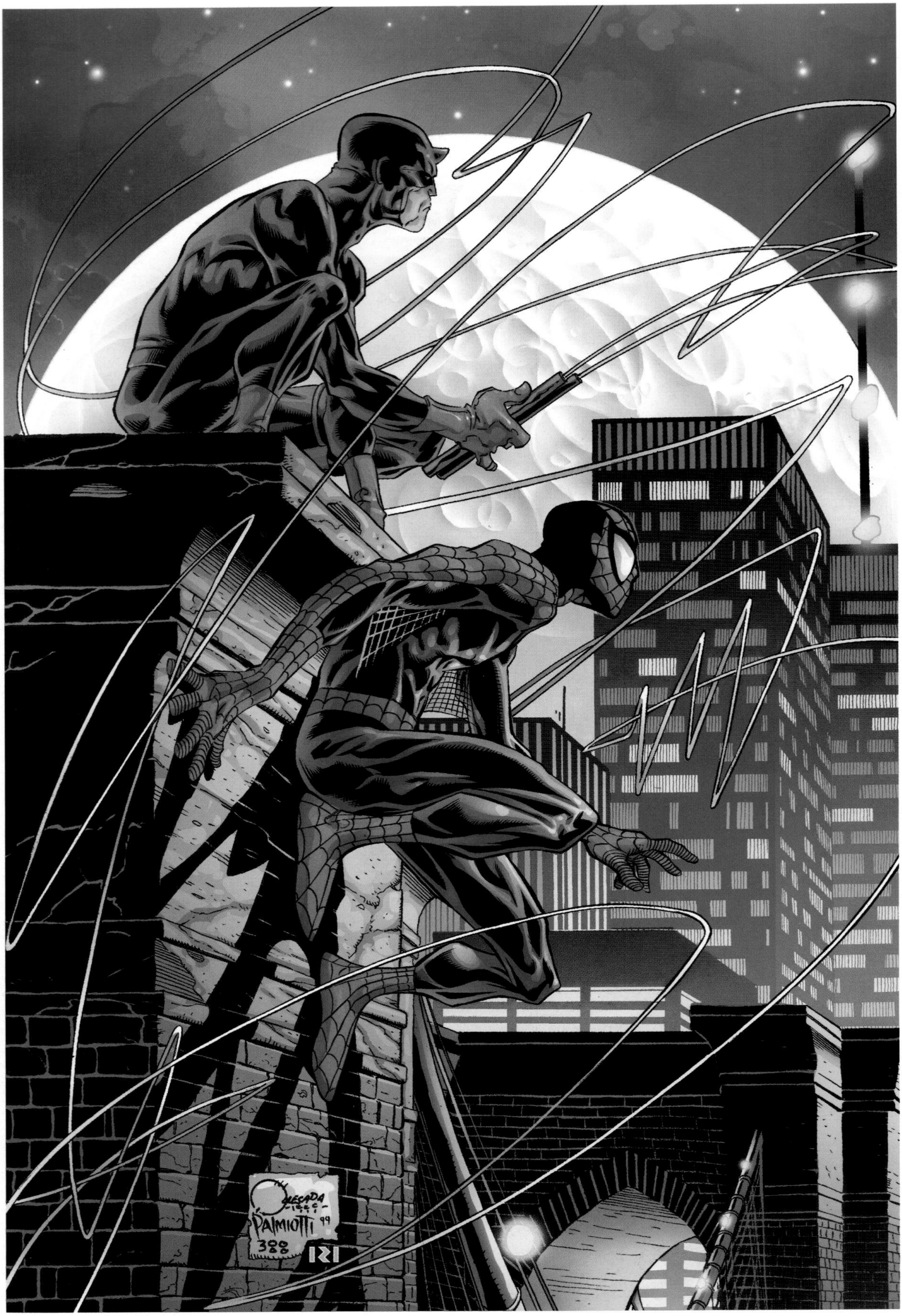

Art by Joe Quesada

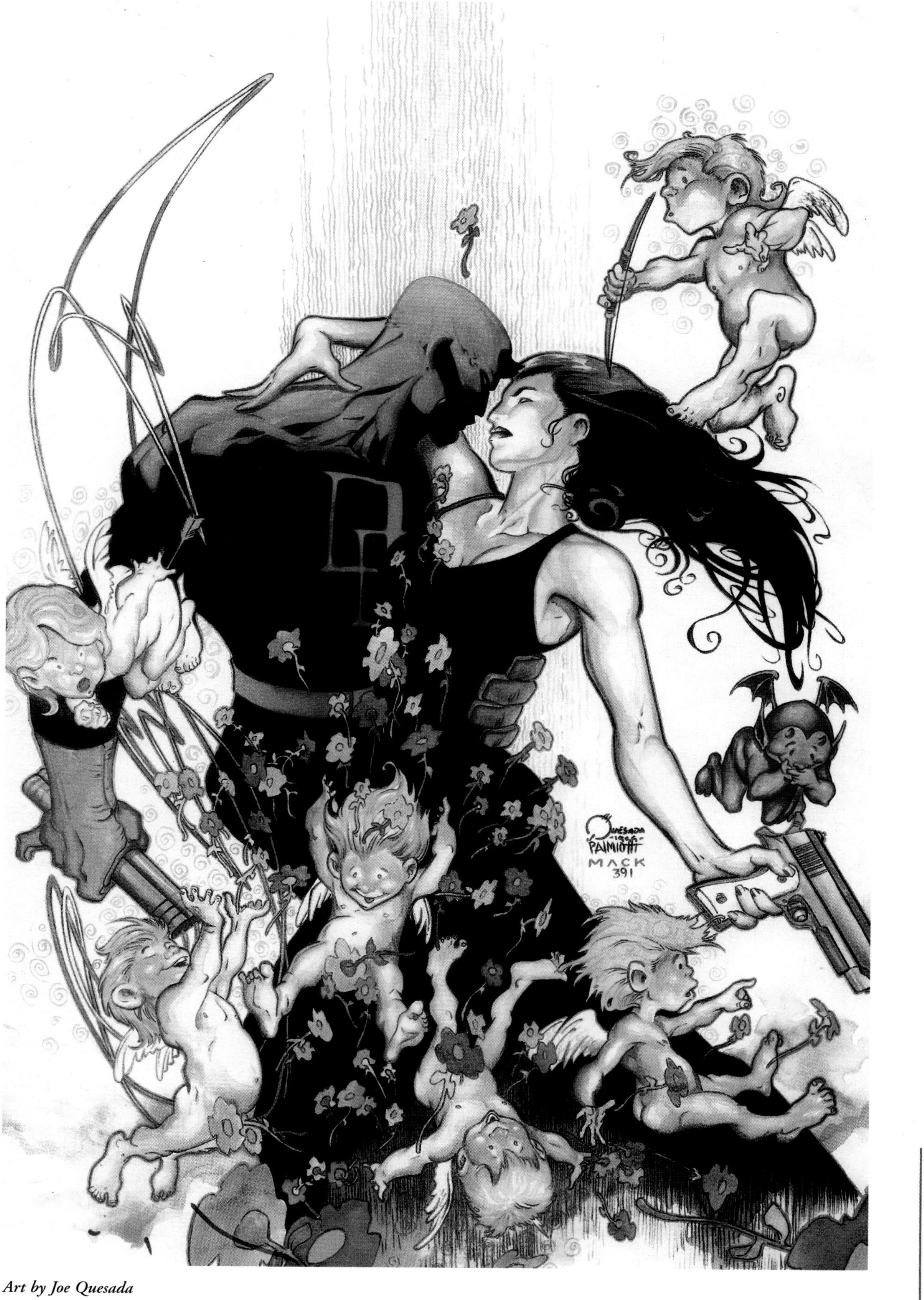
QUESADA
PALMIOTTI
MACK
391

Art by Joe Quesada

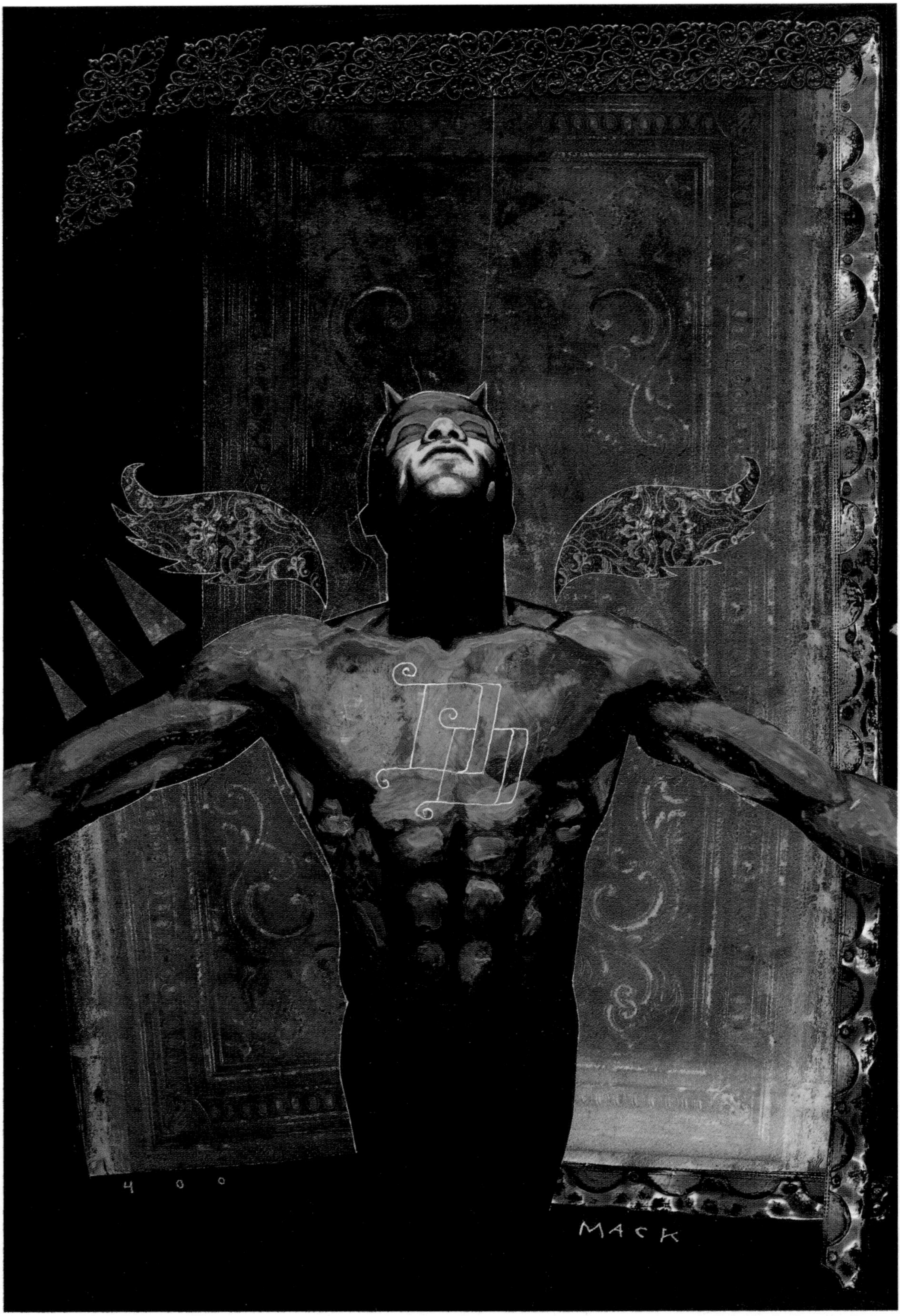
400
MACK

Art by David Mack

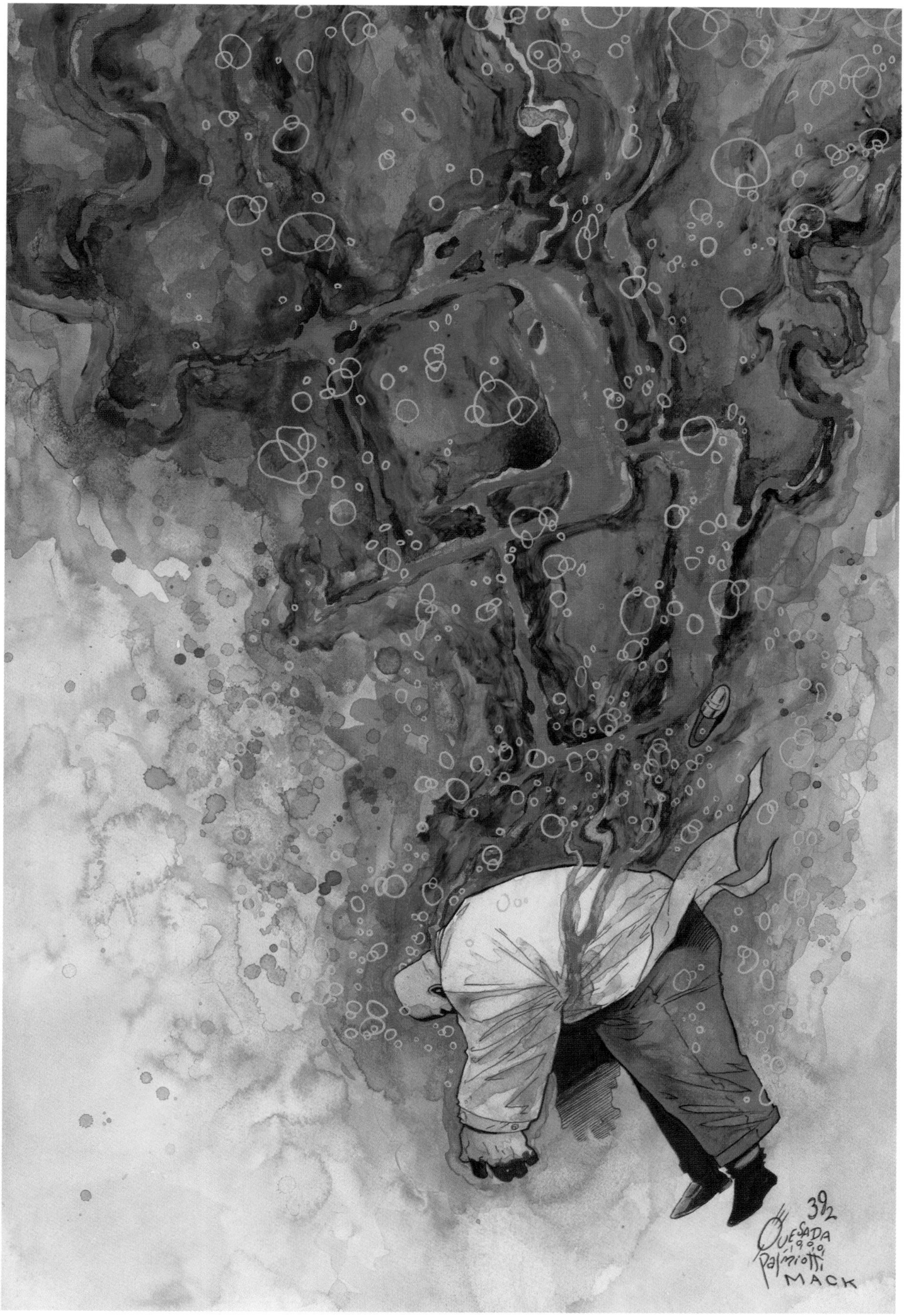
39/2
QUESADA
1999
Palmiotti
MACK

Art by Joe Quesada

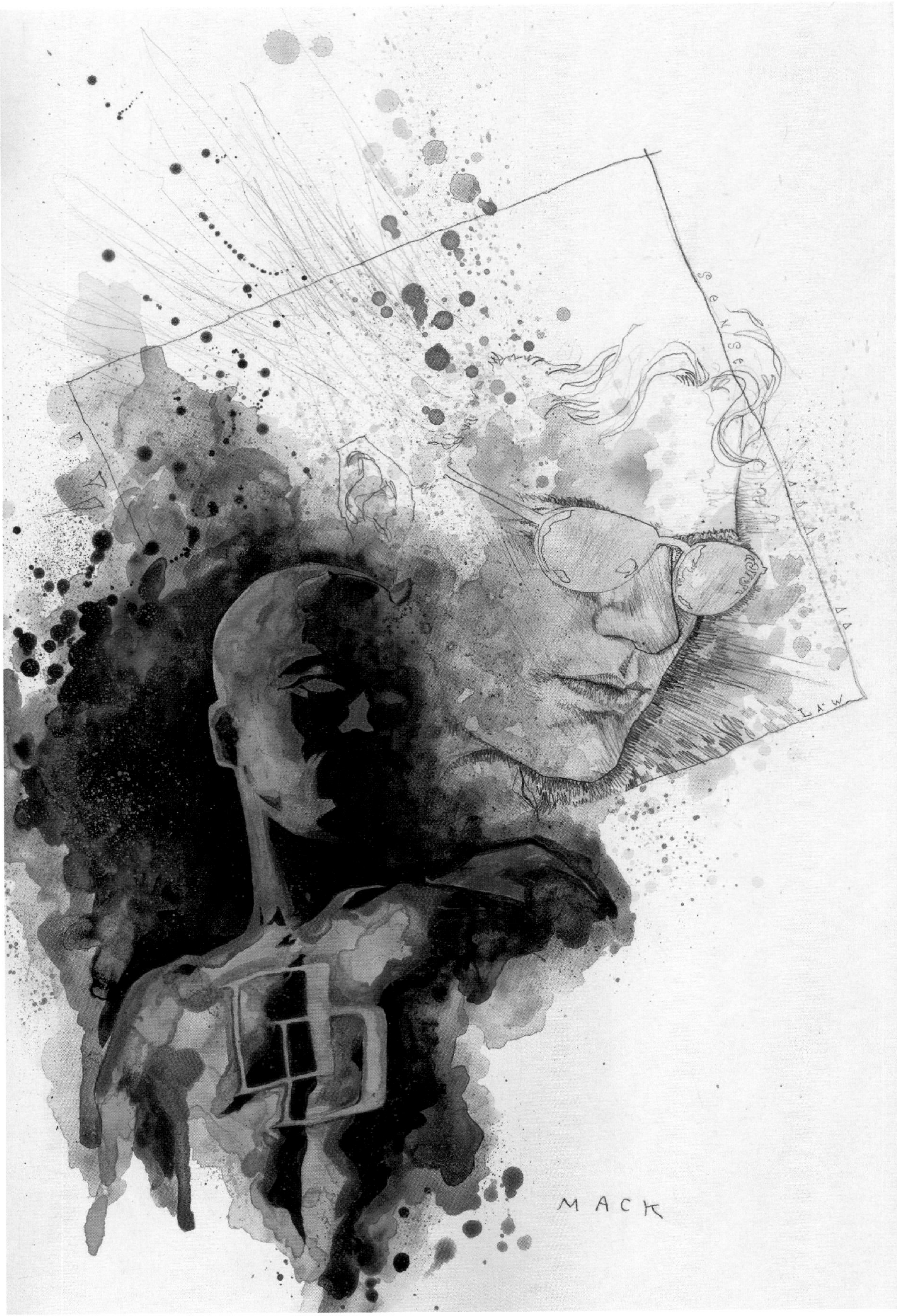
MACK

Art by David Mack

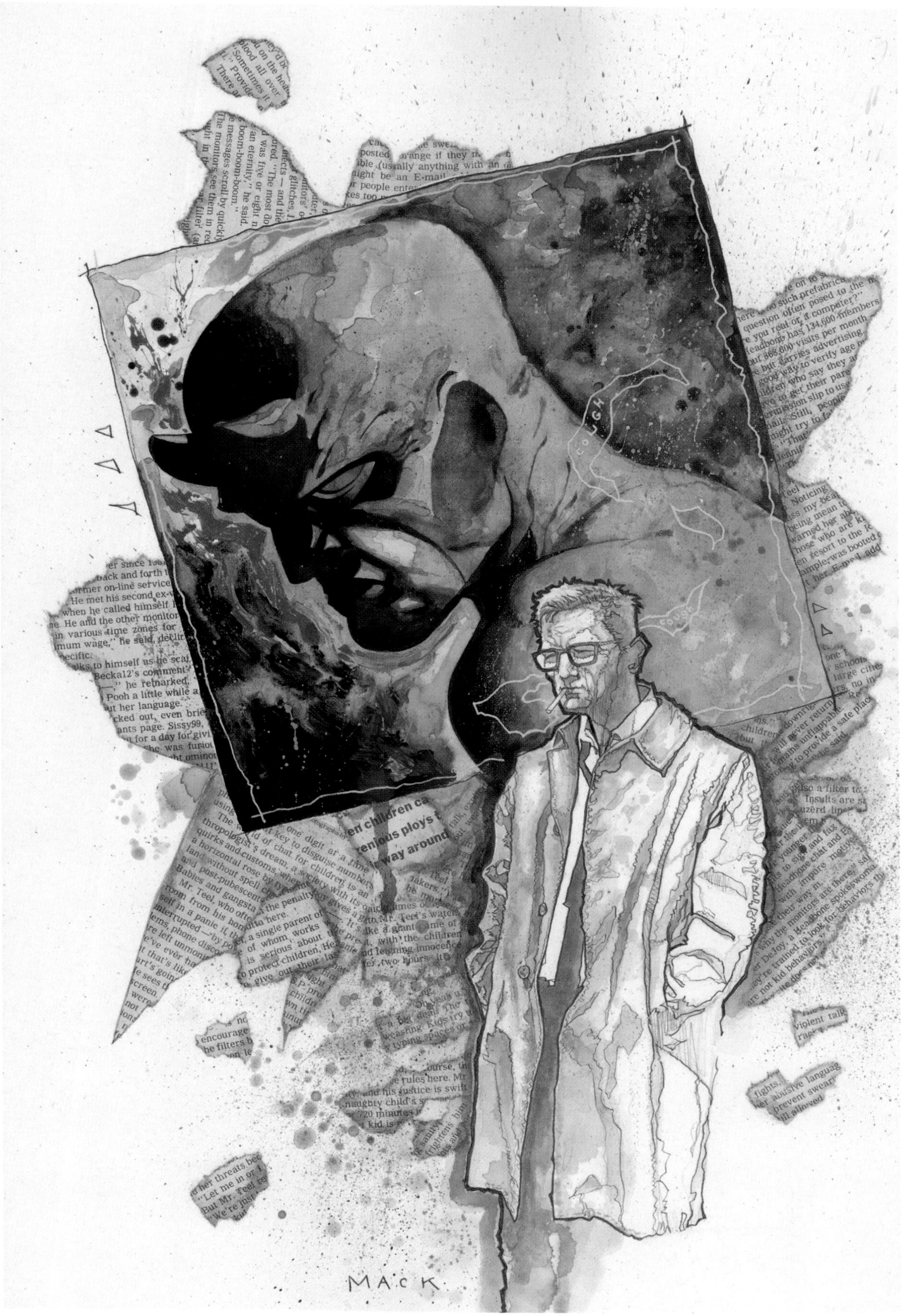
MACK

Art by David Mack

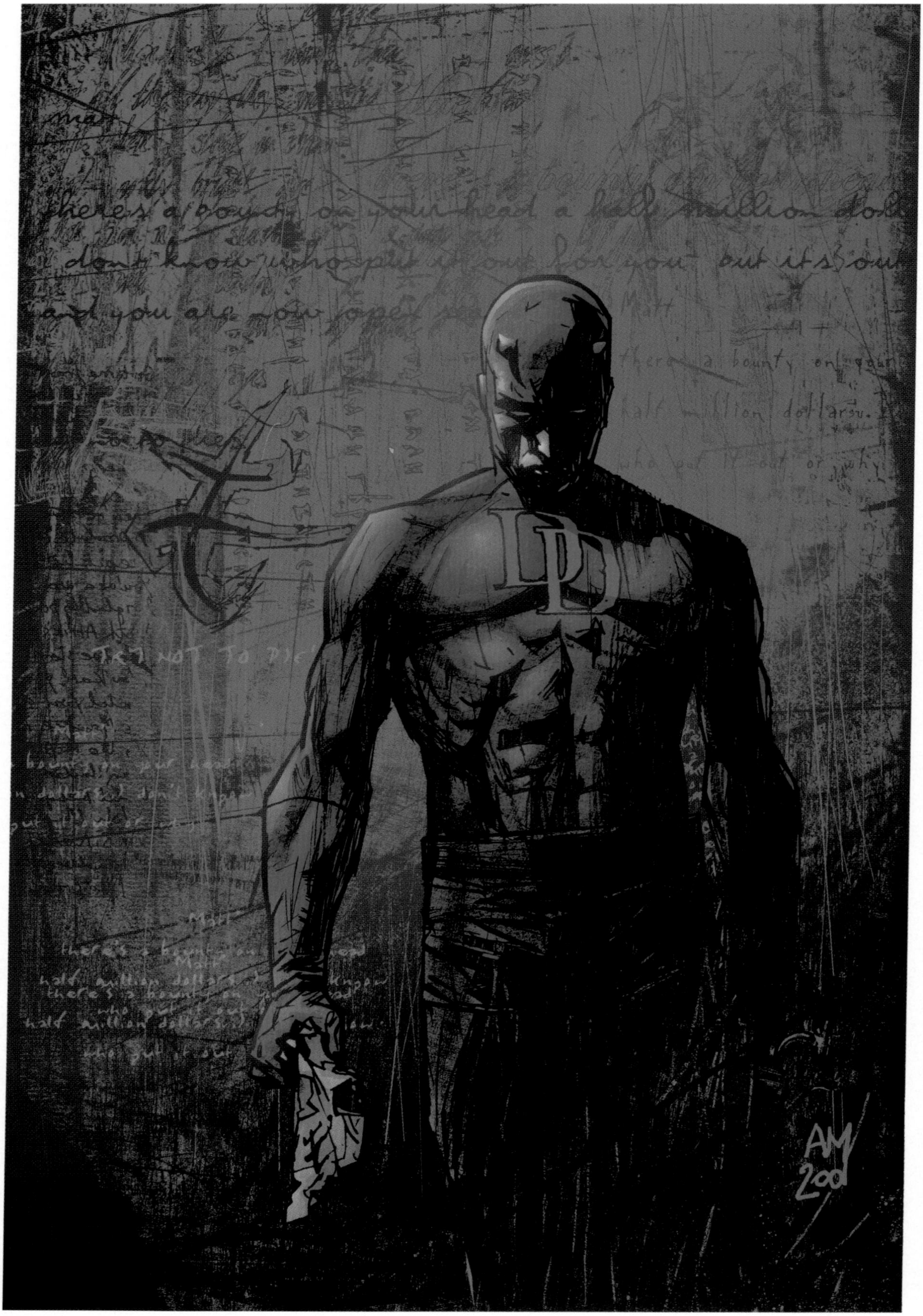
there's a bounty on your head a half million dol
Matt
half million dollars
TRY NOT TO DIE
AM
200

Art by Alex Maleev

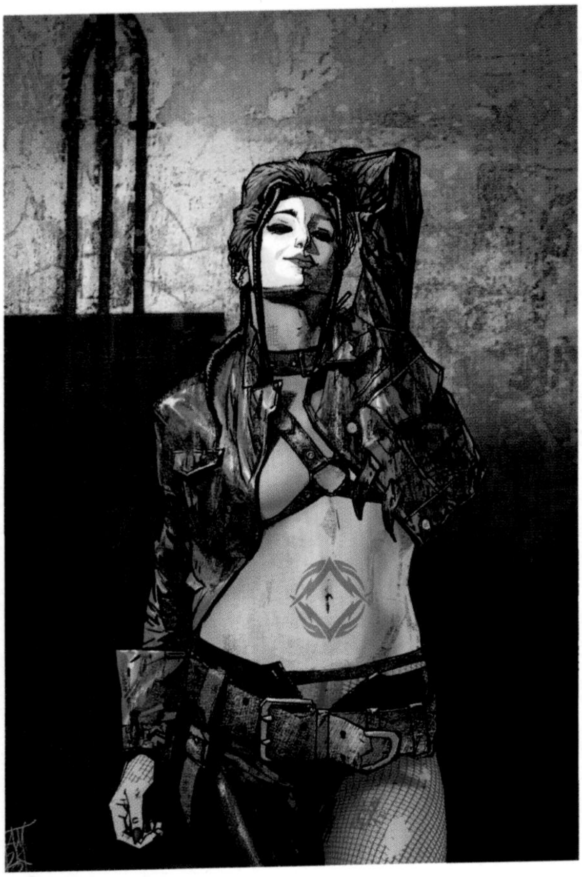

"Brian Michael Bendis and Alex Maleev have created what is already considered a classic run on the Daredevil legacy. These stories were more than a source of inspiration to me throughout the long and grueling process of writing, shooting and editing the *Daredevil* movie. They were validation. Validation that Daredevil still remains the most interesting, most tragic, most thrilling character in all of comics ... Alex Maleev's stark, haunting imagery brings you into a world where anything can happen."

Mark Steven Johnson
Director
Daredevil

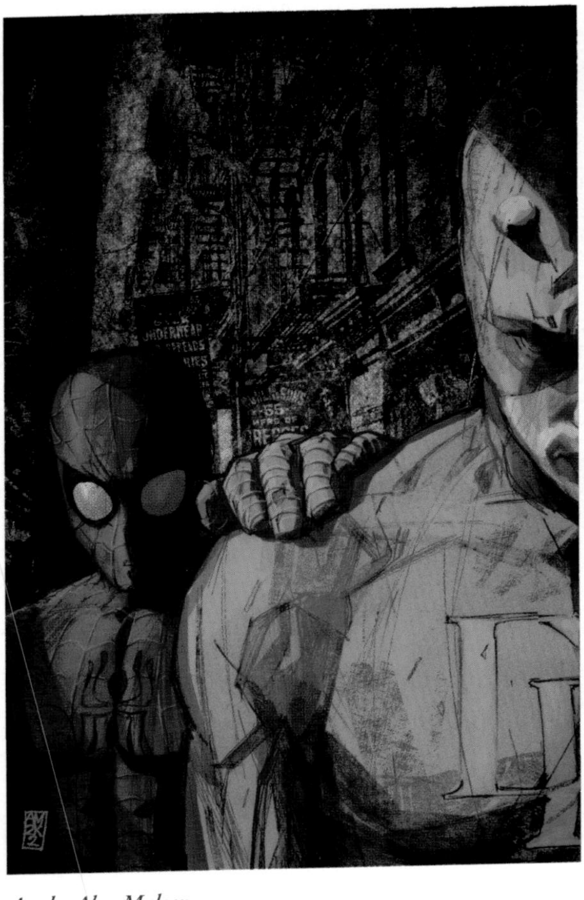

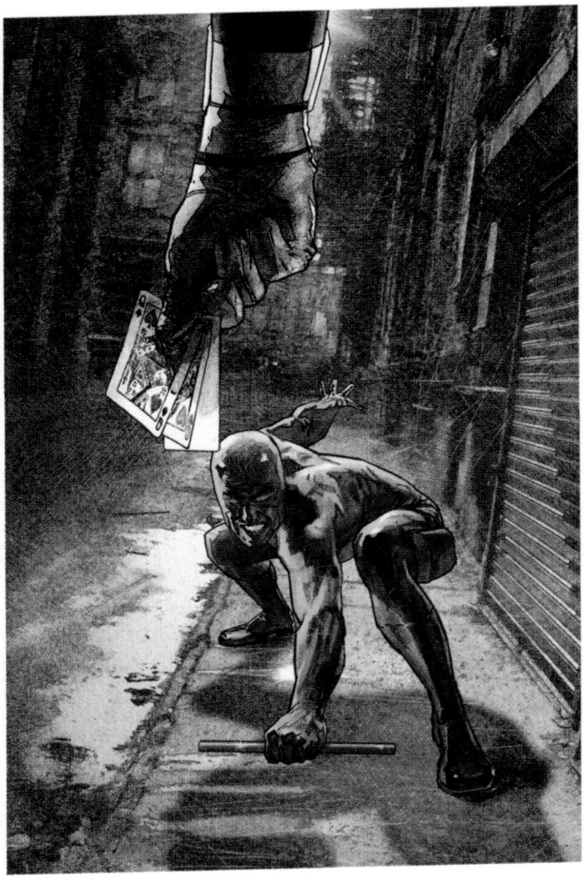

Art by Alex Maleev

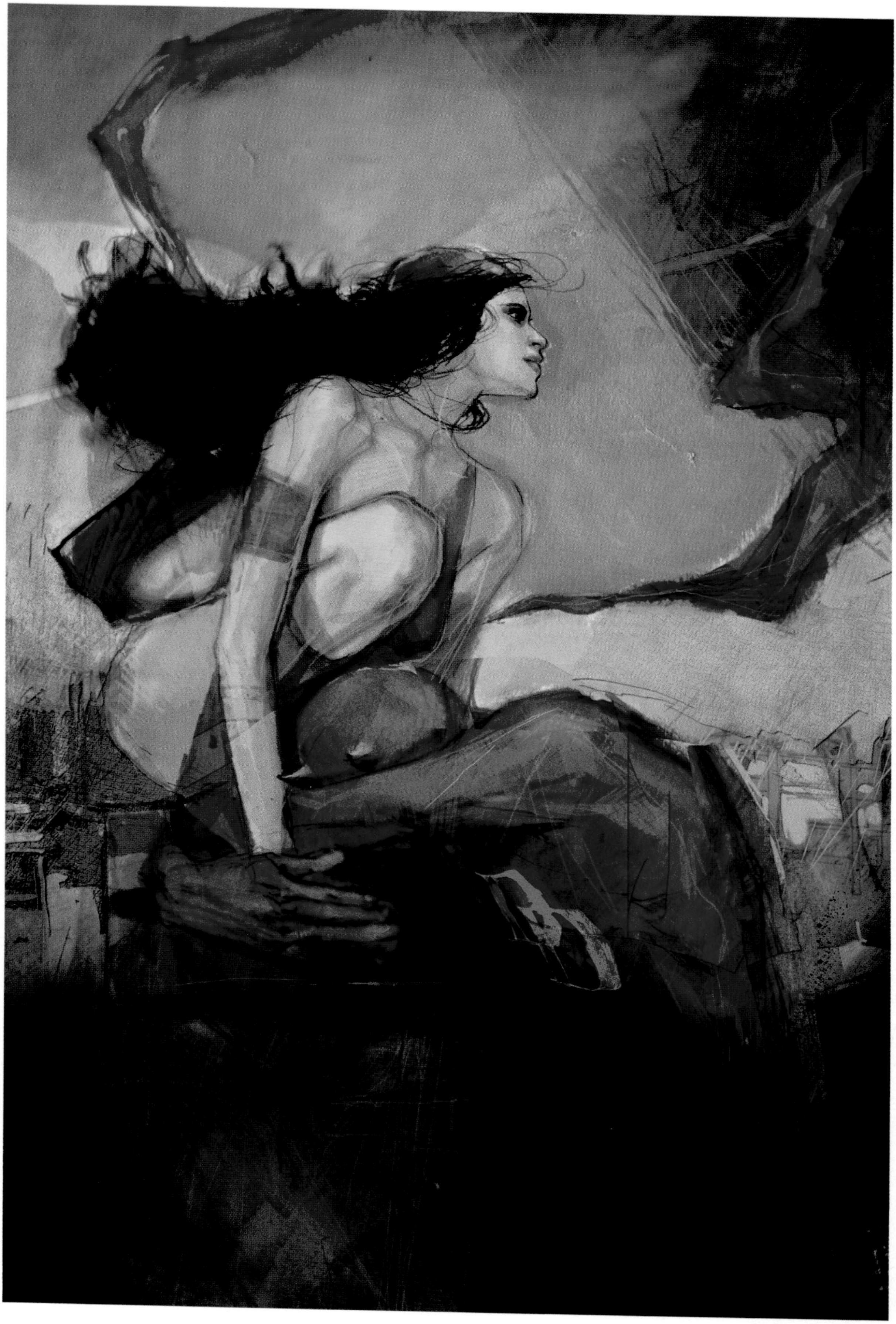

Art by Alex Maleev

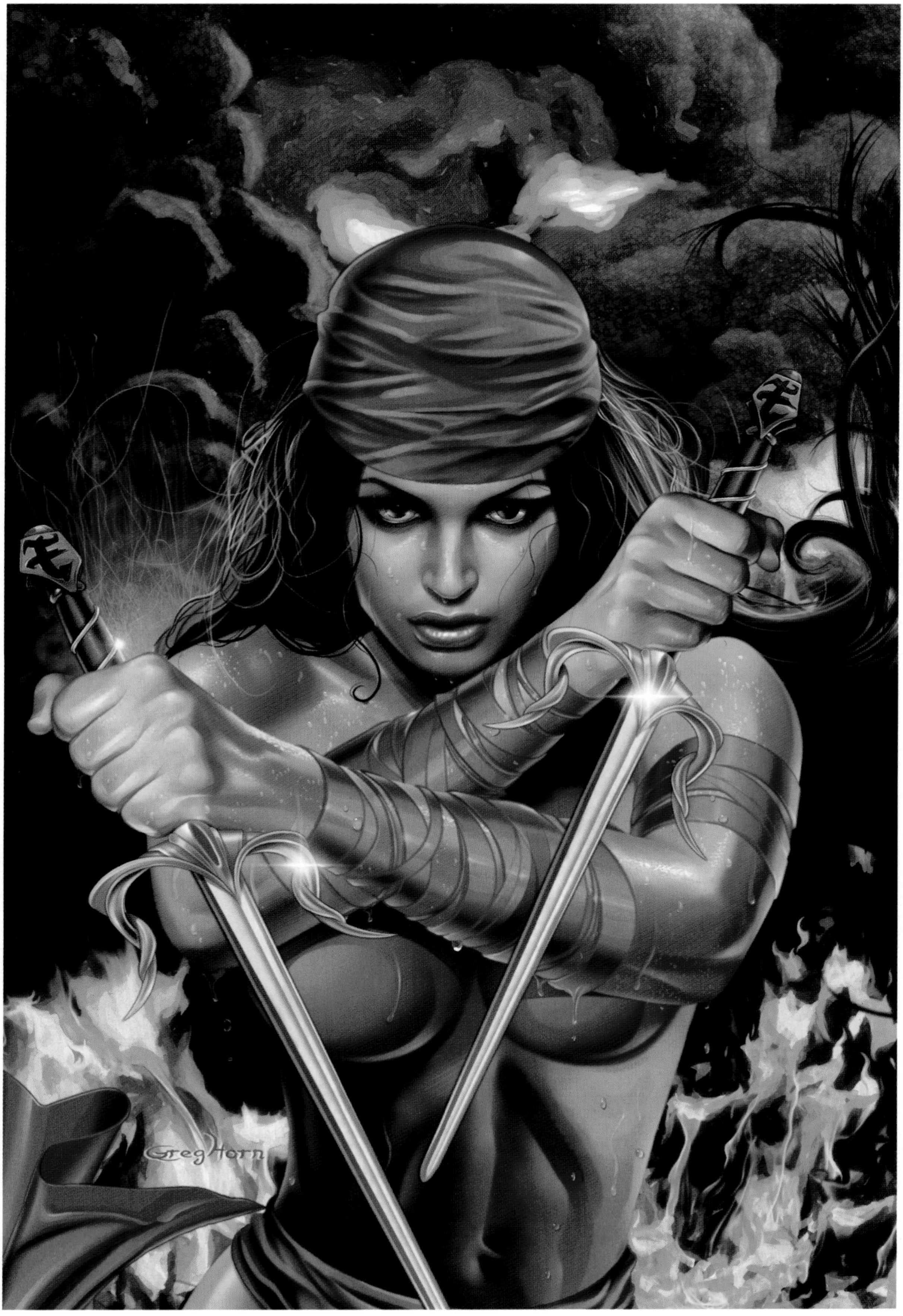
Greg Horn

Art by Greg Horn

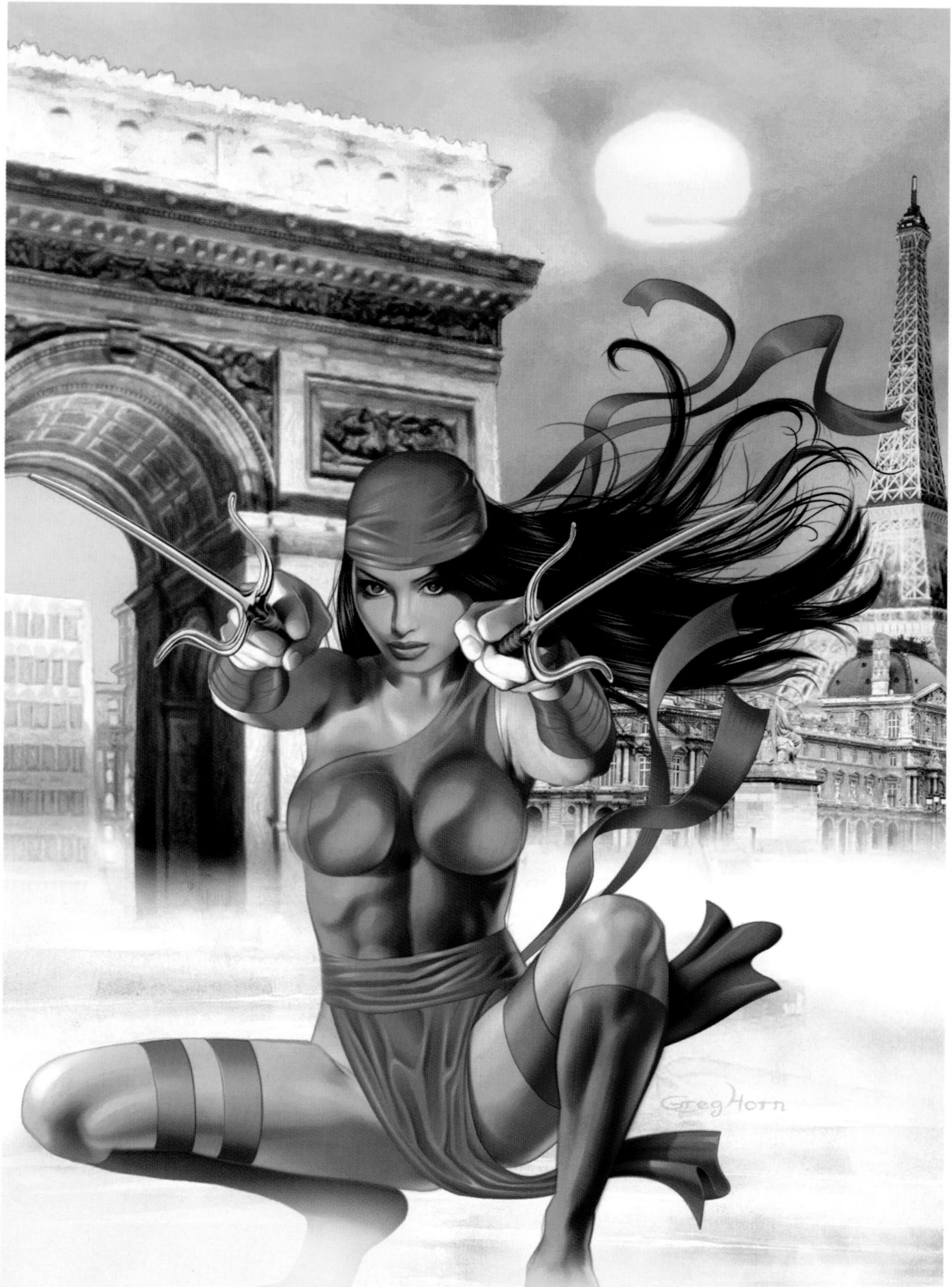
Greg Horn

Art by Greg Horn

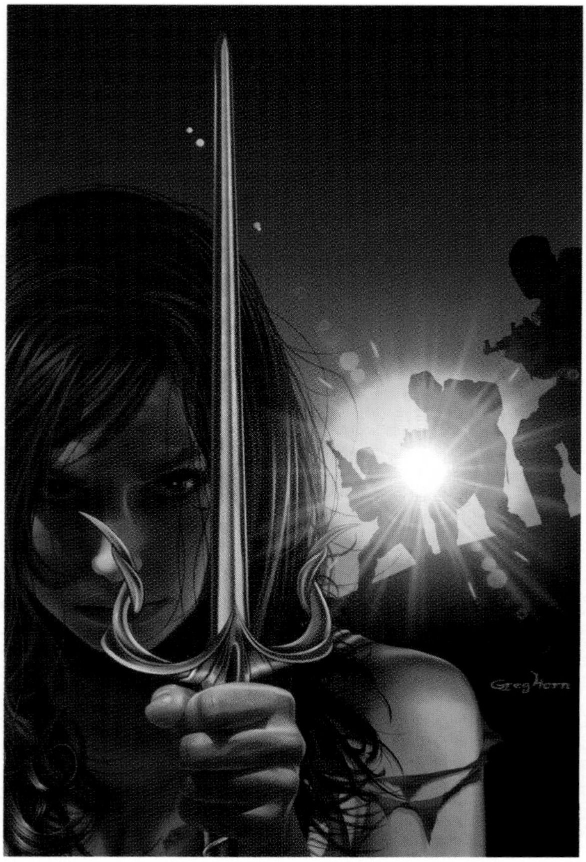

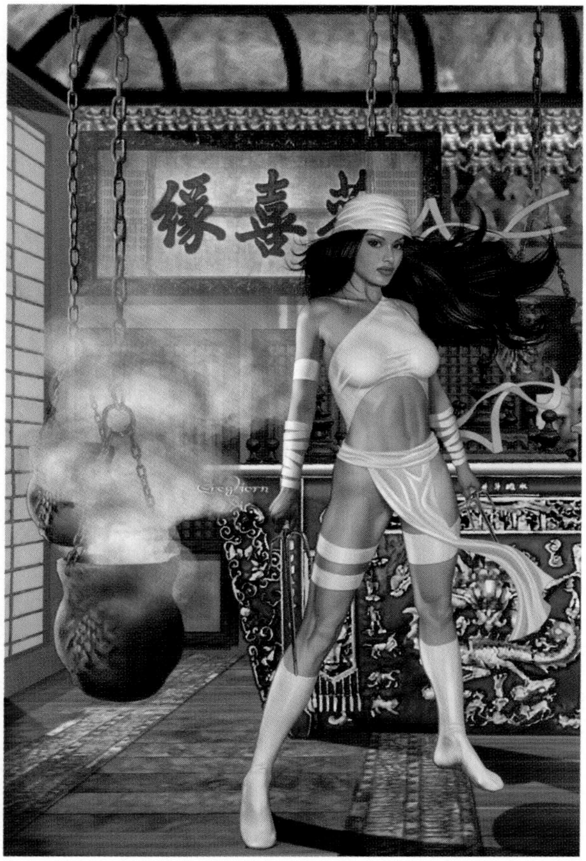

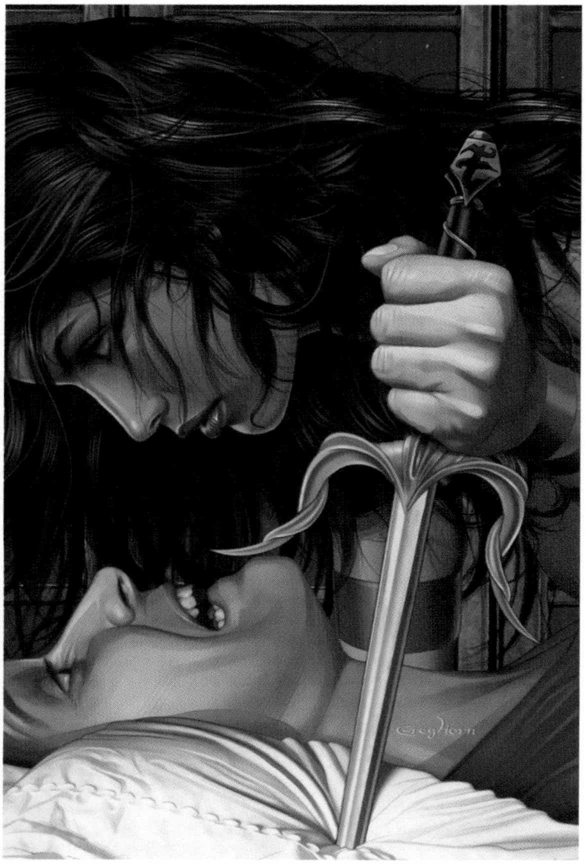

Art by Greg Horn

"I love [*Elektra* cover artist] Greg Horn's art. I saw one of his Elektra drawings in black leather and thought it was sexy as hell. I thought that it made sense for the real world."

Mark Steven Johnson
Director
Daredevil

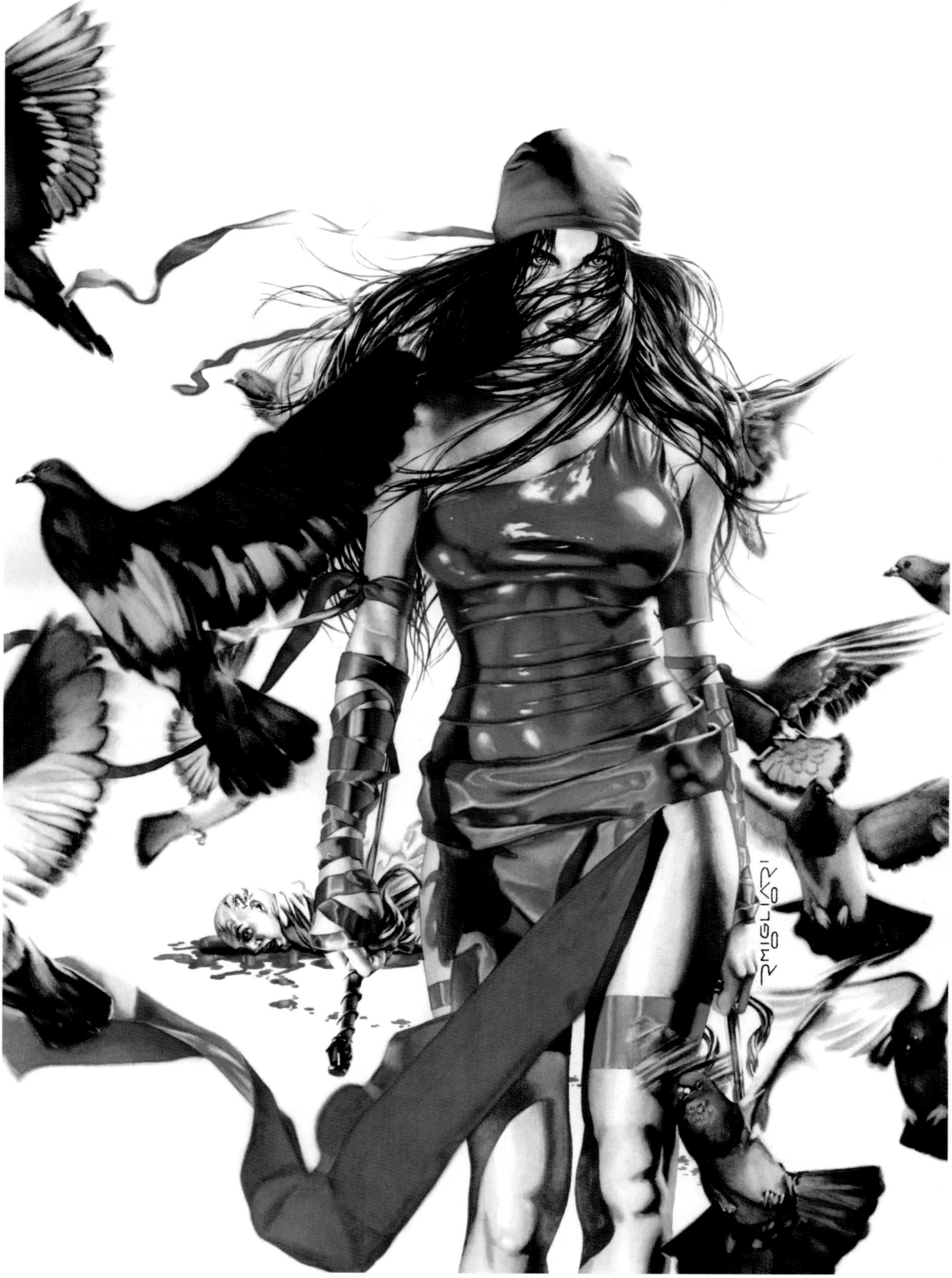
R MIGLIARI
00
Art by Rudolfo Migliari

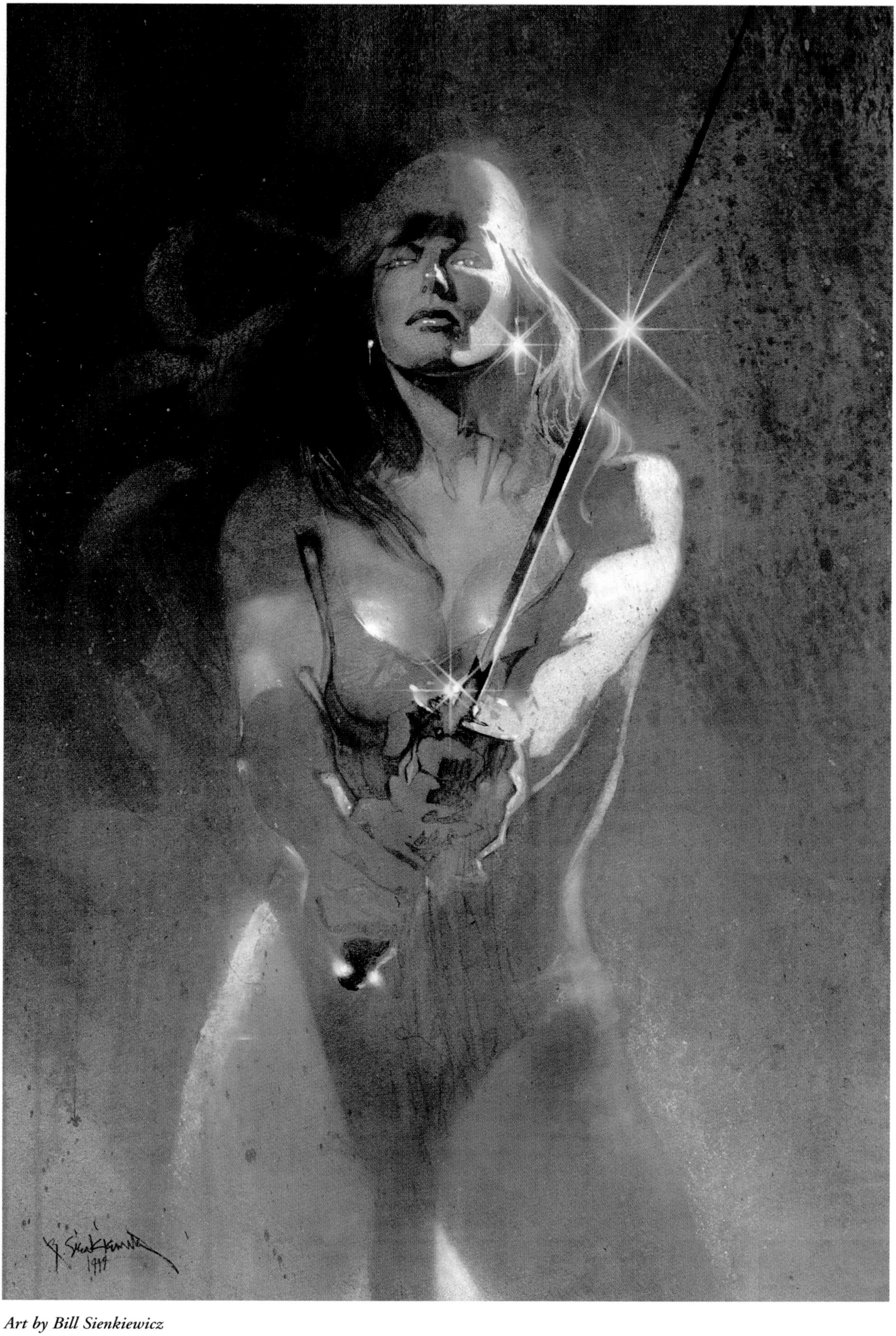

Art by Bill Sienkiewicz

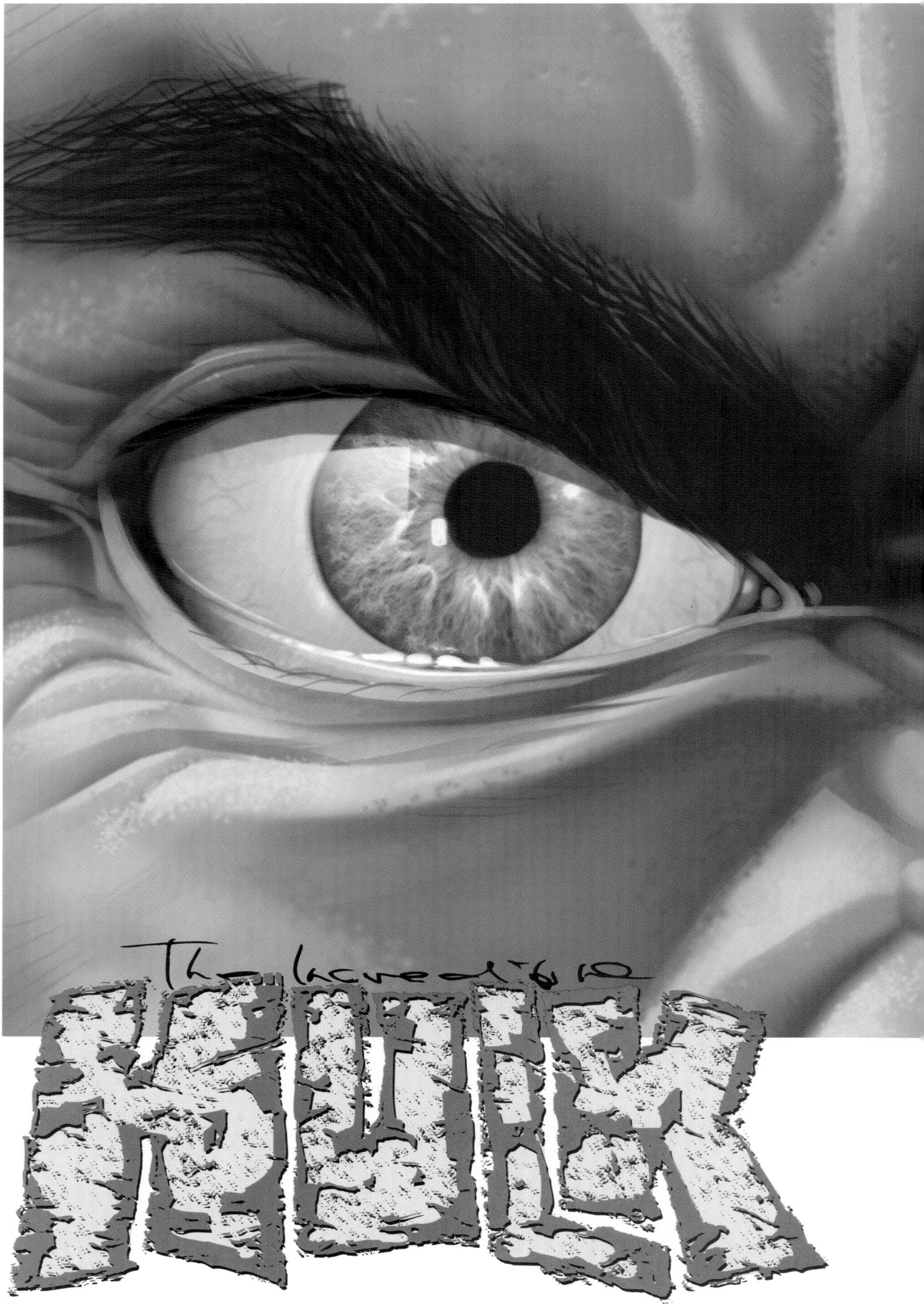
The Incredible
HULK

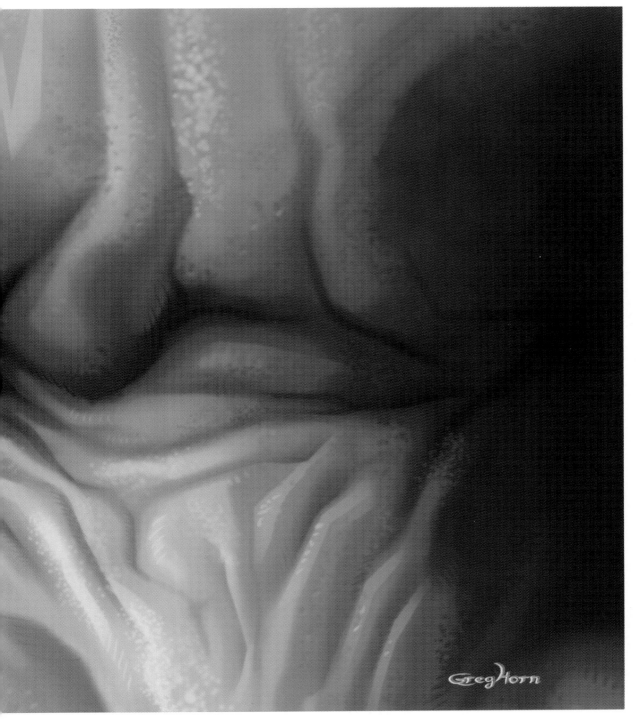

Art by Greg Horn

Caught in the heart of a nuclear explosion of gamma radiation, Dr. Bruce Banner now finds himself transformed into the dark personification of his repressed rage and fury. On the run — from the police, the government, clandestine forces faceless and compassionless, and the unbridled beast within men call the Hulk — Banner knows the dread of the hunted, the terror of a mind never completely his, never entirely sane.

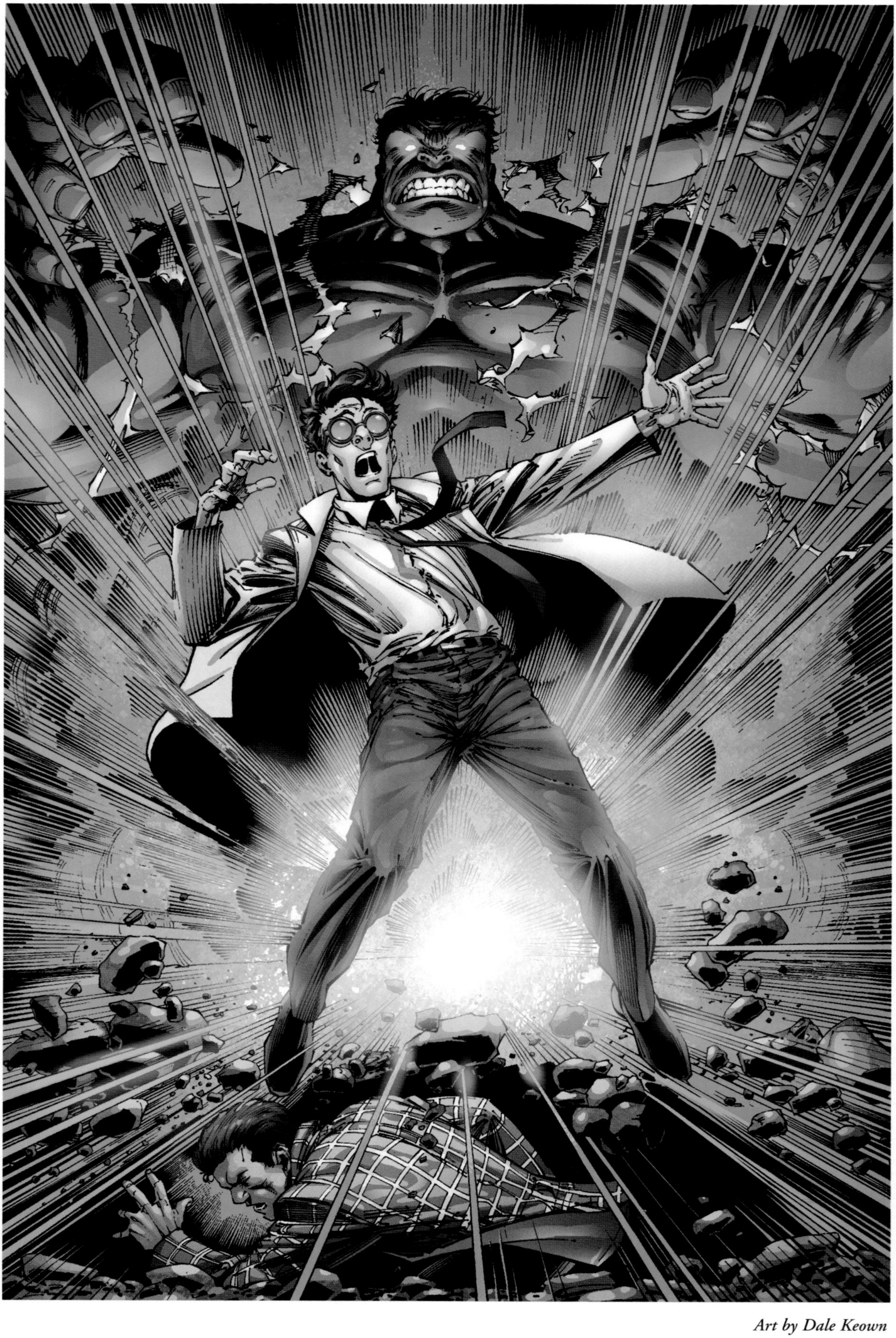

Art by Dale Keown

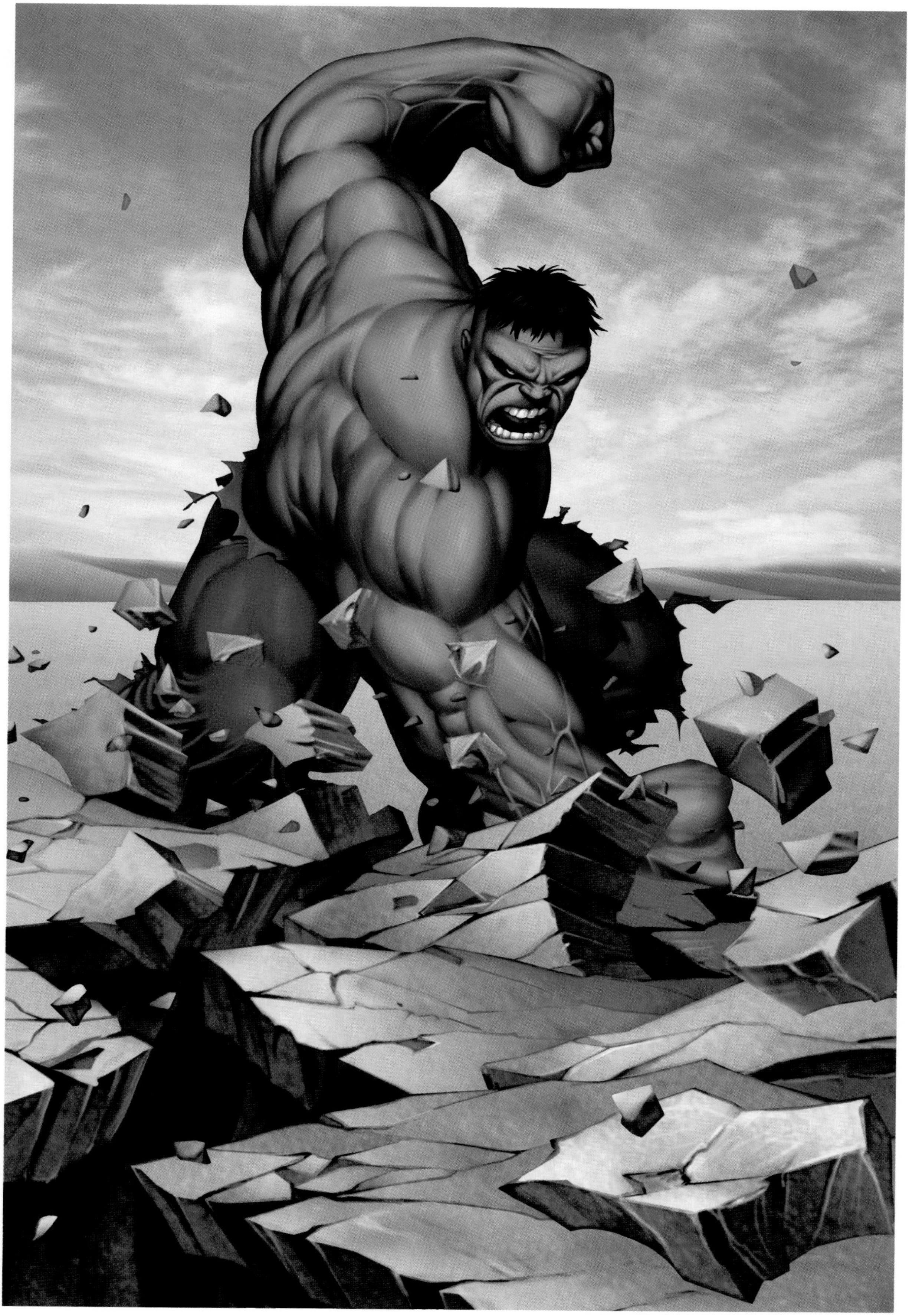

Art by Dale Keown

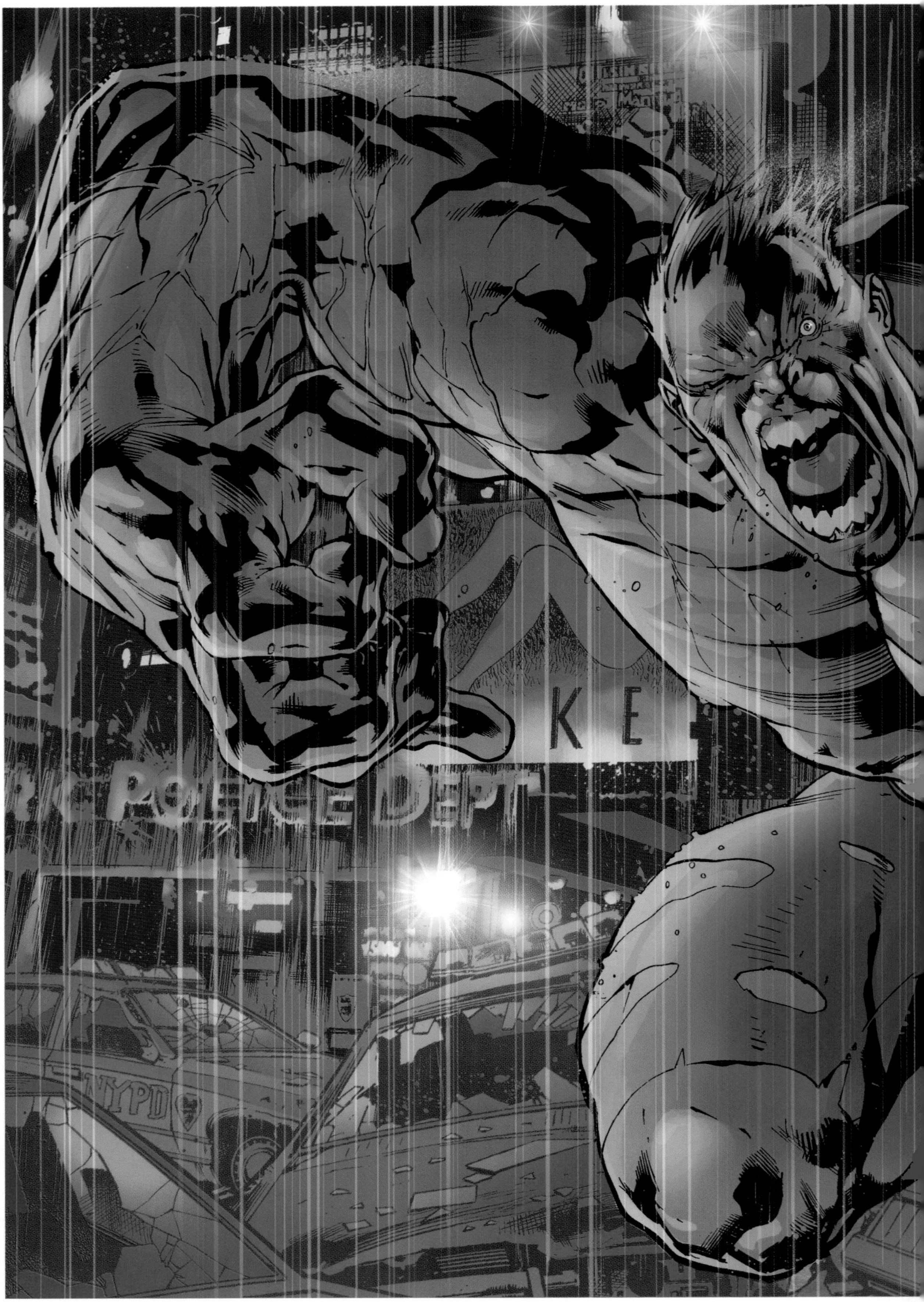
KE
POLICE DEPT
NYPD

Art by Bryan Hitch

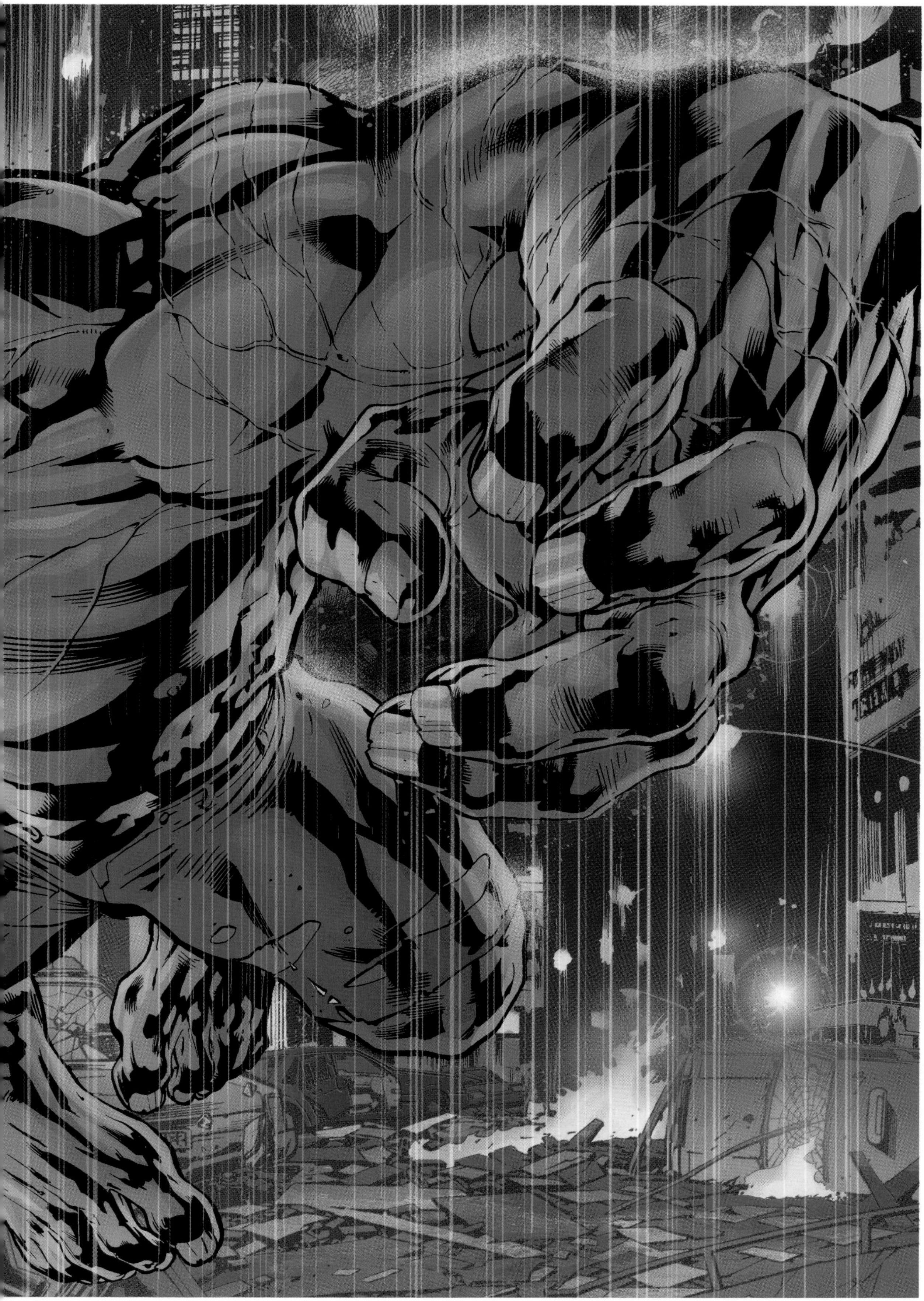

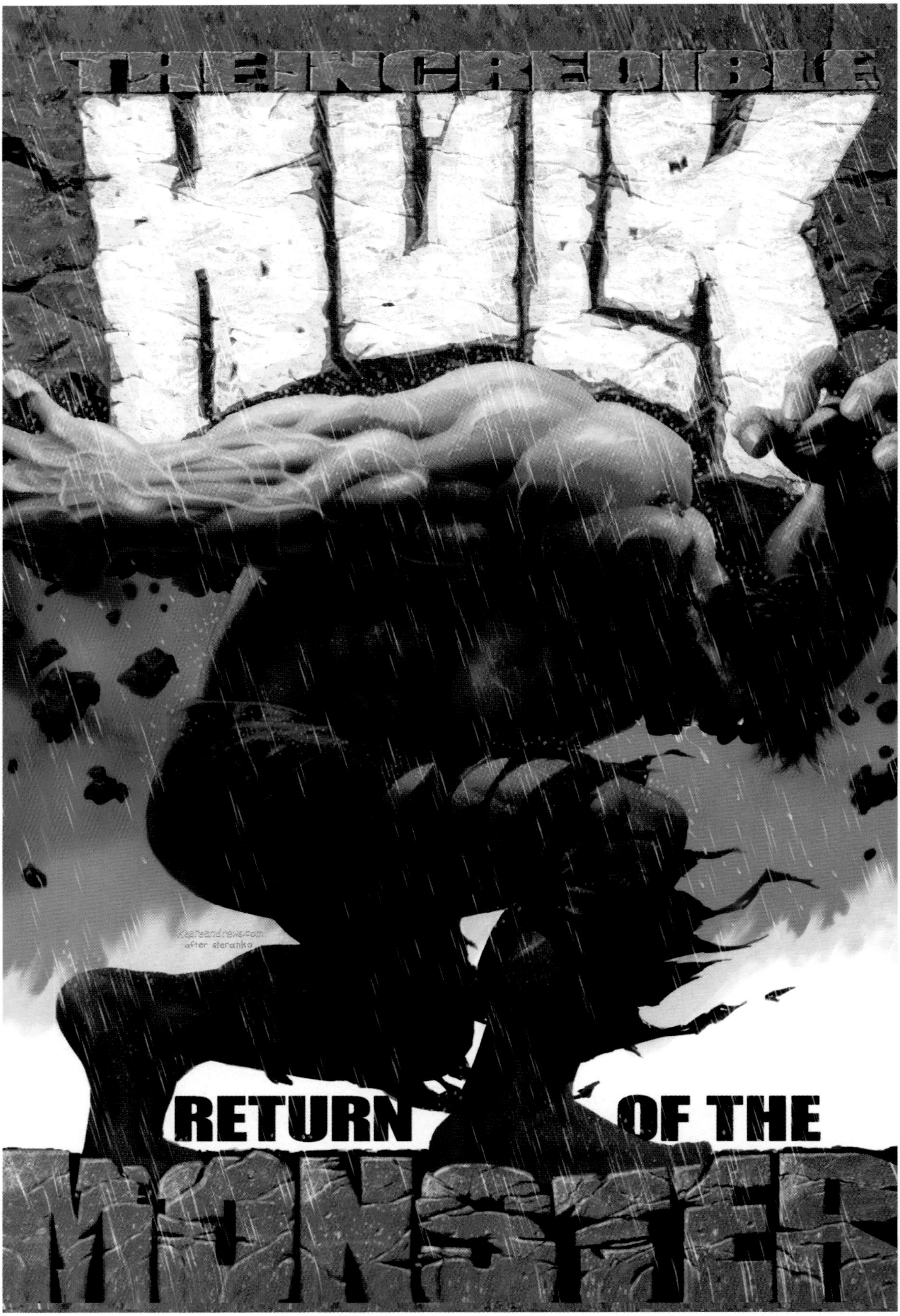
THE INCREDIBLE
HULK
kaareandrews.com
after steranko
RETURN OF THE
MONSTER

Art by Kaare Andrews

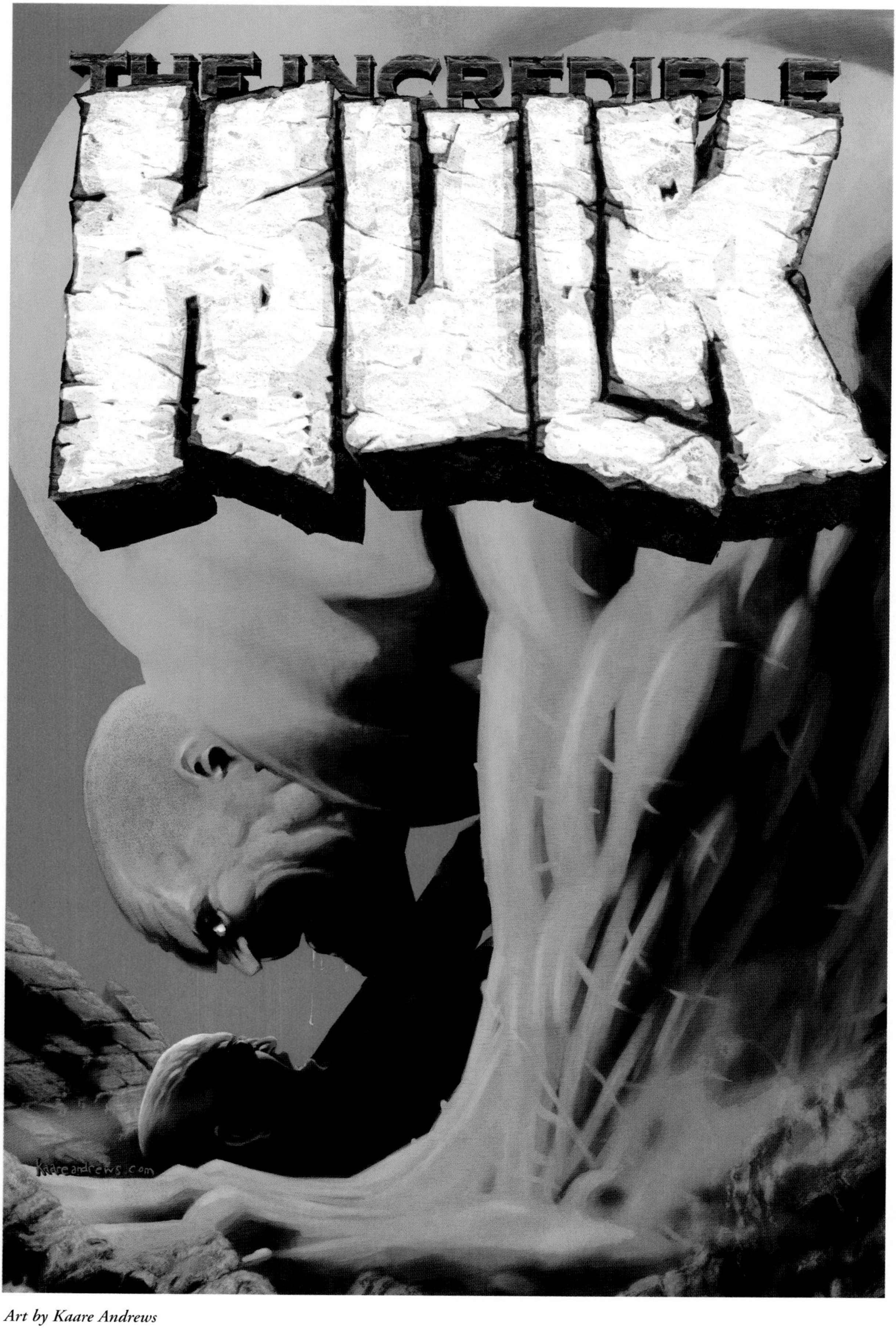
THE INCREDIBLE
HULK
kaareandrews.com

Art by Kaare Andrews

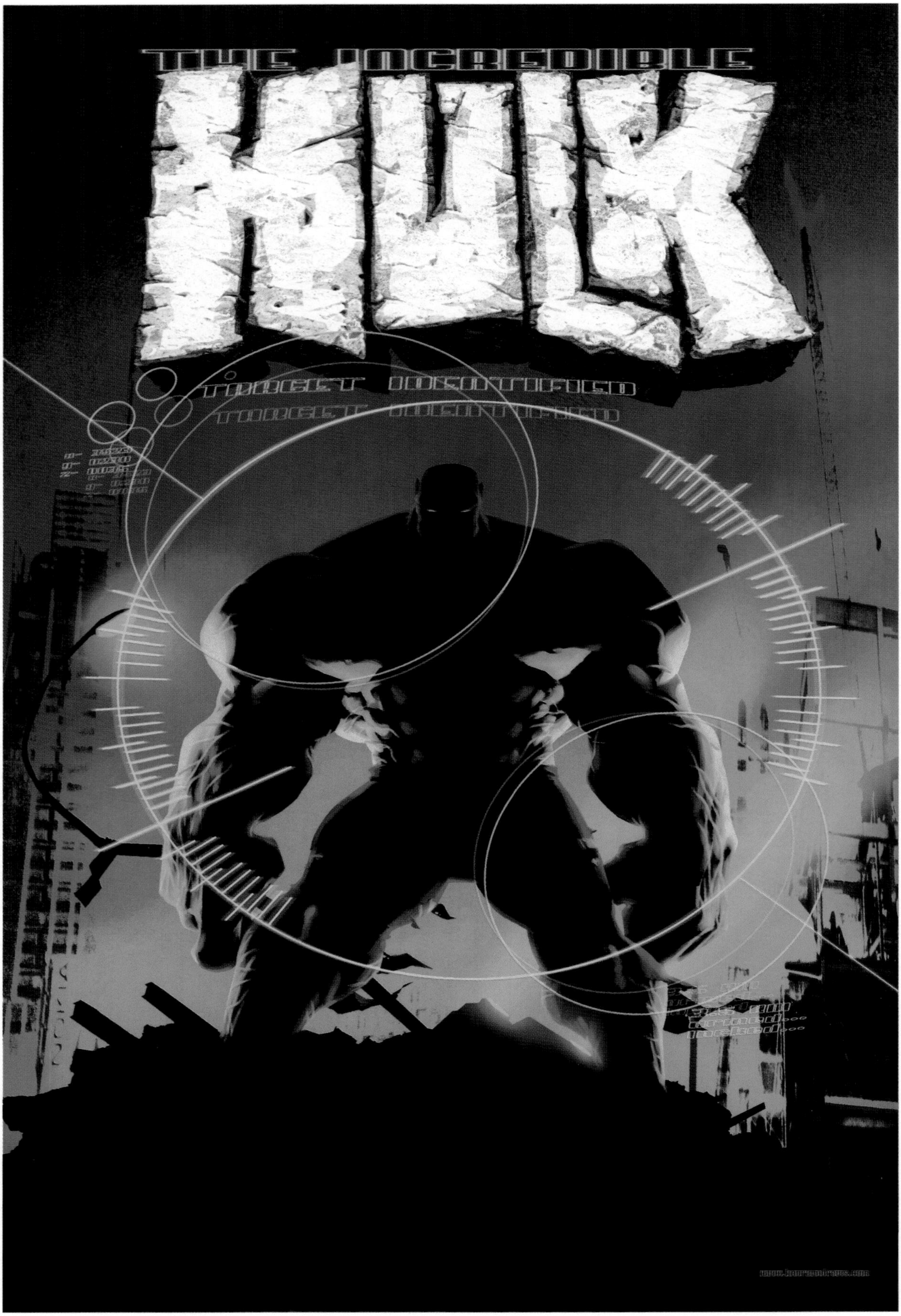
THE INCREDIBLE
HULK

Art by Kaare Andrews

"Unlike Spider-Man or Daredevil, Banner doesn't spend his days as the Hulk-in-disguise. One of the most singular aspects of Banner's personality is his utter repugnance regarding his destructive counterpart—equaled only, perhaps, by the Hulk's hatred for Banner."

Bruce Jones
Writer
Incredible Hulk

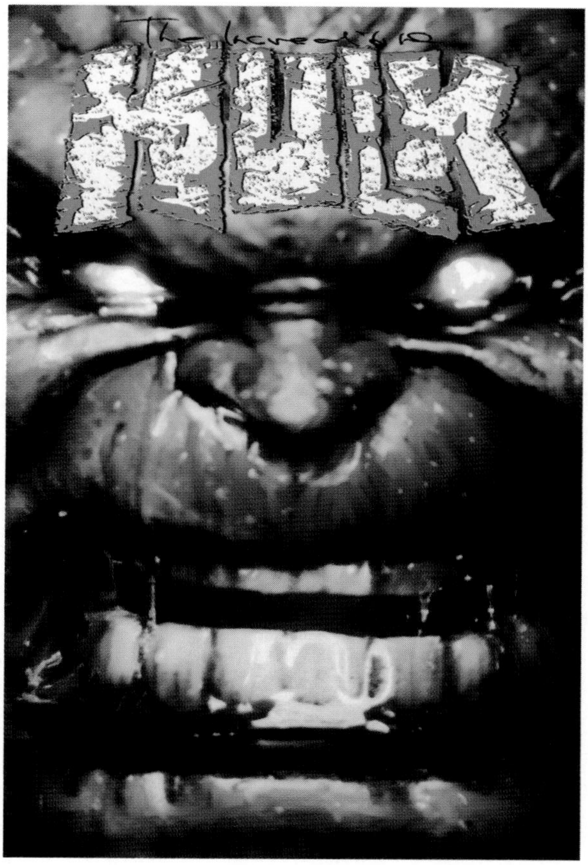
HULK

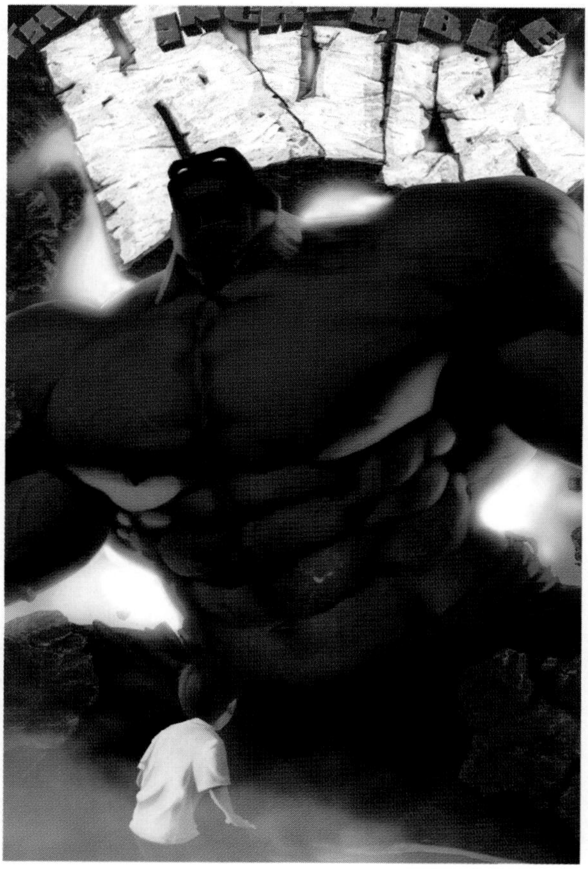
HULK

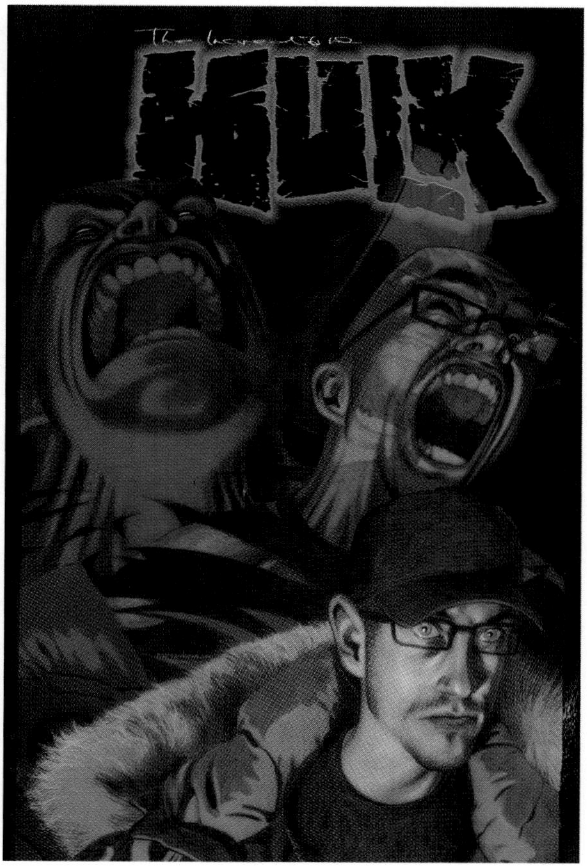
HULK

Art by Kaare Andrews

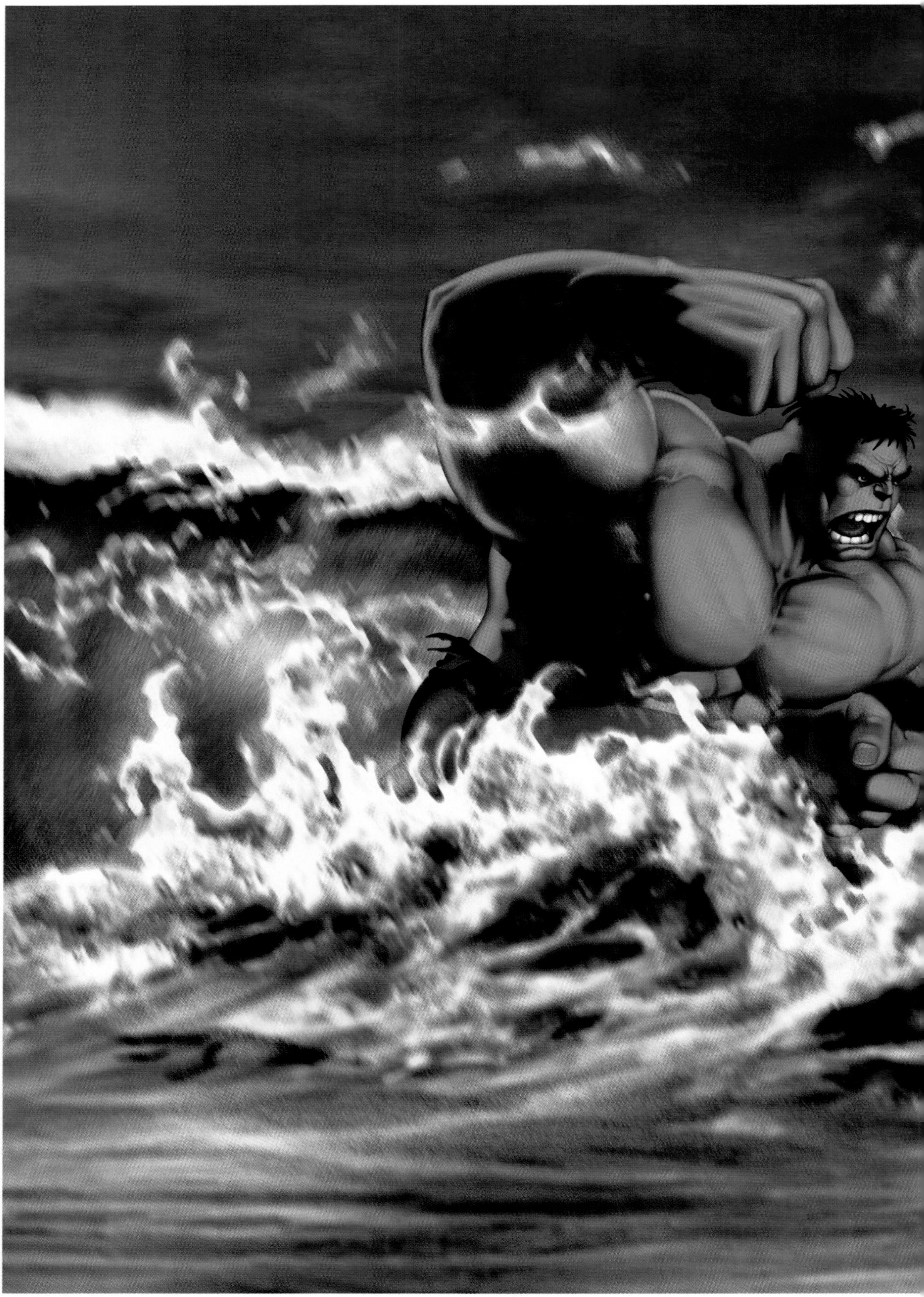

Art by Stuart Immonen

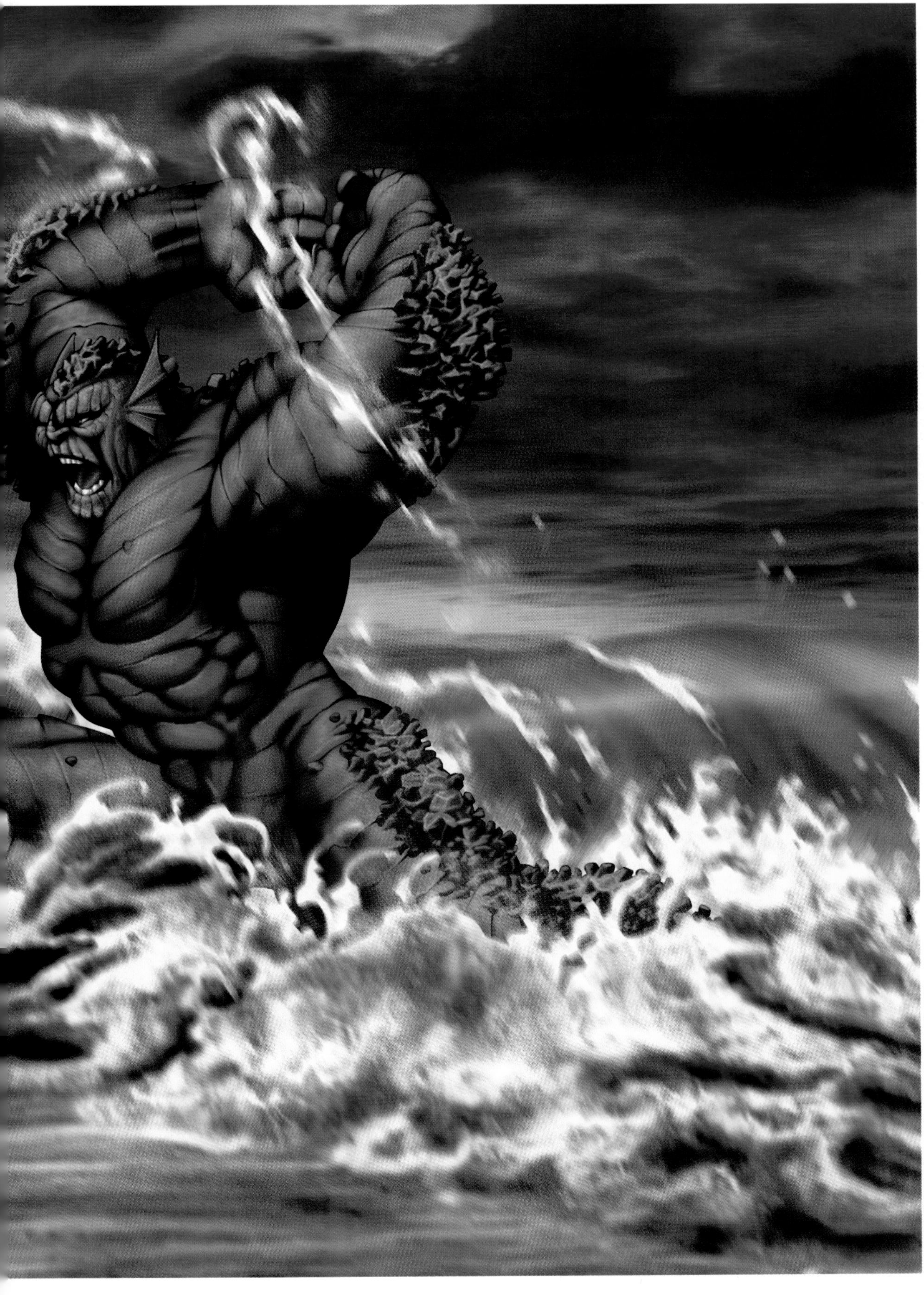

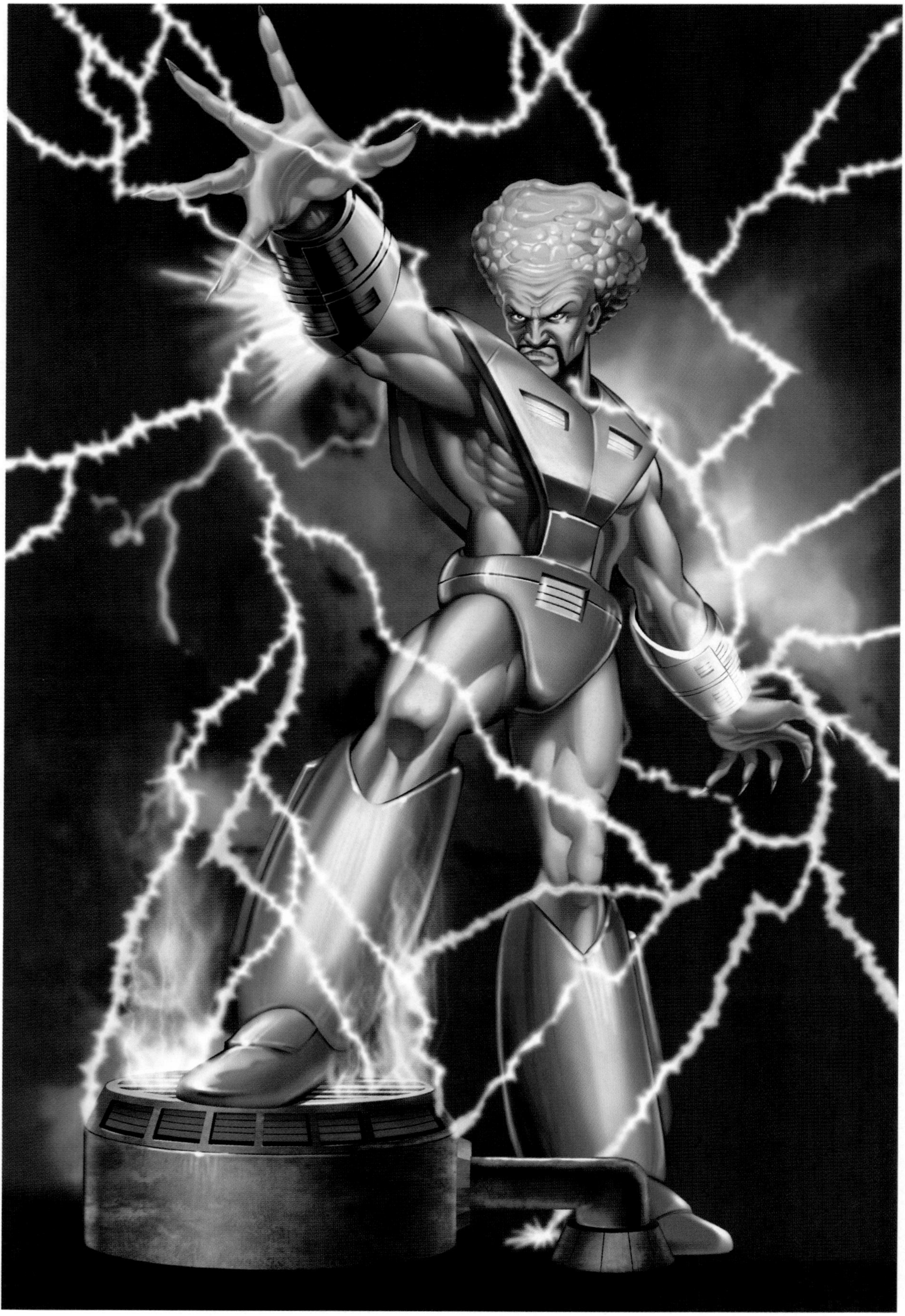

Art by Tom Marvelli

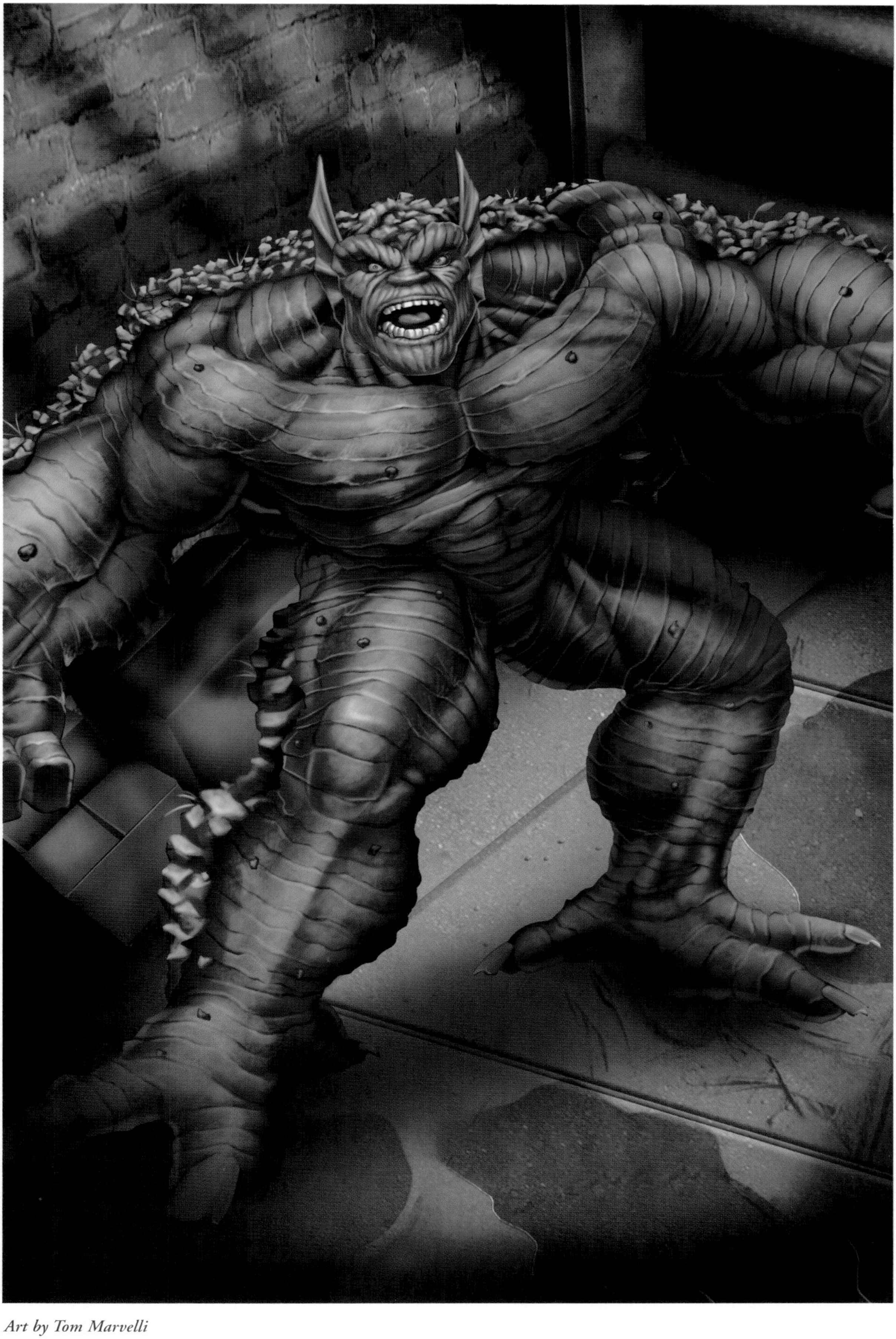

Art by Tom Marvelli

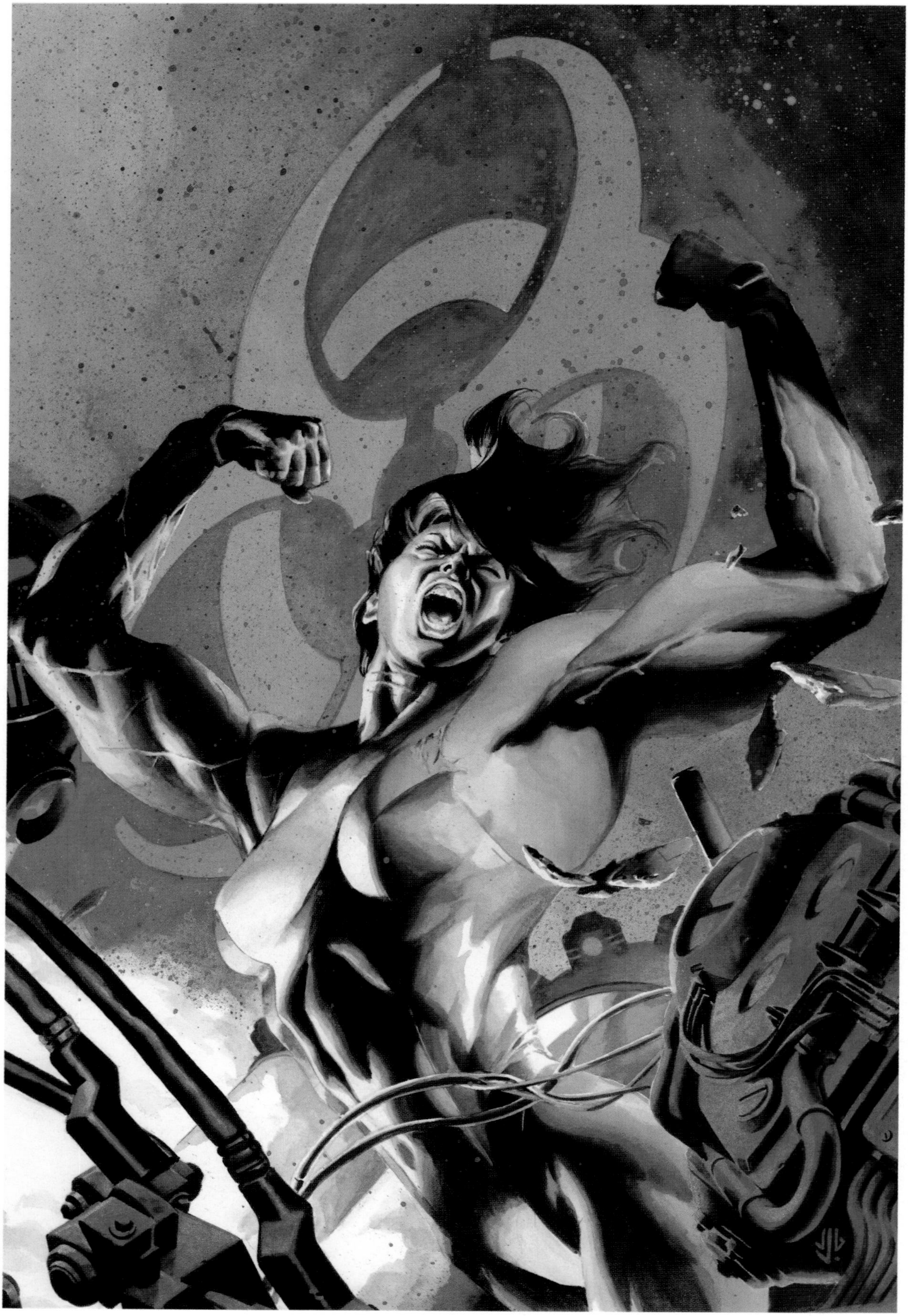

Art by J.G. Jones

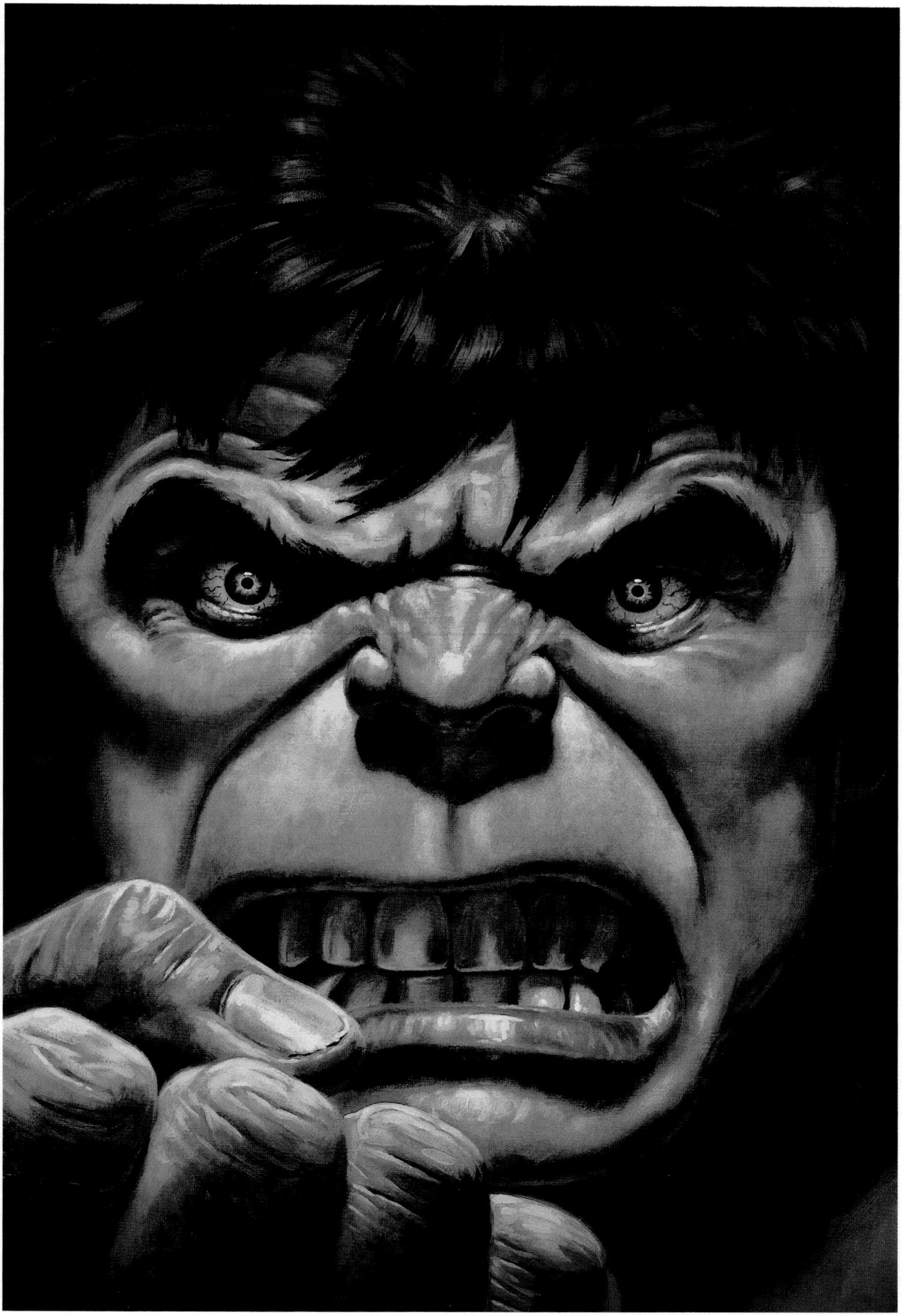

Art by Bob Larkin

Art by John Romita Jr.

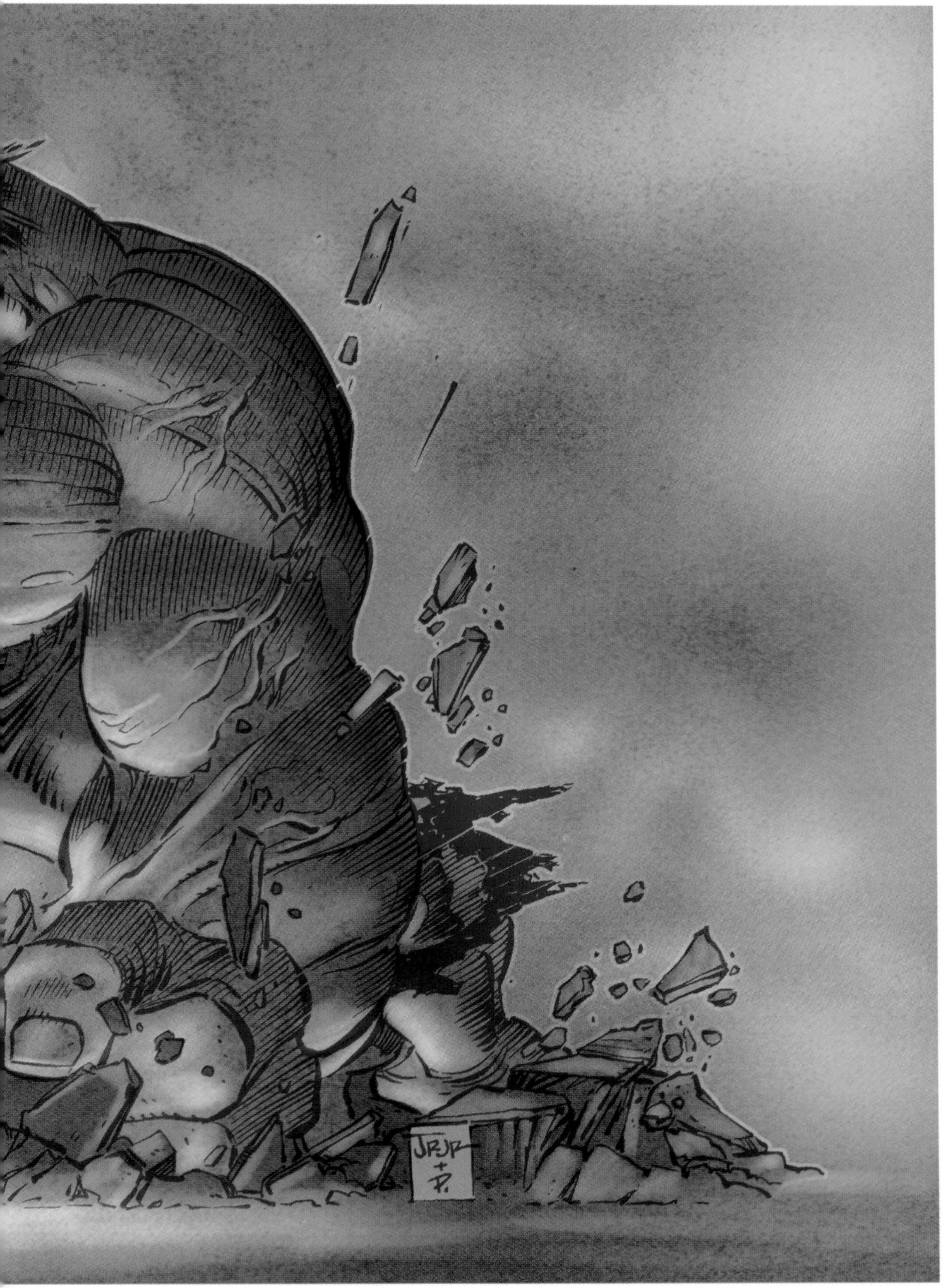
JRJR
+
P.

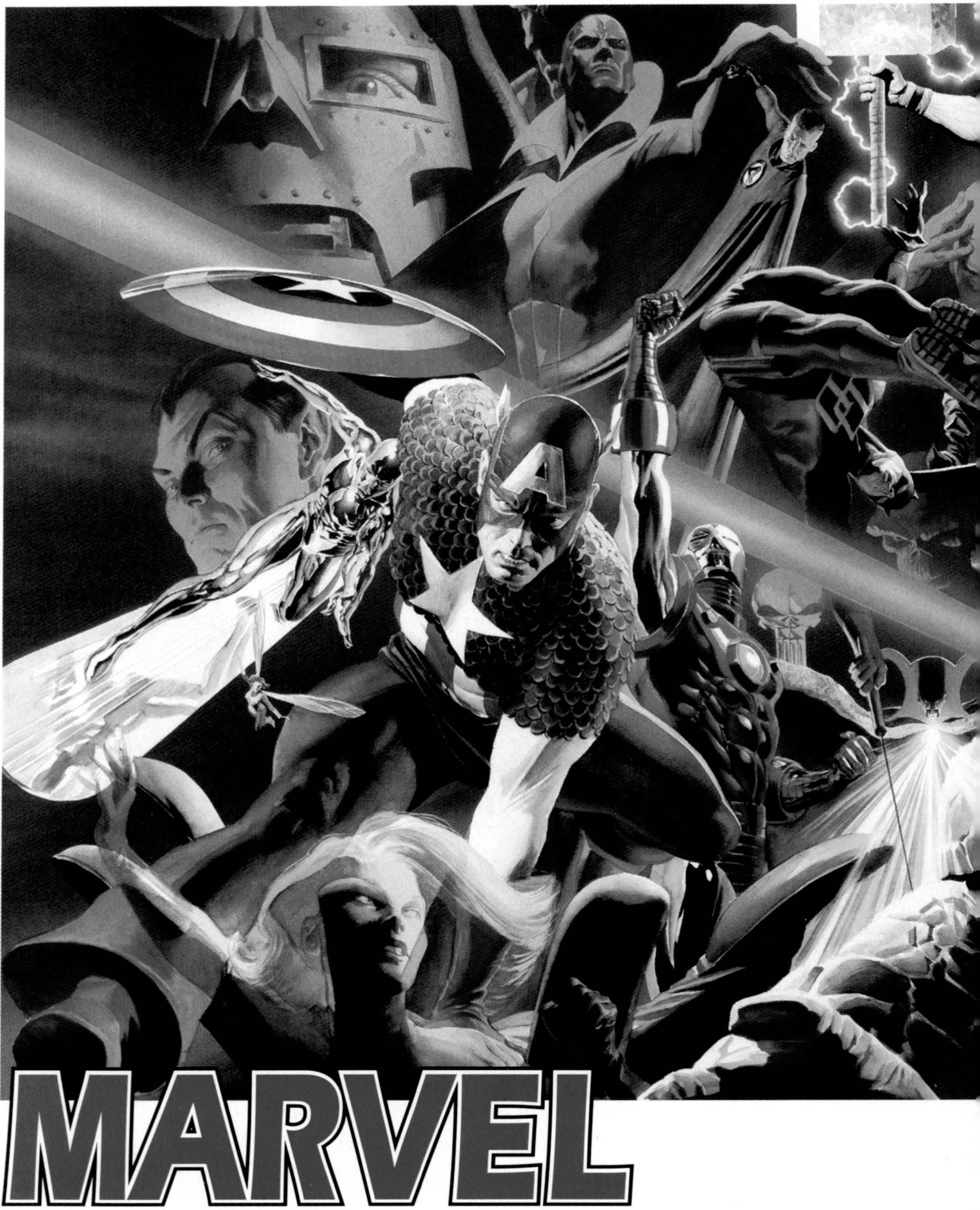

MARVEL HEROES

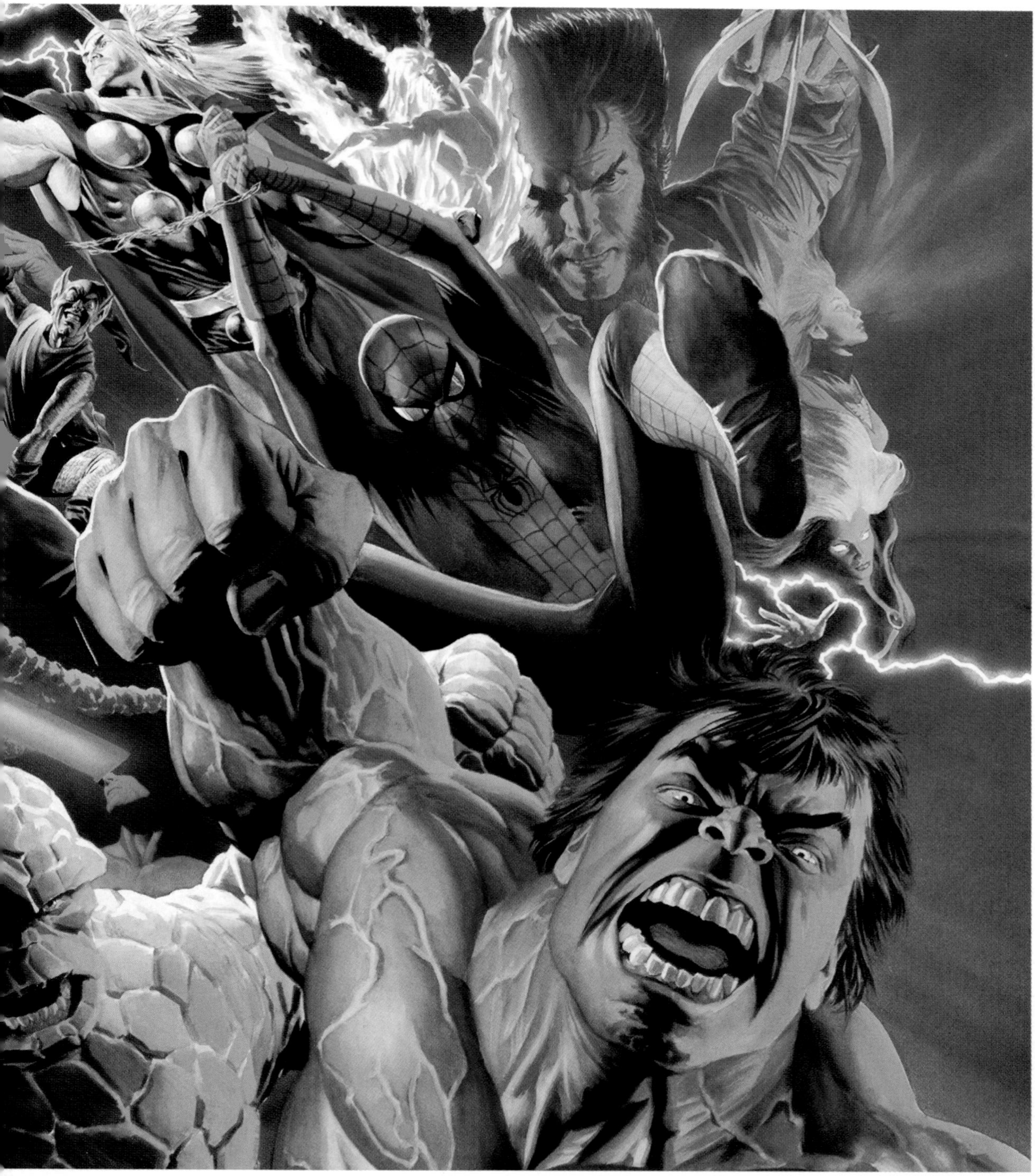

Art by Alex Ross

There came a day, unlike any other, when Earth's mightiest heroes found themselves united against a common threat ...

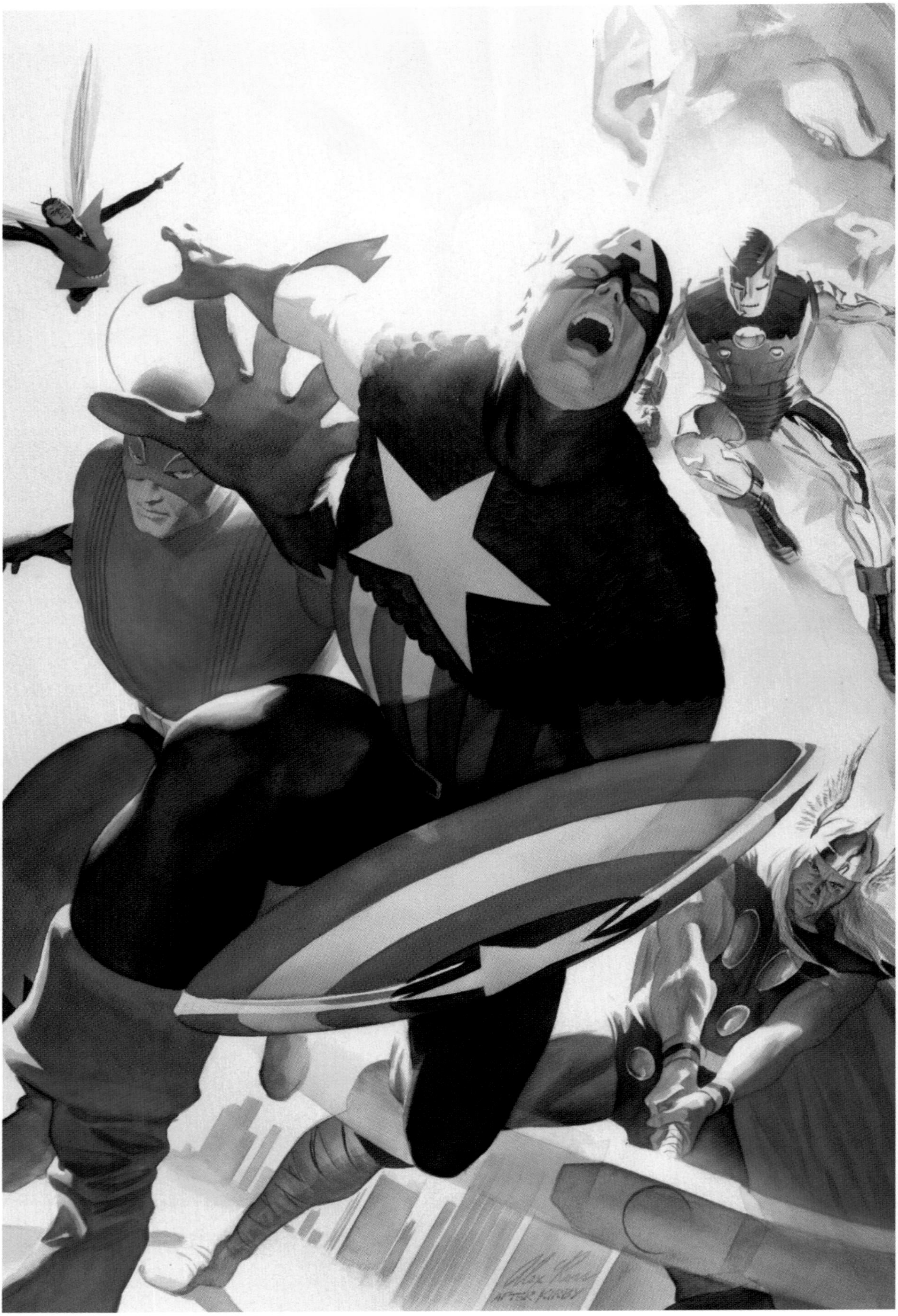
Alex Ross
AFTER KIRBY

Art by Alex Ross

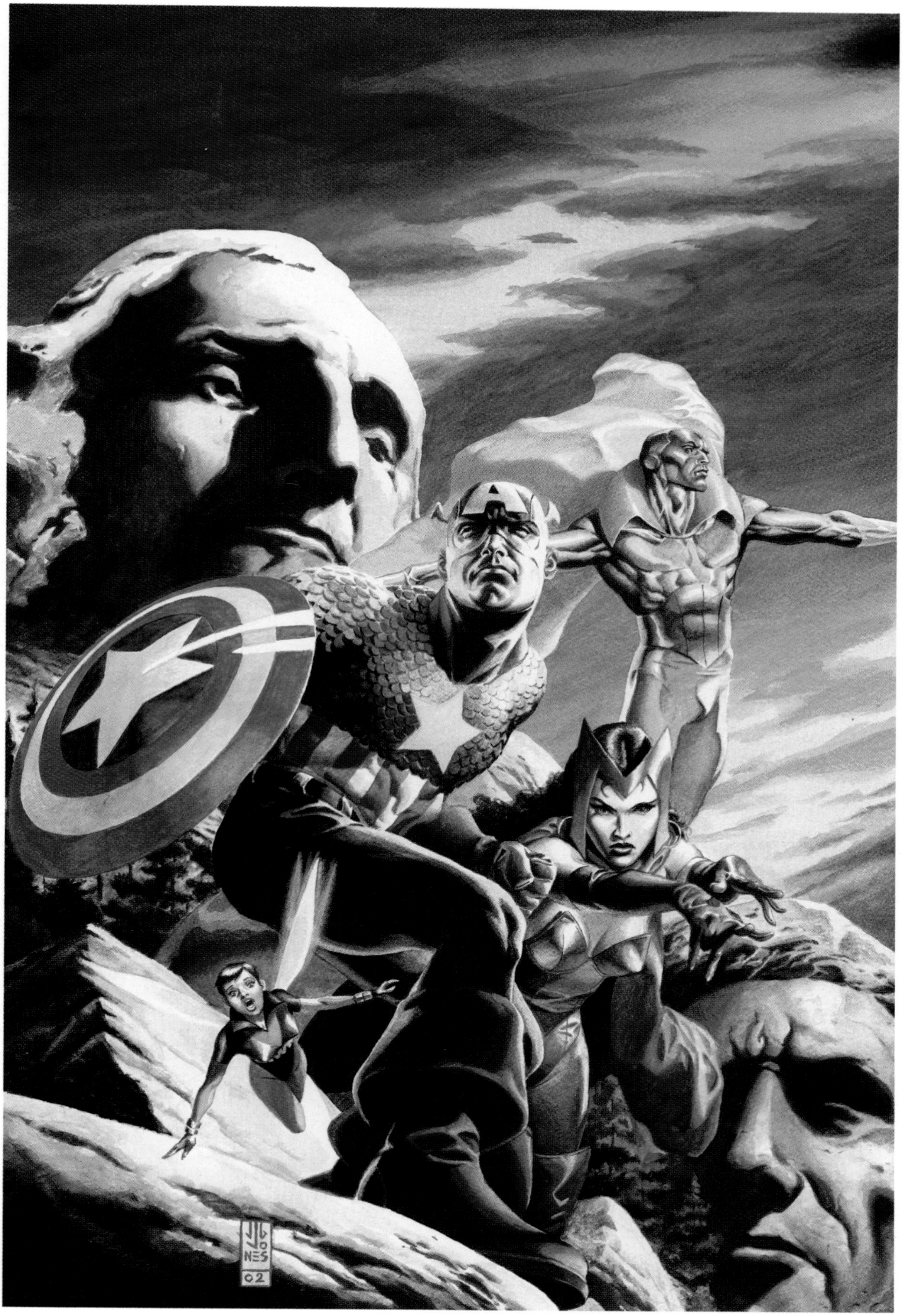
JG JONES 02
Art by J.G. Jones

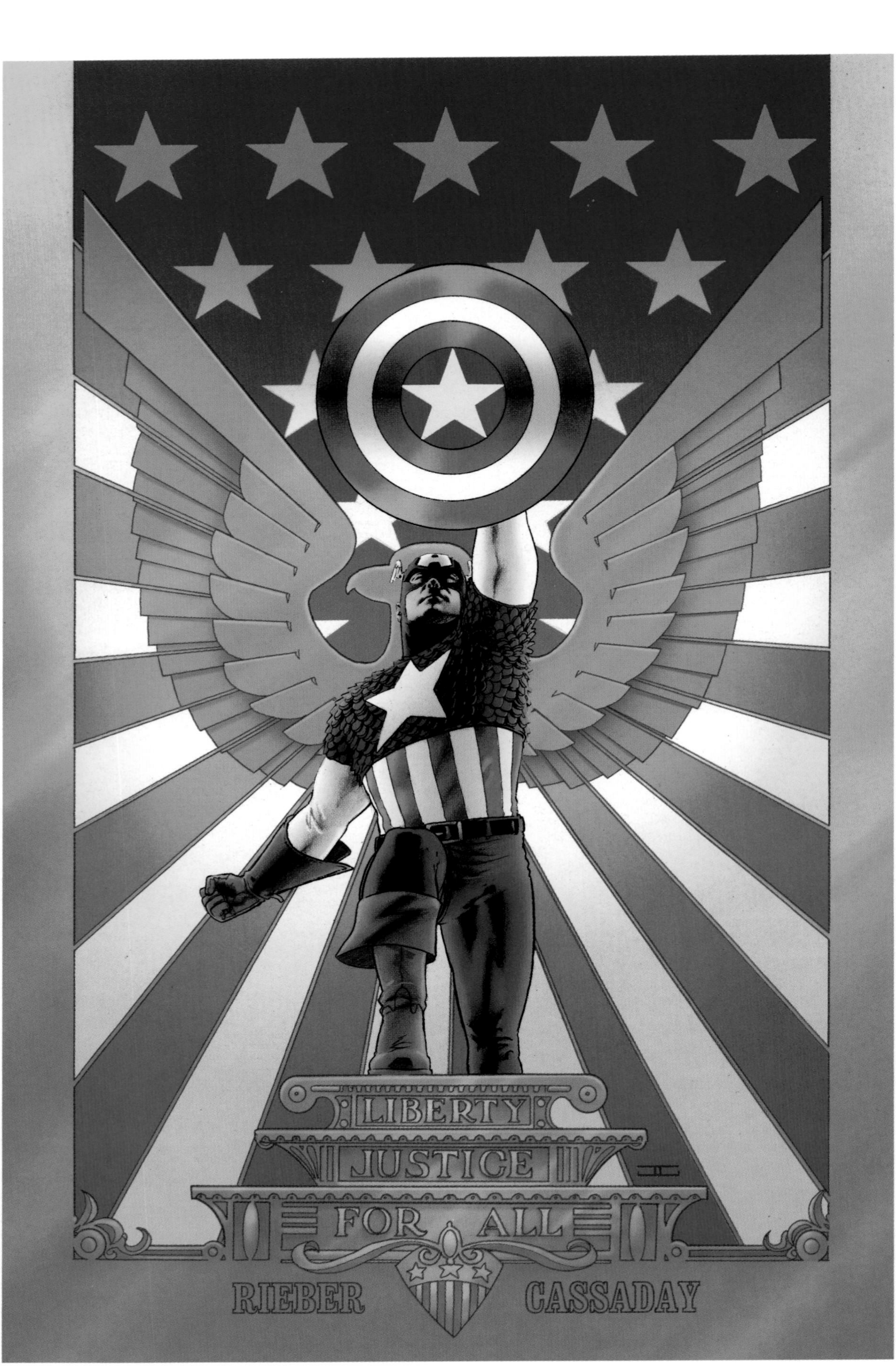
LIBERTY
JUSTICE
FOR ALL
RIEBER
CASSADAY

Art by John Cassaday

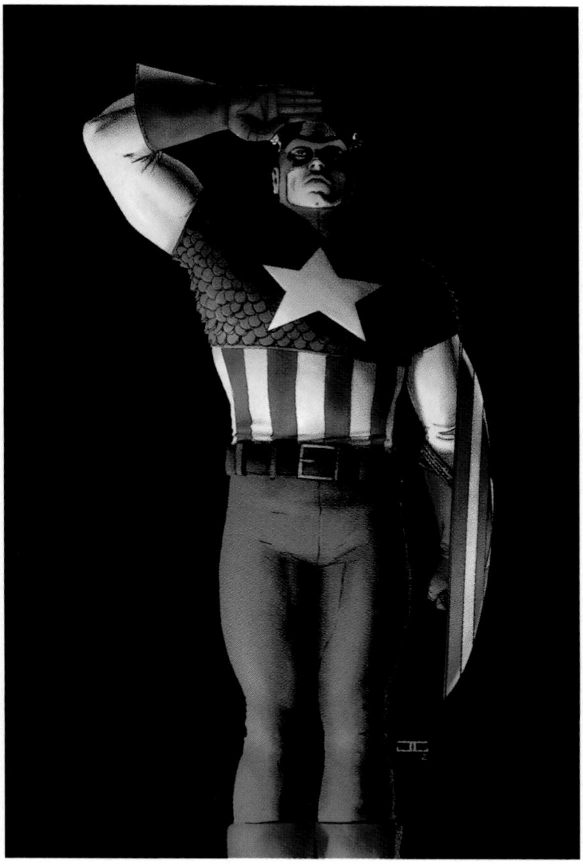

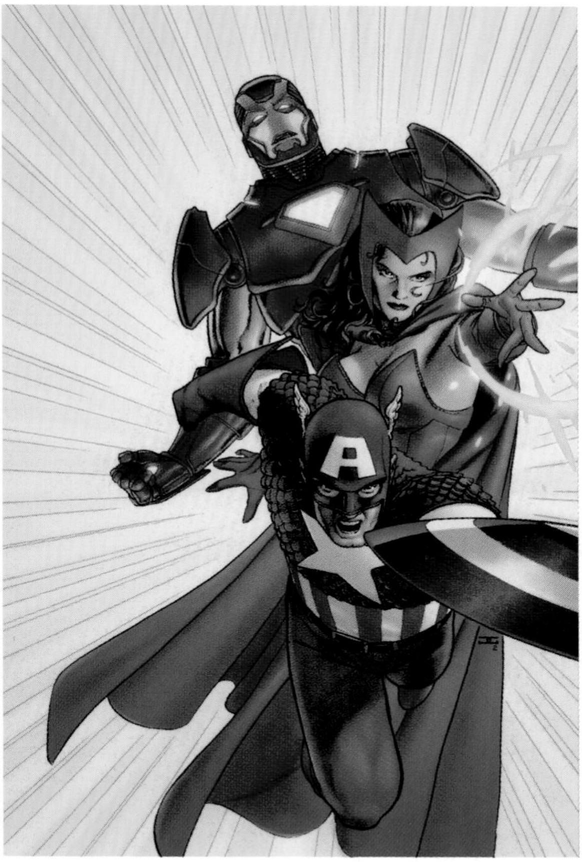

"Writer John Ney Rieber and artist John Cassaday may have faced the most formidable of all modern Captain America challenges in attempting to take this classic character of a simpler time into the smoky aftermath of September 11th. They succeed heroically and not by stooping to jingoistic nonsense."

Max Allan Collins
Author
Road to Perdition

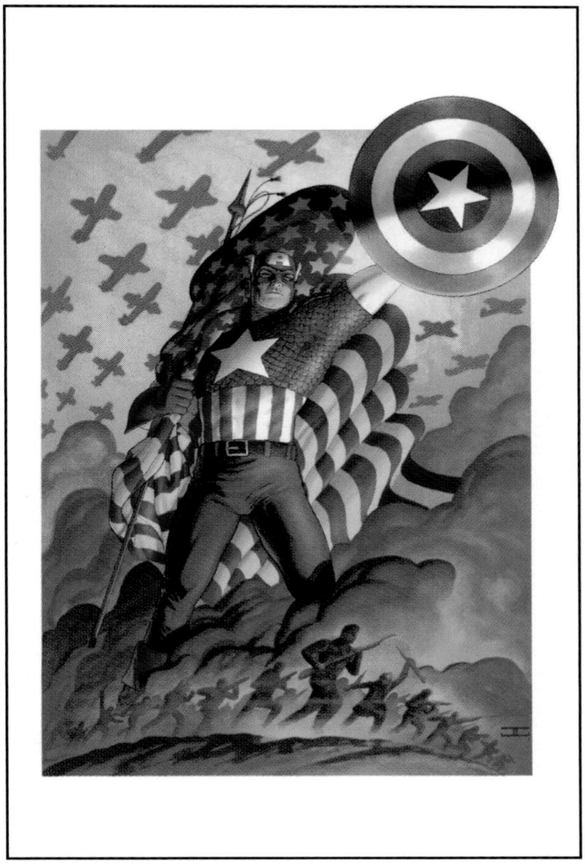

Art by John Cassaday

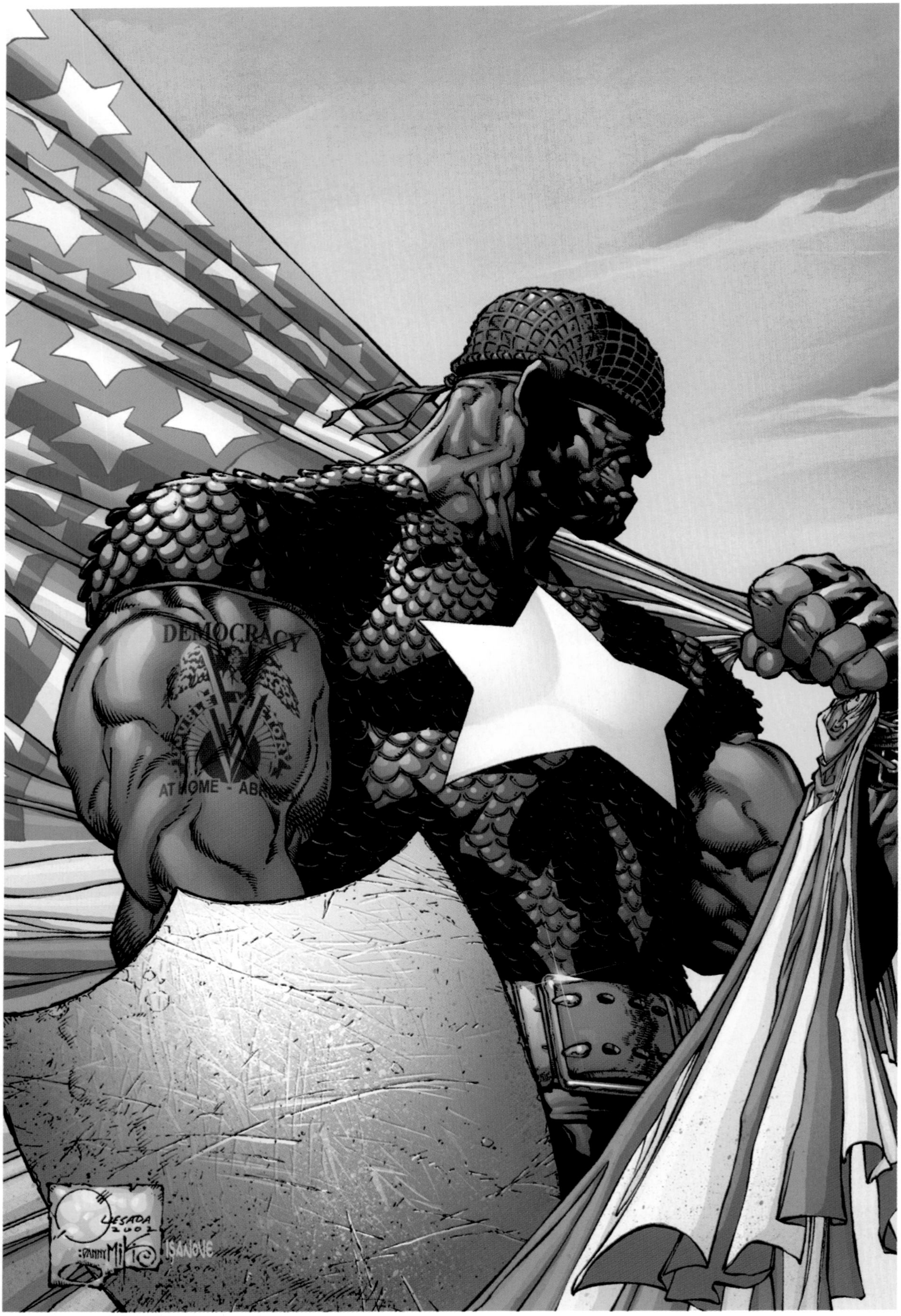
DEMOCRACY

Art by Joe Quesada

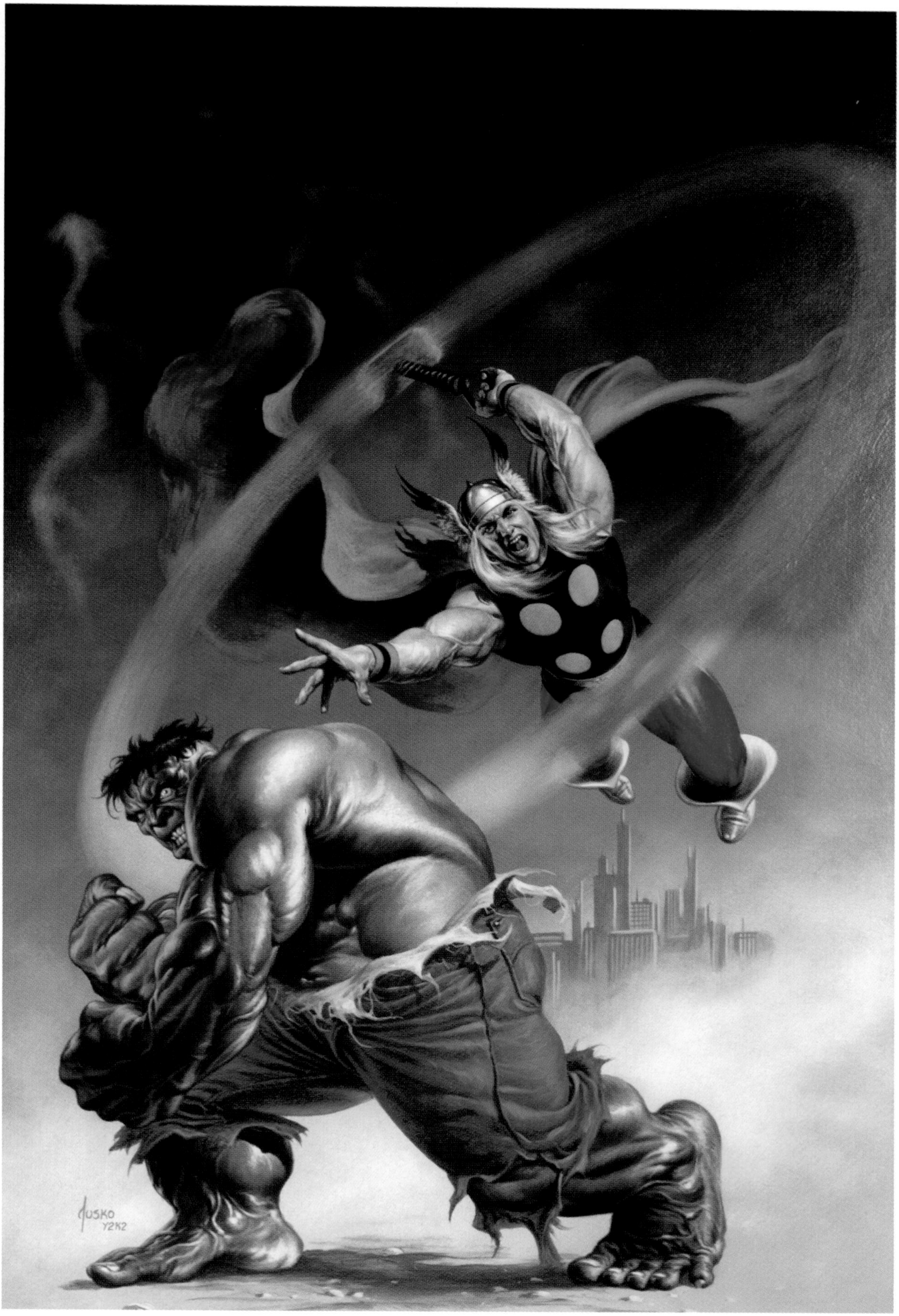
JUSKO
Y2K2

Art by Joe Jusko

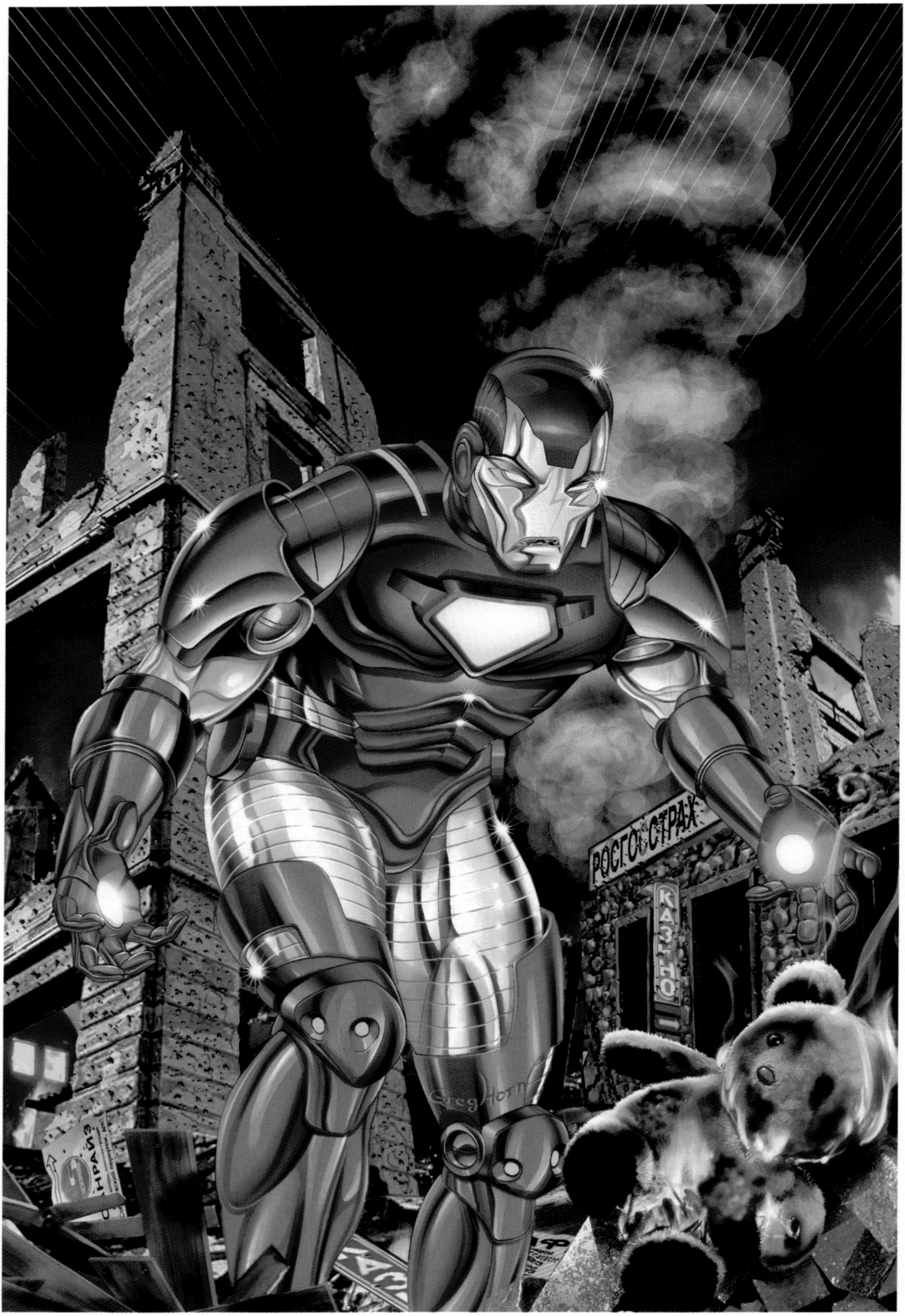
РОСГОССТРАХ
КАЗИНО
Greg Horn

Art by Greg Horn

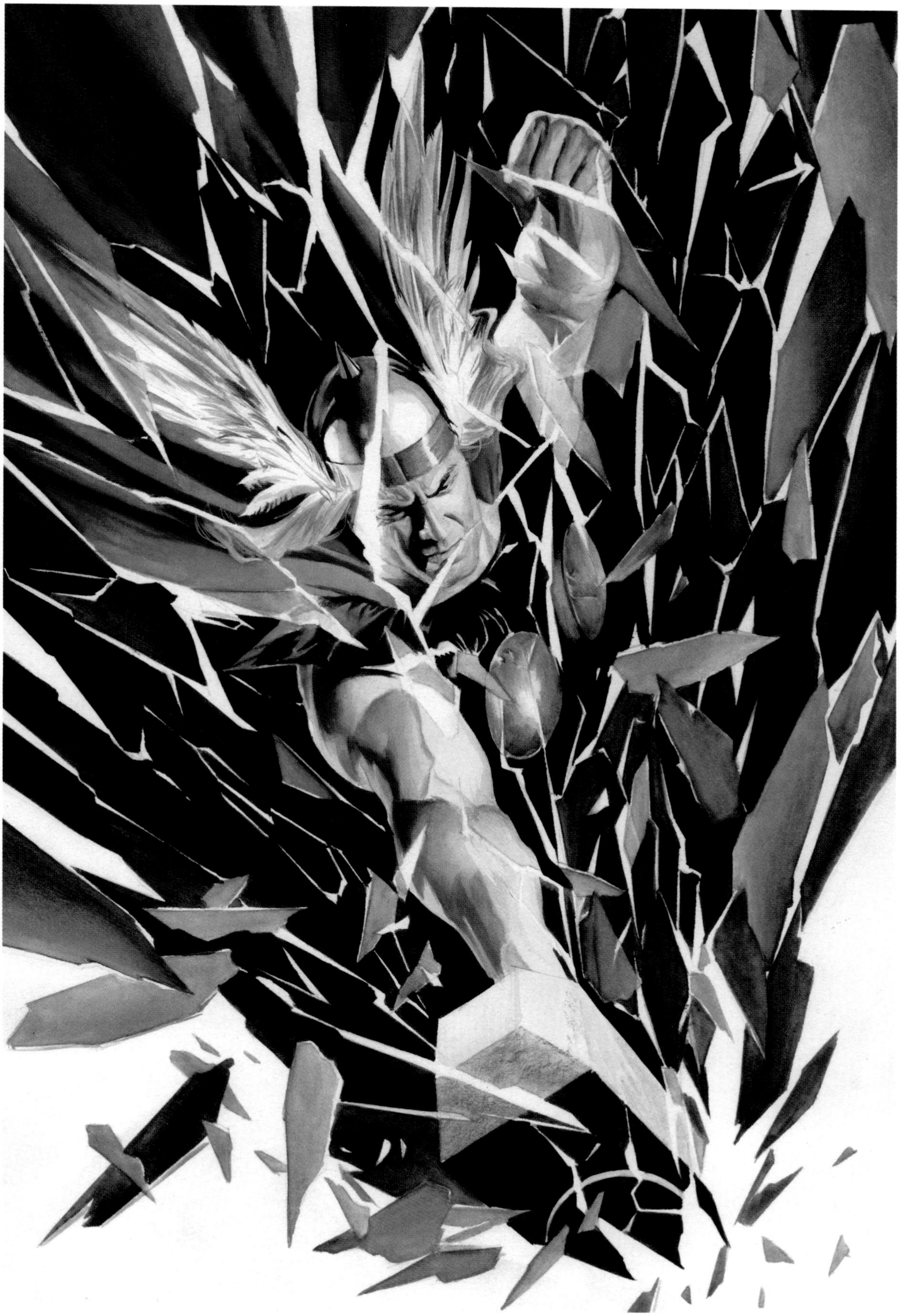

Art by Alex Ross

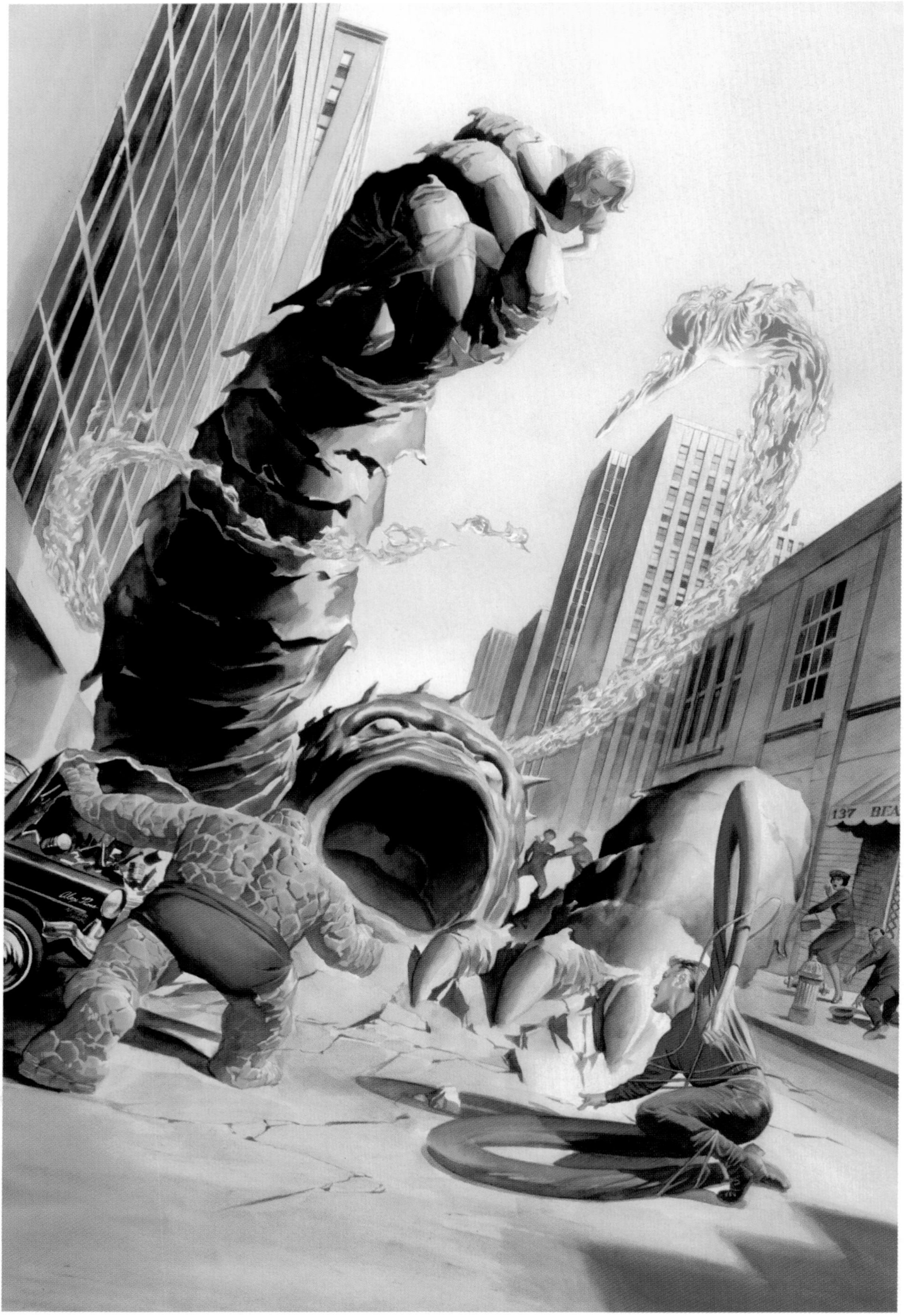
137 BEA

Art by Alex Ross

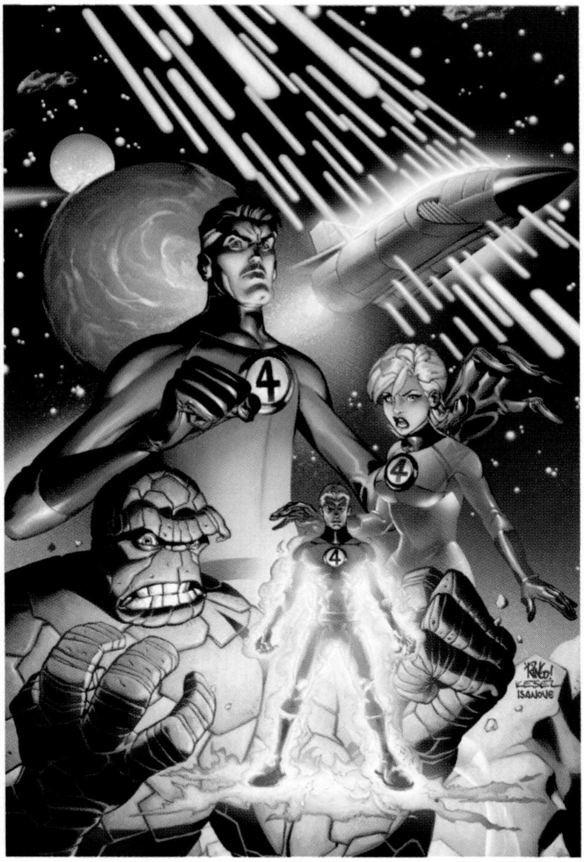

"During the entire decade of the 1960s, if you read comics and wanted to see something new, something fresh and exciting, something innovative and unlike anything you'd ever seen before in a comic book, there was only one place to go: the Baxter Building. [Stan Lee and Jack Kirby's] *Fantastic Four* was, at its peak, almost inarguably the richest and most imaginative comic in the history of the medium."

Mark Waid
Writer
Fantastic Four

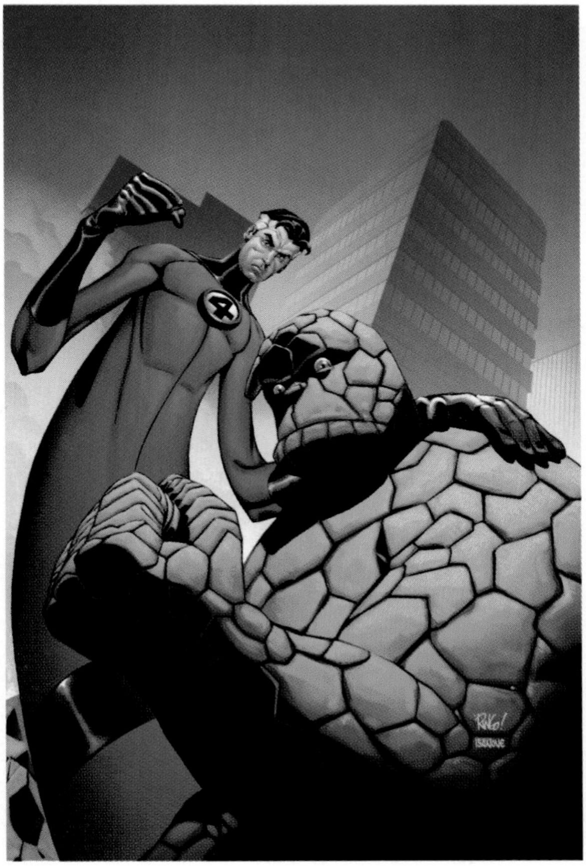

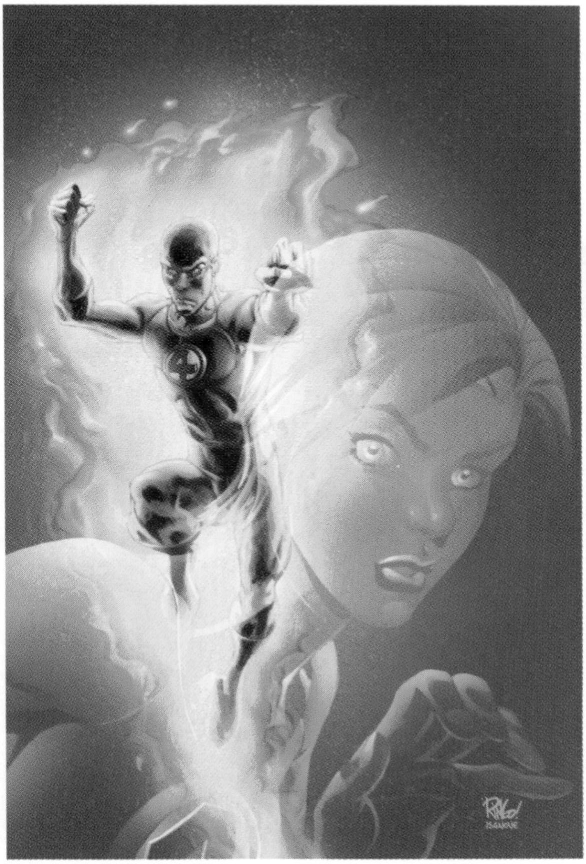

Art by Mike Weiringo

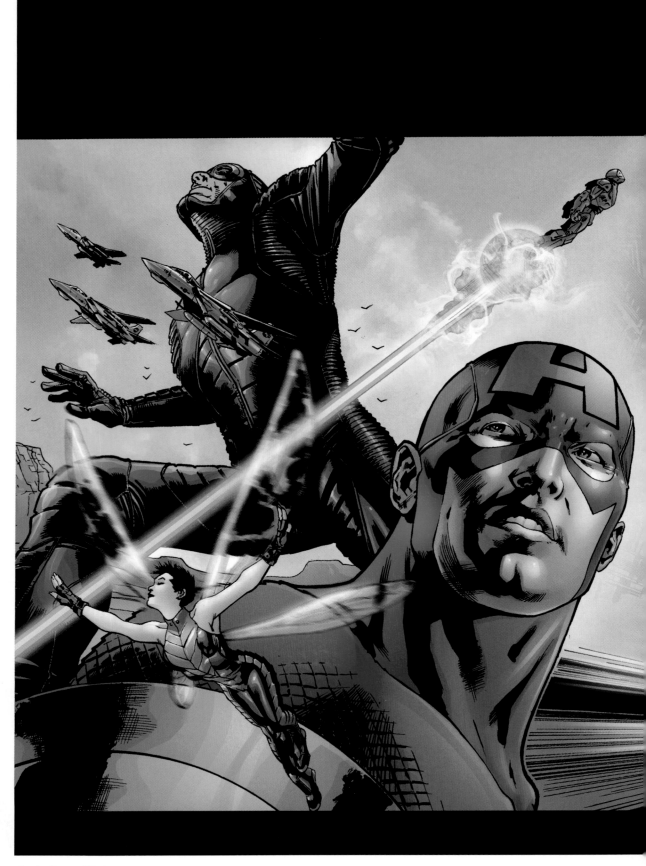

Art by Bryan Hitch

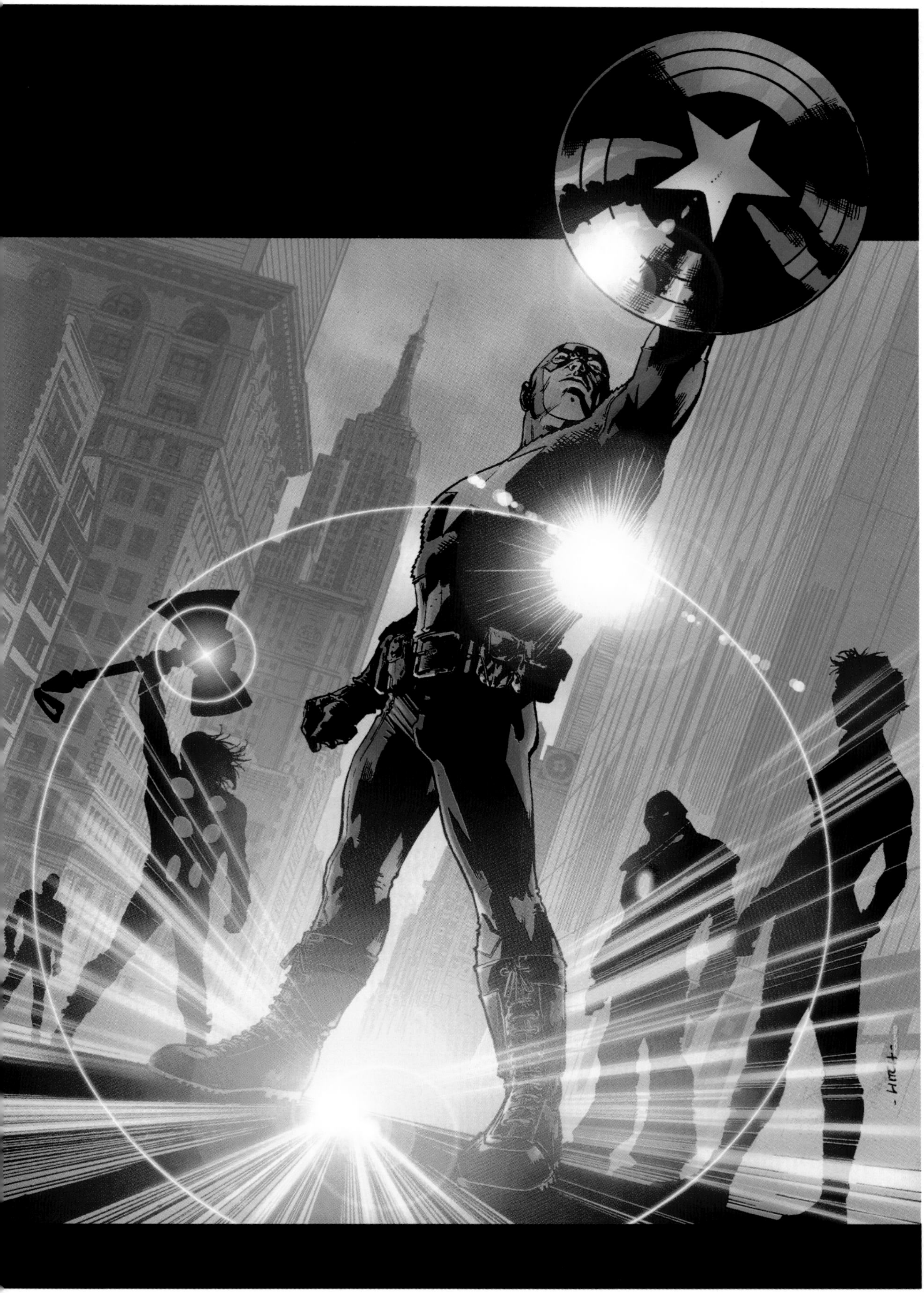

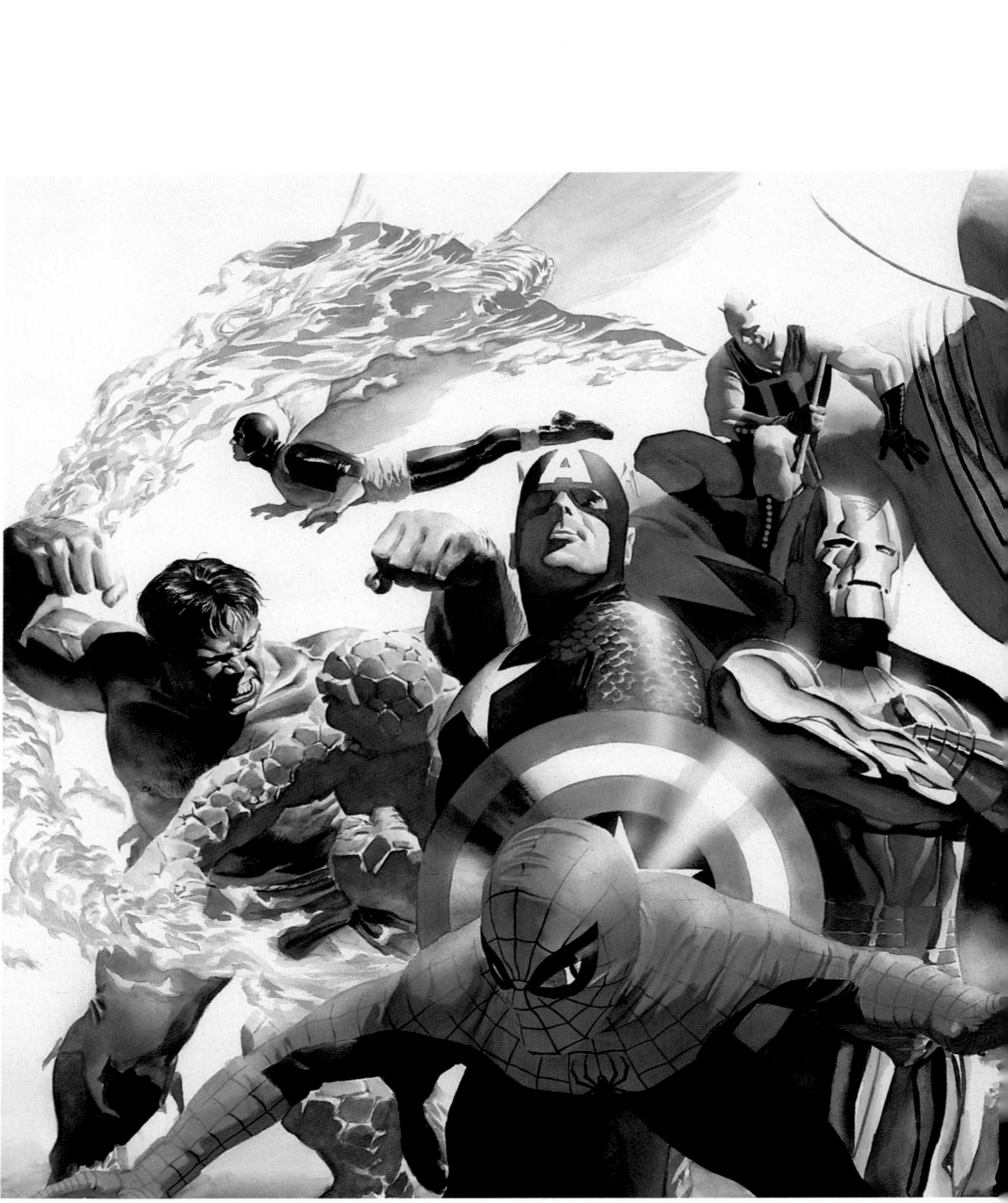
Art by Alex Ross

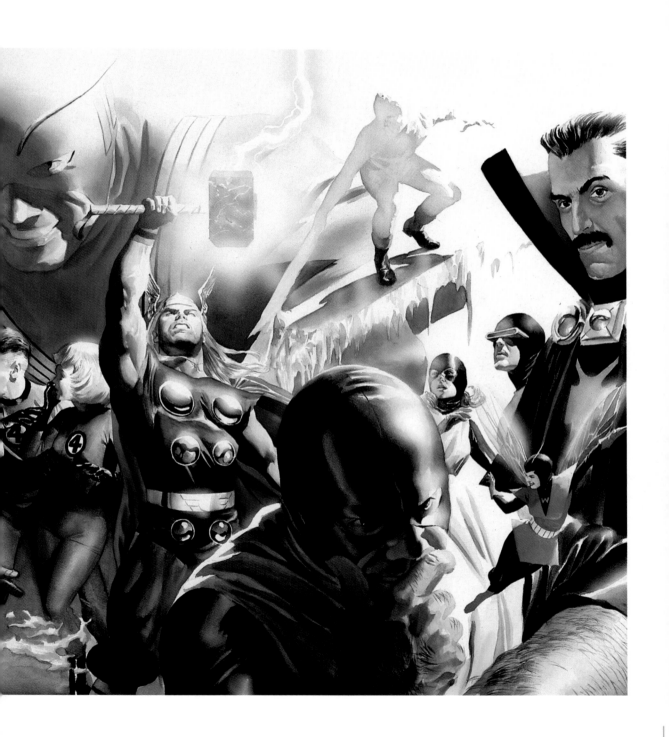

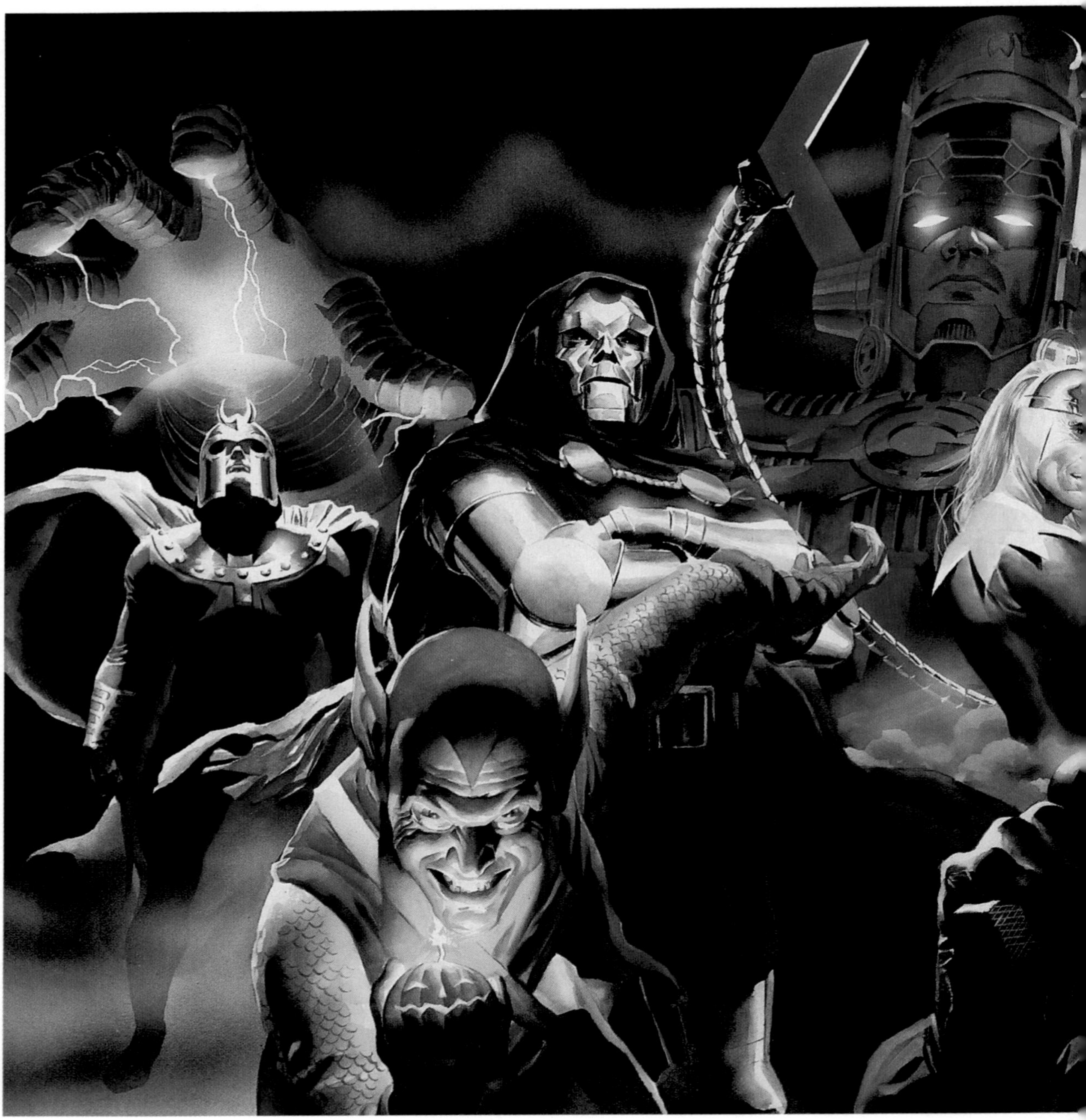

Art by Alex Ross

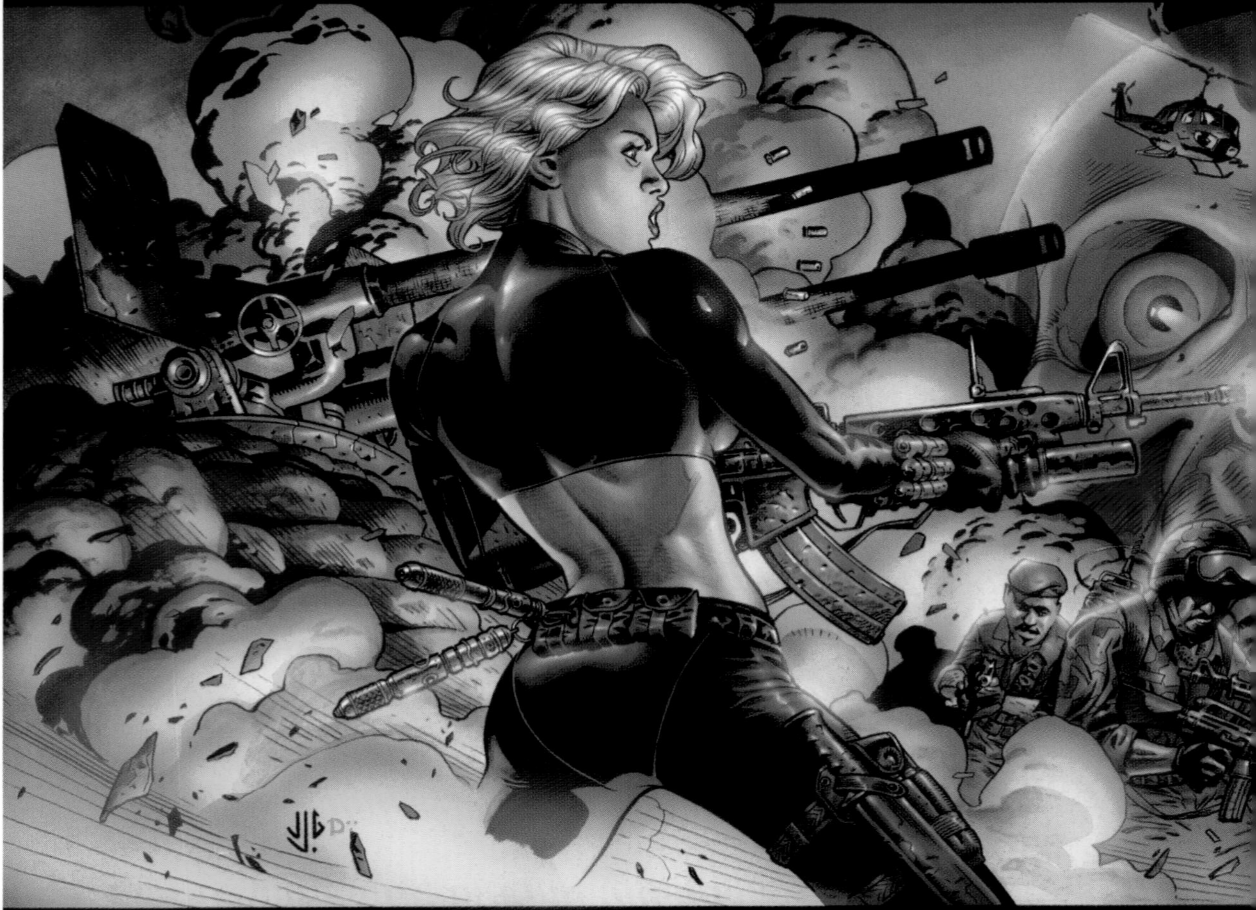

MARVEL KNIGHTS

MAX COMICS

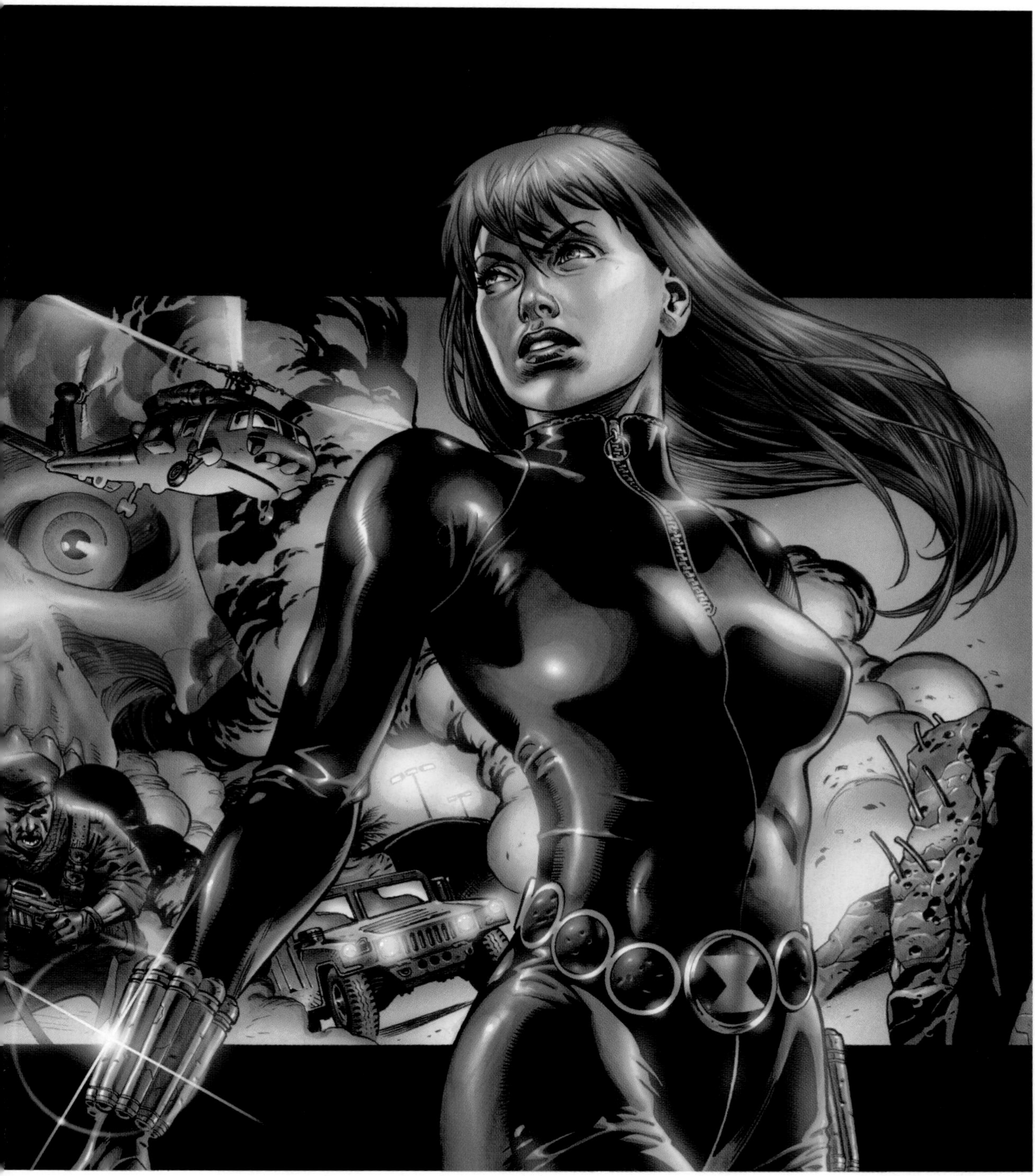

Art by J.G. Jones

On the mean streets of Marvel Knights, the kid gloves come off. Guardian devils, vengeance-crazed vigilantes and enigmatic assassins stalk the city's dark underbelly, and the urban action unfolds with gritty intensity.

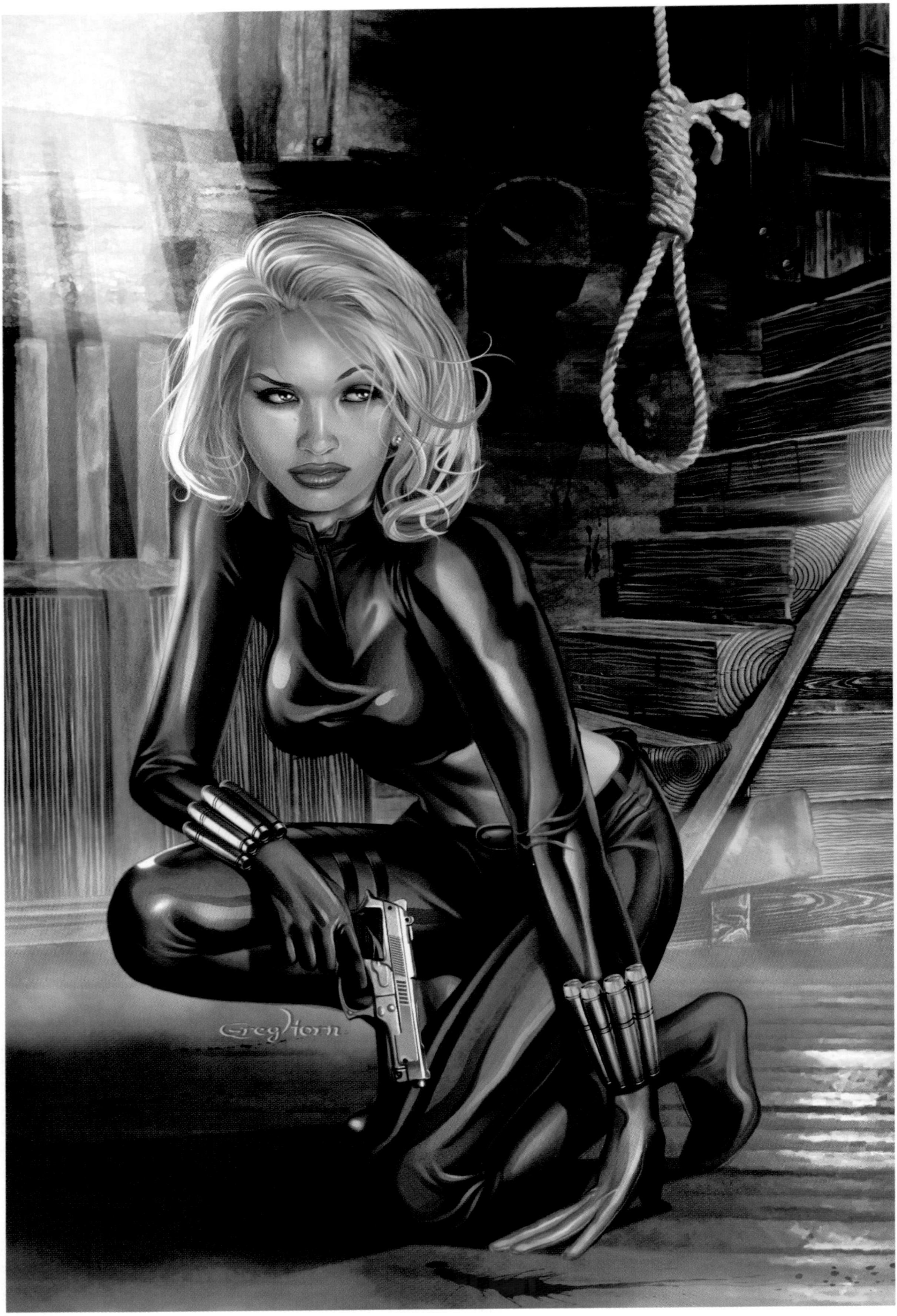
Greg Horn

Art by Greg Horn

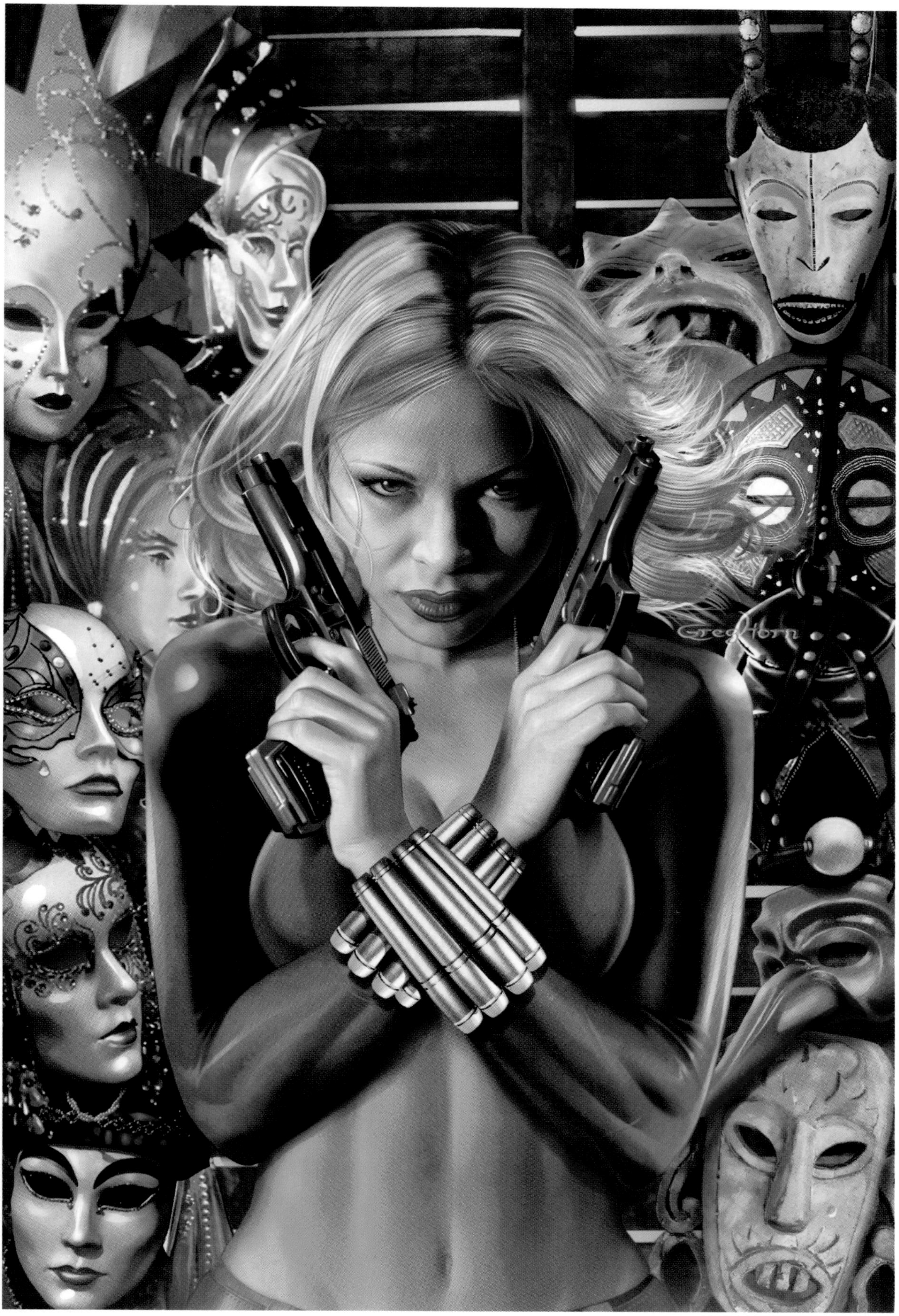
Greg Horn

Art by Greg Horn

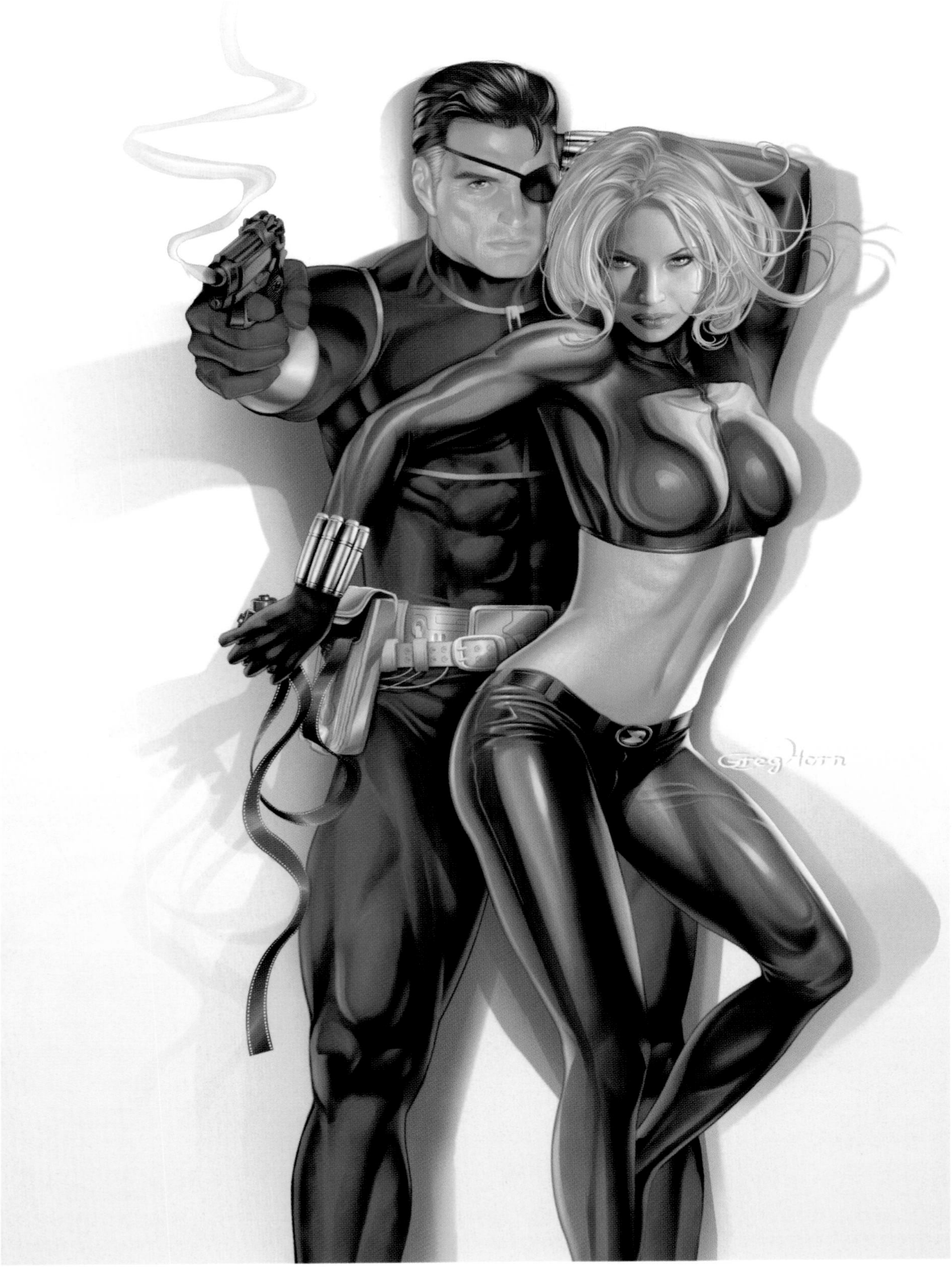
Greg Horn

Art by Greg Horn

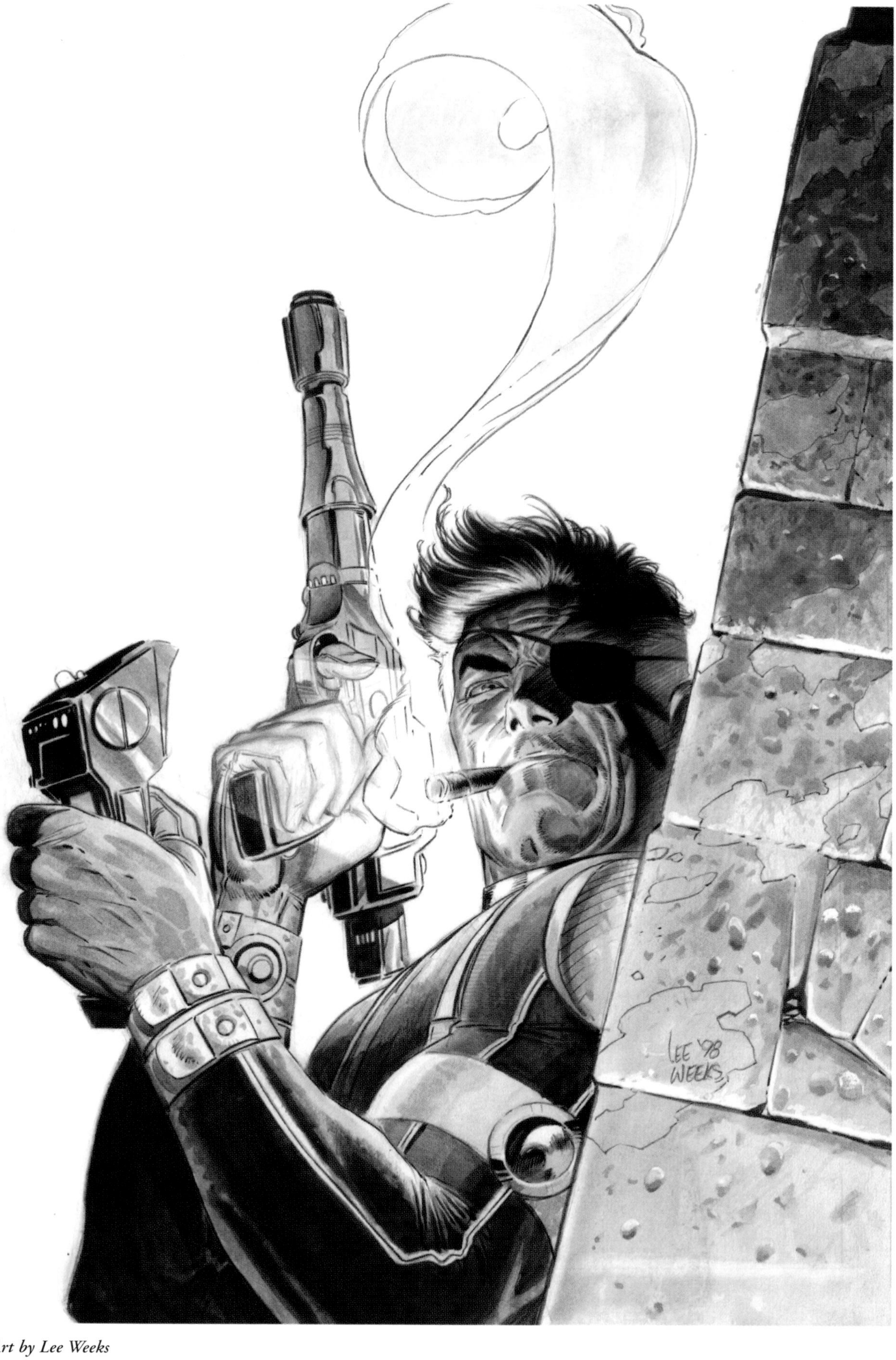
LEE '98
WEEKS

Art by Lee Weeks

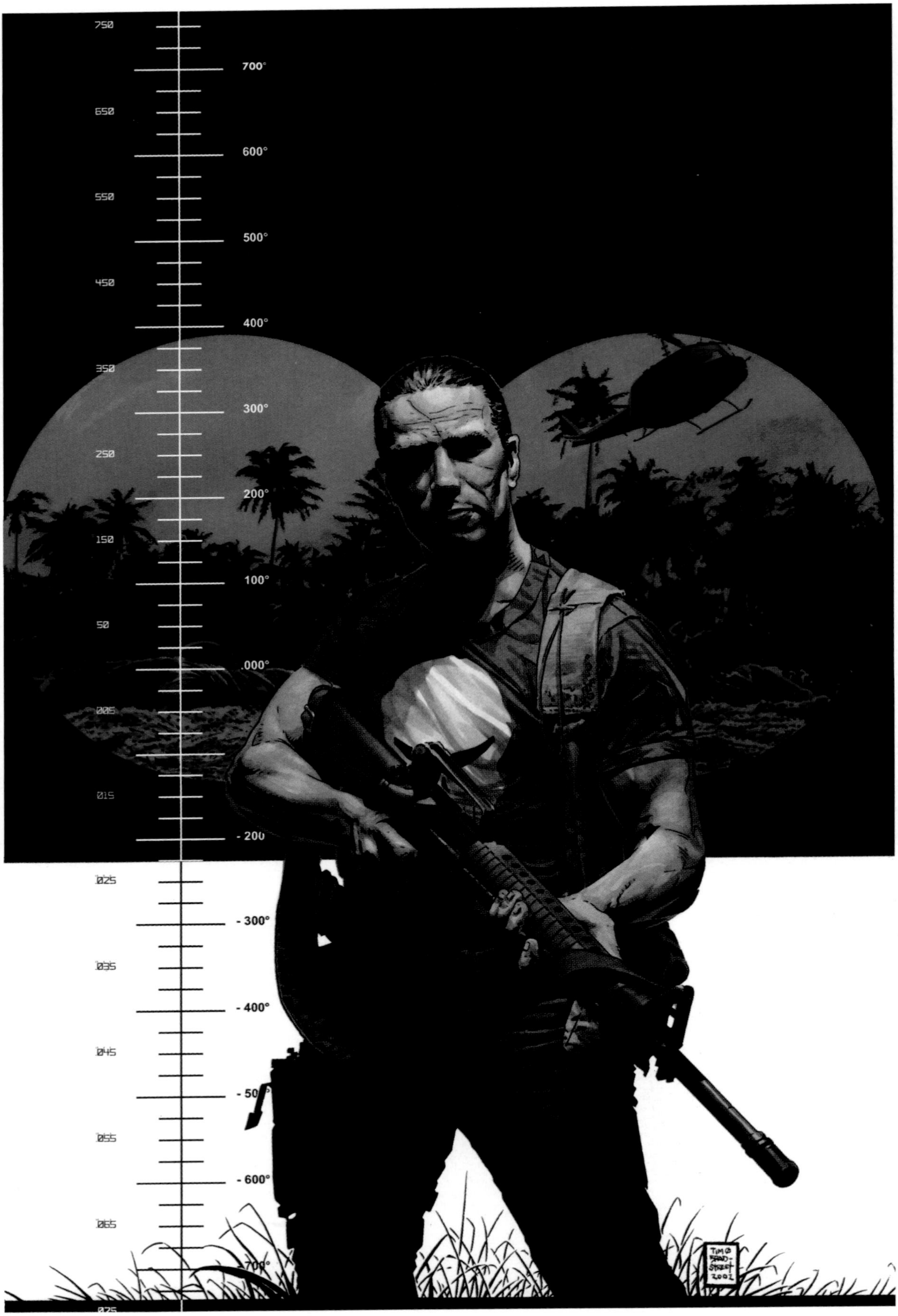
750
700°
650
600°
550
500°
450
400°
350
300°
250
200°
150
100°
50
.000°
005
015
- 200
025
- 300°
035
- 400°
045
055
- 600°
065

Art by Tim Bradstreet

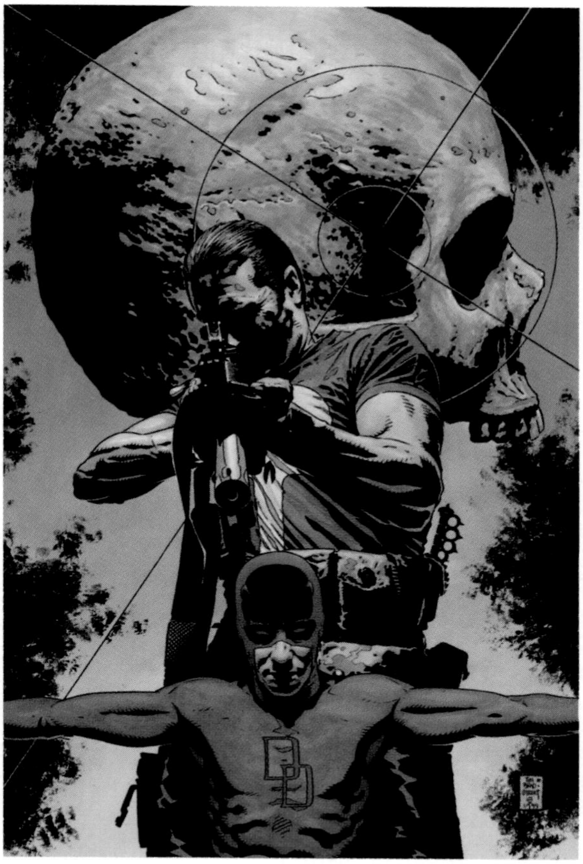

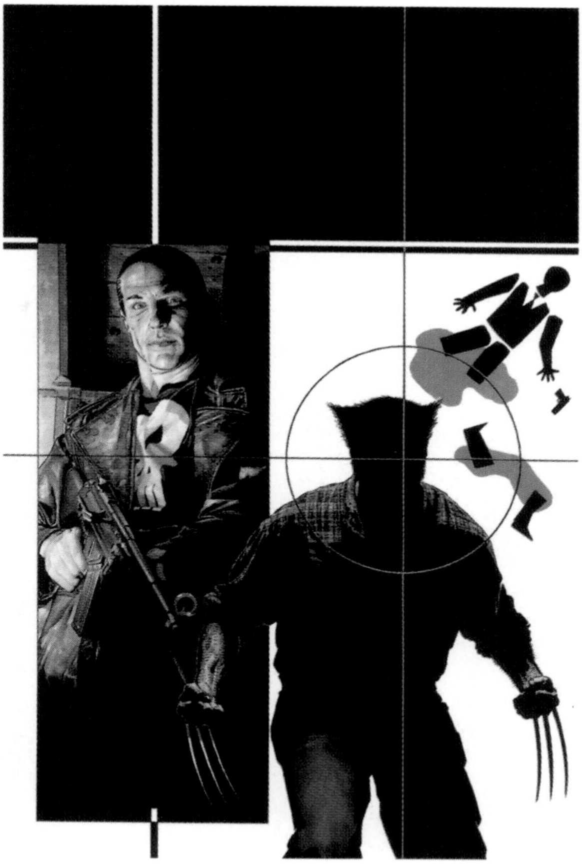

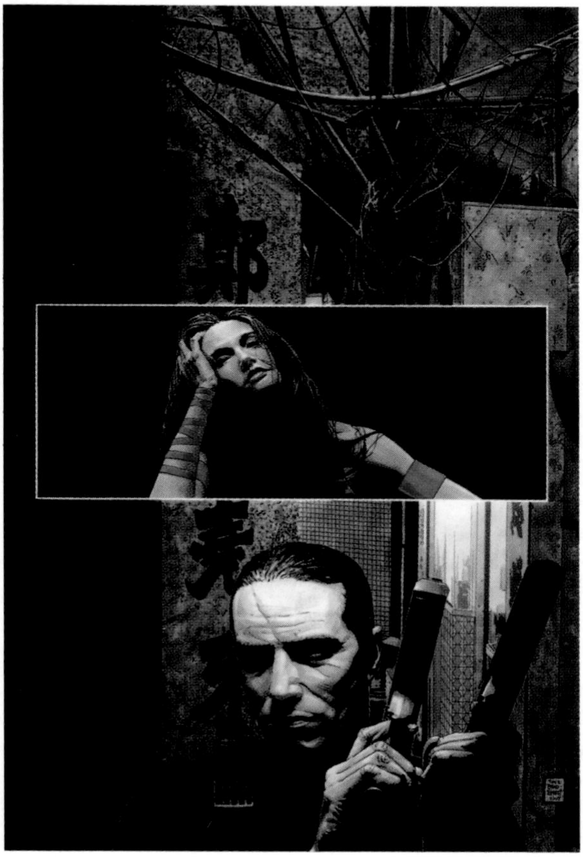

"[Tim Bradstreet's] perfect, seedy action-movie-style covers ... take me back in time to every over-18 VHS video I ever faked ID to rent in 1984. Never has the Punisher looked creepier, more sadistic or more deranged."

Mark Millar
Writer
The Ultimates

Art by Tim Bradstreet

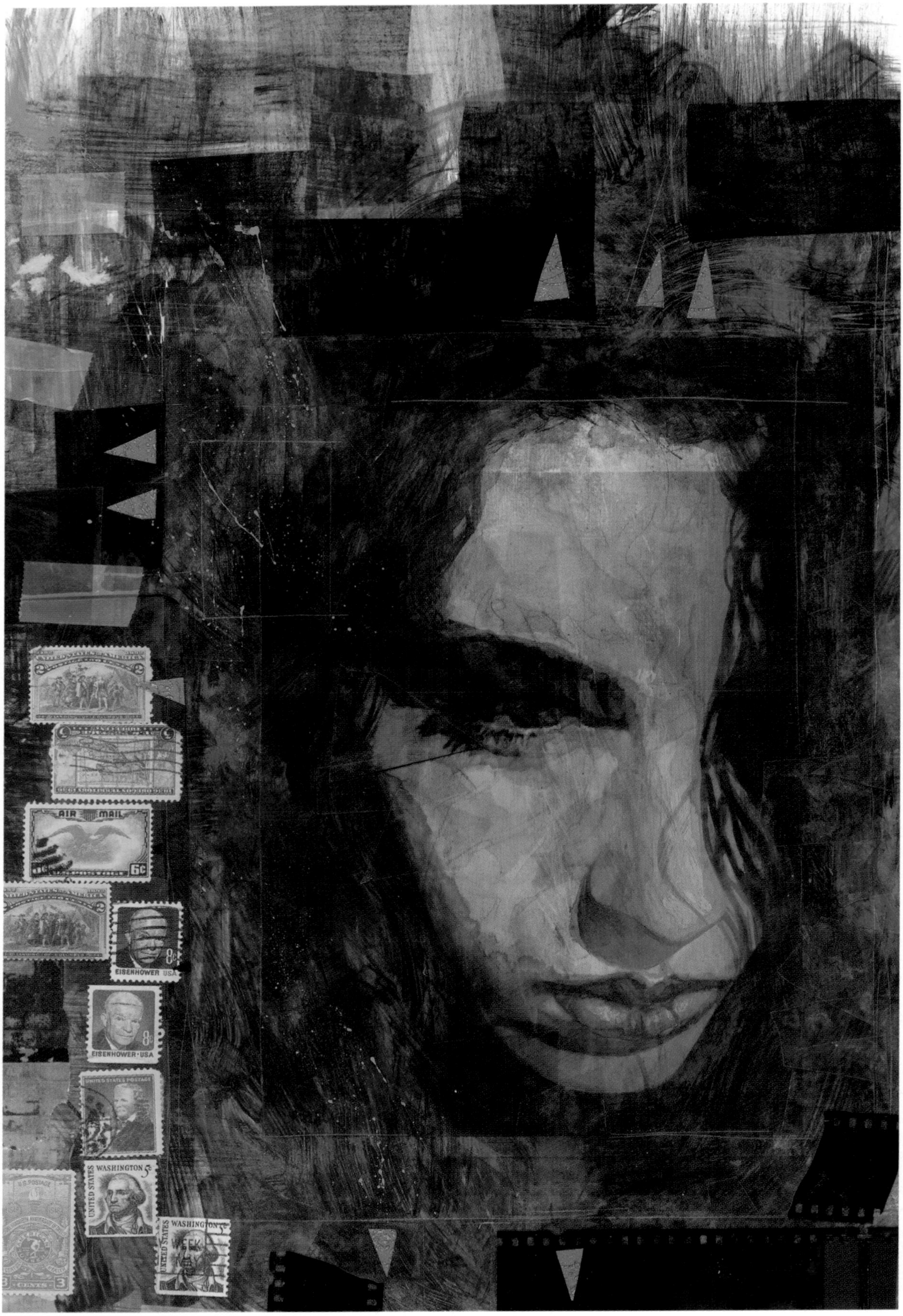
AIR MAIL
6c
EISENHOWER USA
EISENHOWER·USA
WASHINGTON
UNITED STATES
WASHINGTON
UNITED STATES

Art by David Mack

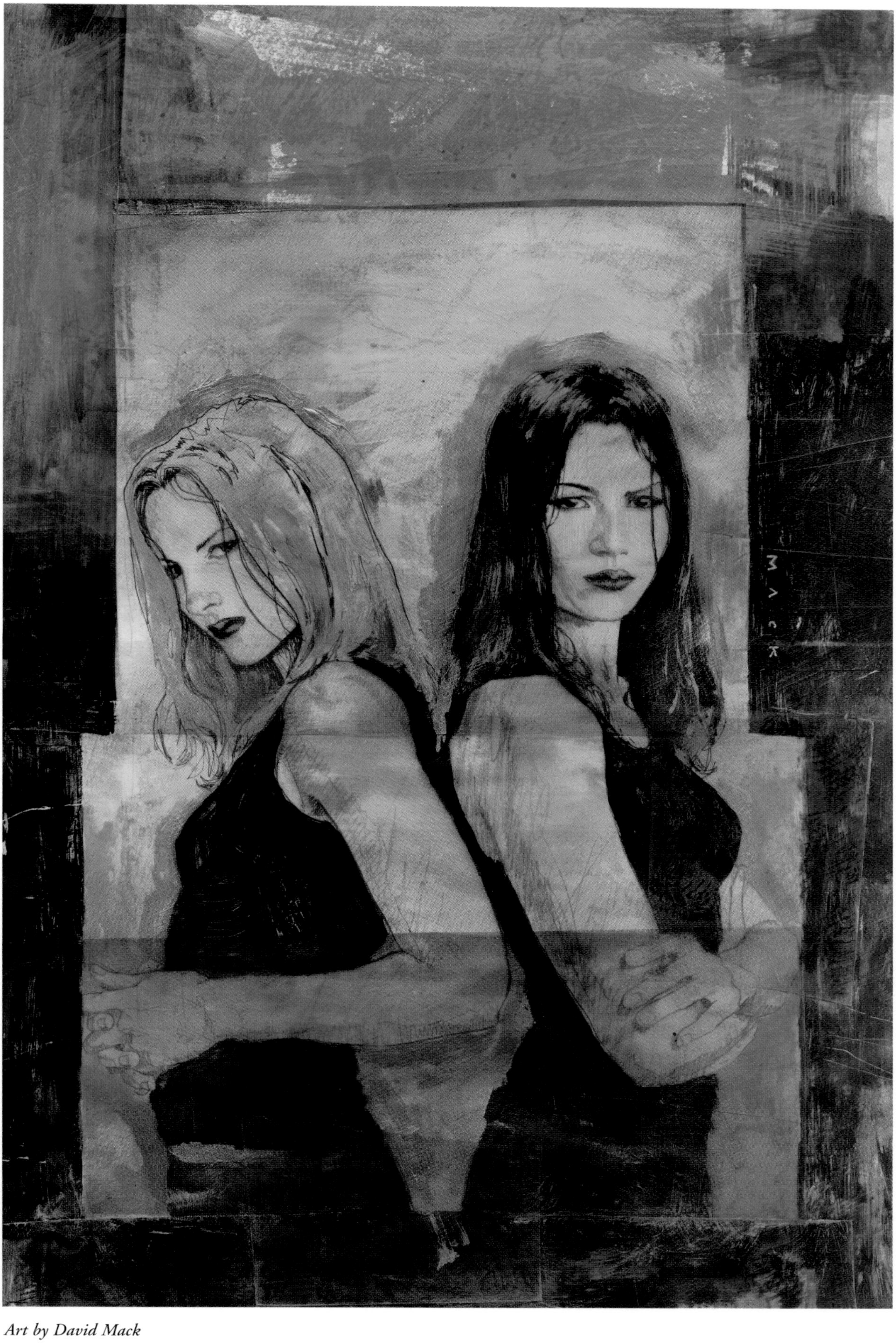
MACK
Art by David Mack

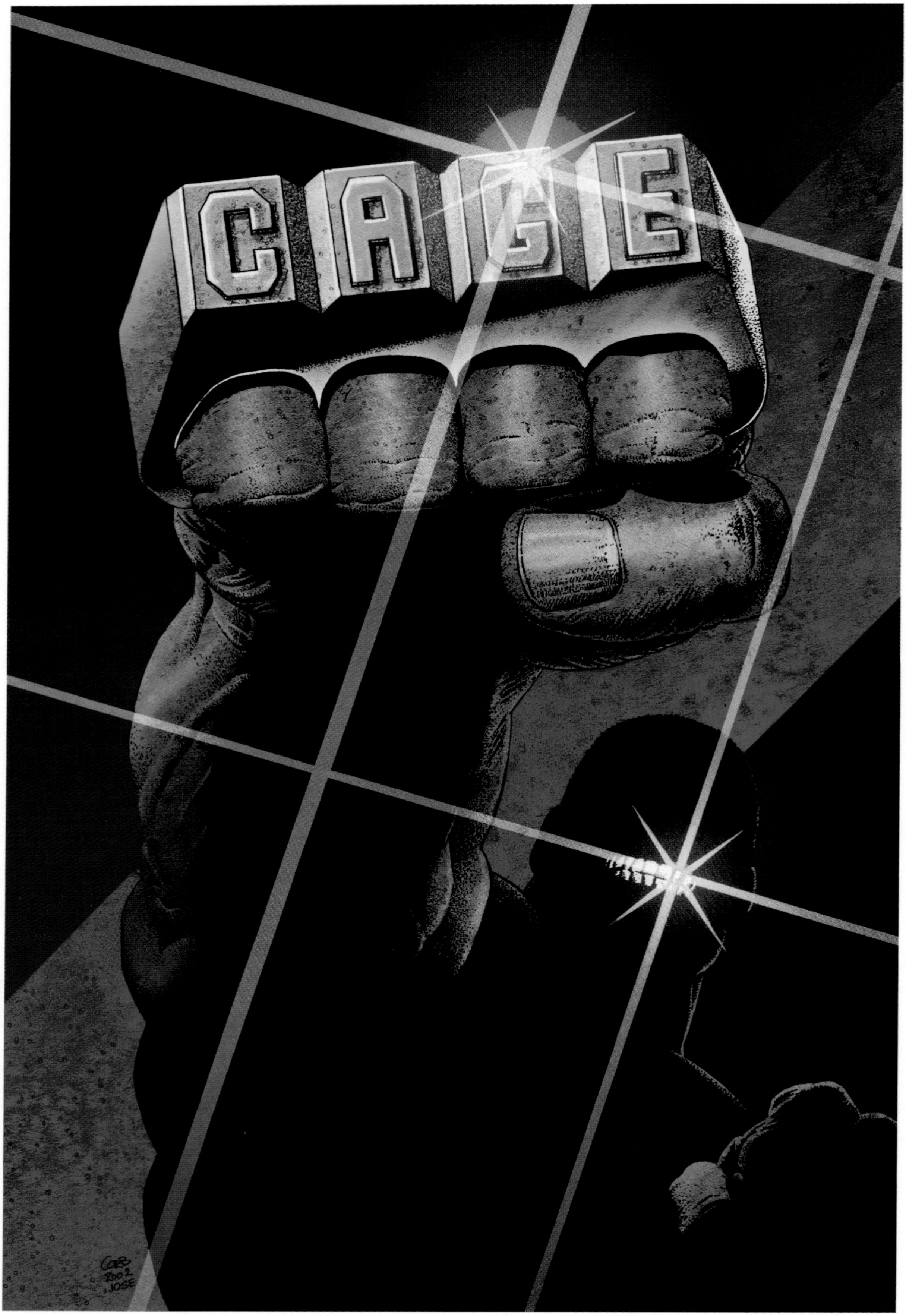
CAGE
CORB
2002
JOSE

Art by Richard Corben

"This Cage is less smiles and jive talk, more 'speak softly and carry big-ass biceps.' With his skullcap, headphones and sunglasses, he could reduce P. Diddy's entire entourage to tears with just one look."

Maxim Online

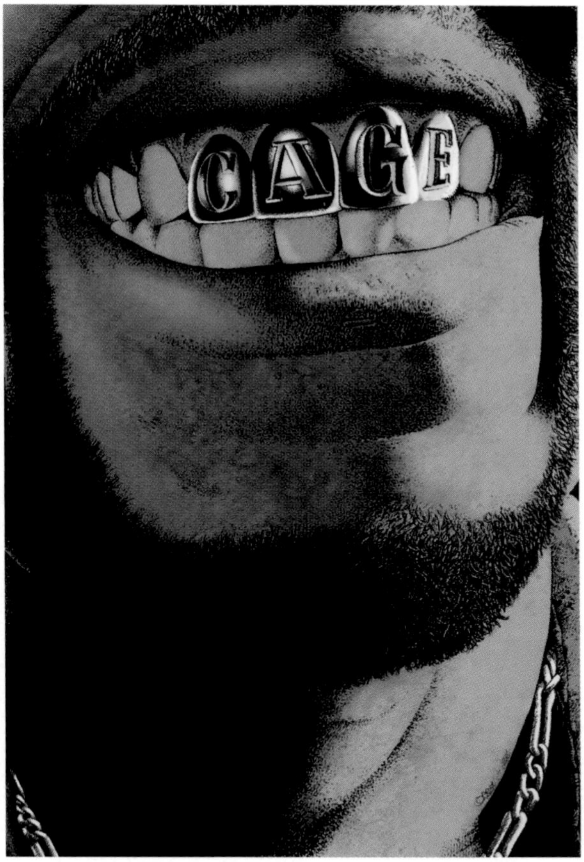
CAGE

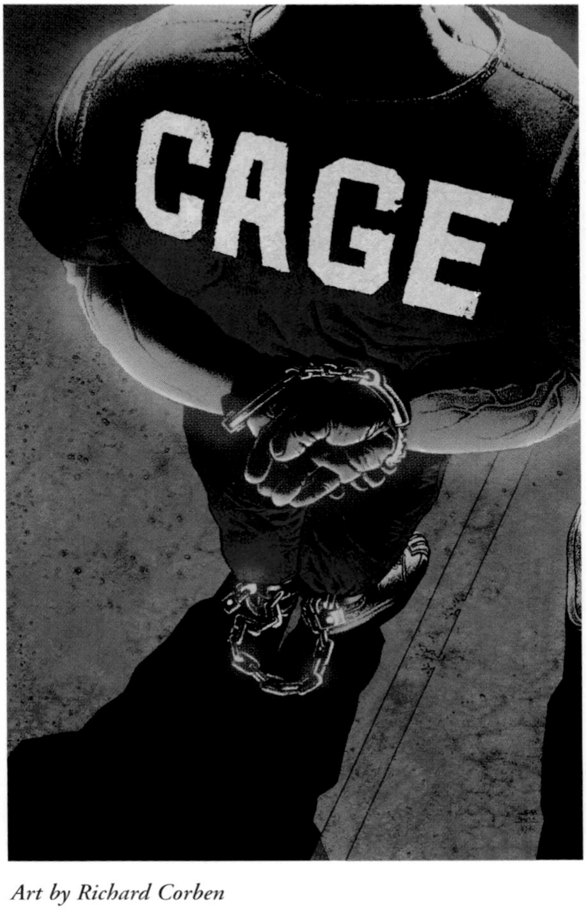
CAGE

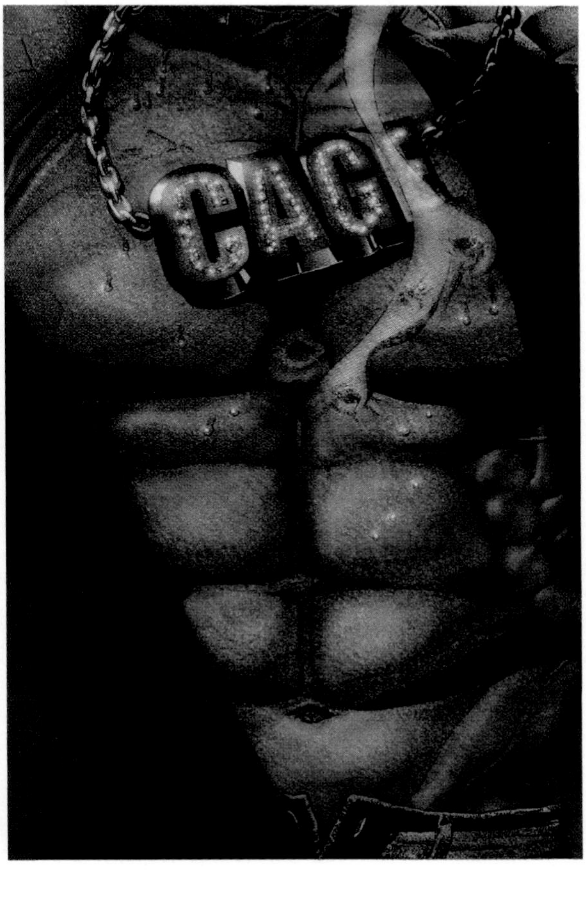
CAGE

Art by Richard Corben

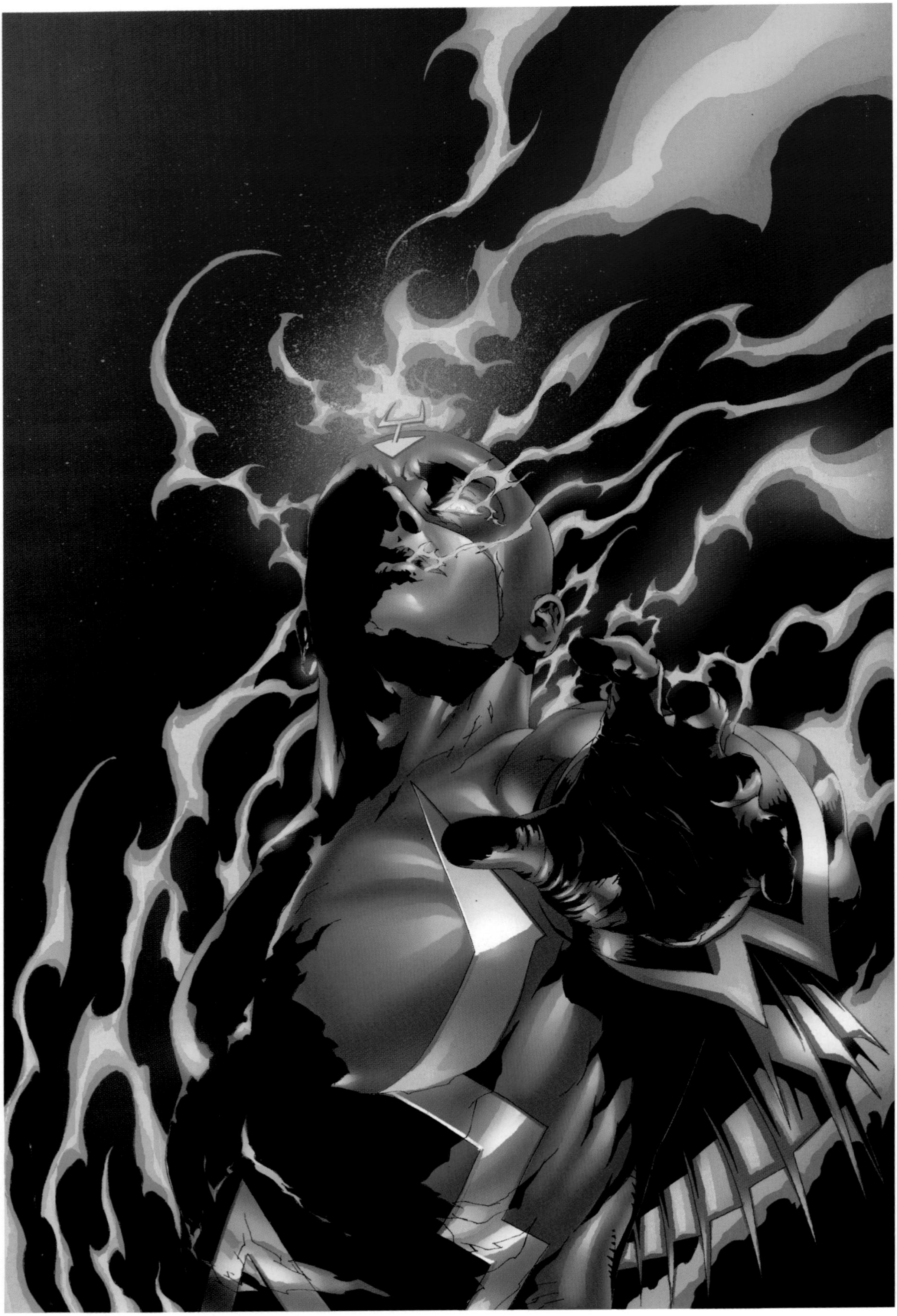

Art by Jae Lee

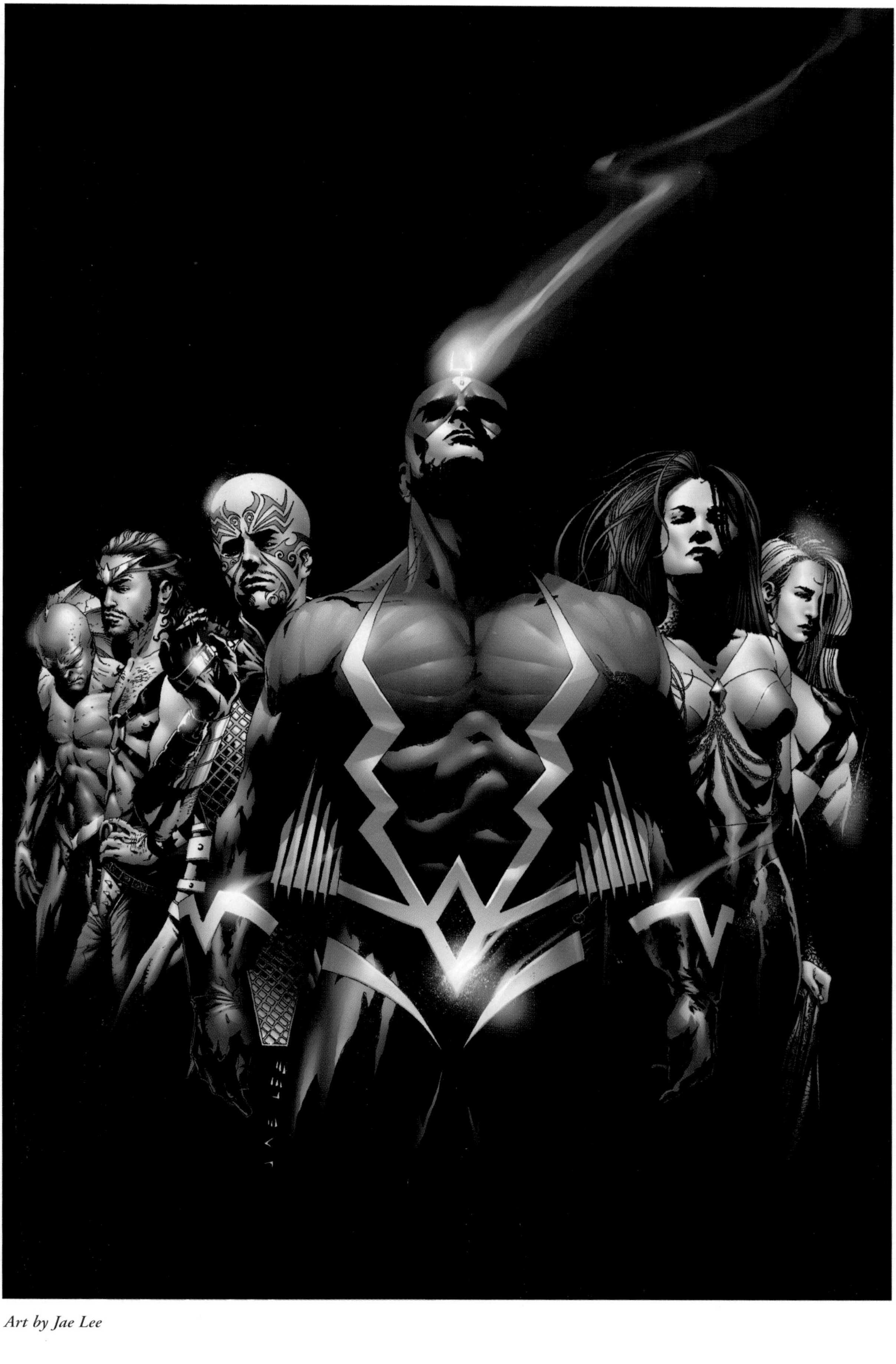

Art by Jae Lee

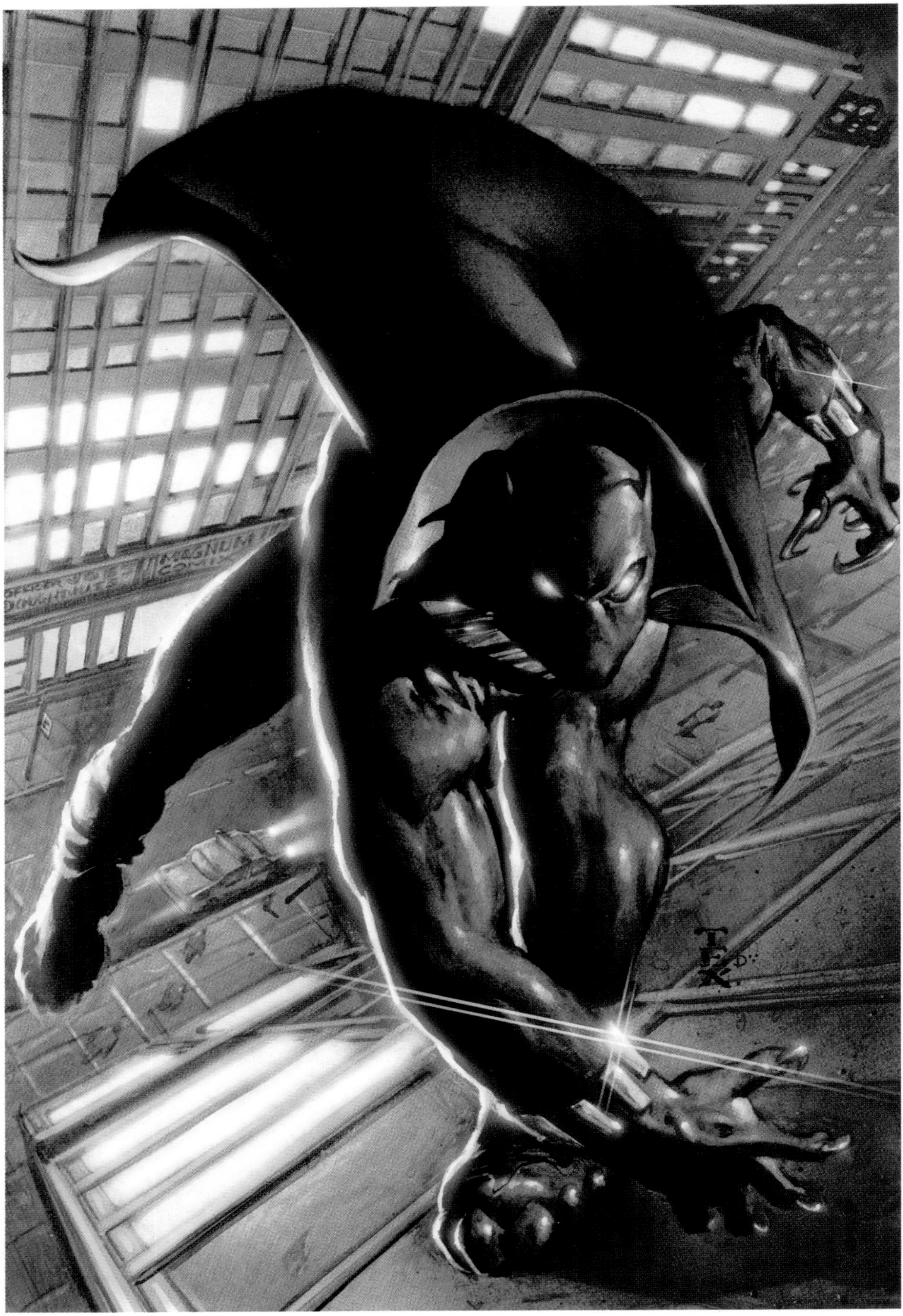
OFFICER
MAGNUM
COMIX

Art by Mark Texeira